A Little History of the United States

JAMES WEST

DAVIDSON

A LITTLE

HISTORY

 of the

UNITED STATES

Yale
UNIVERSITY PRESS
New Haven & London

Lines from "I Have a Dream" and "Address to 1st Montgomery Improvement
Association (MIA) Mass Meeting, at Holt Street Baptist Church" by Martin Luther
King, Jr., reprinted by arrangement with the Heirs to the Estate of Martin Luther
King, Jr., c/o Writers House as agent for the proprietor, New York, NY. © 1963
Dr. Martin Luther King, Jr. © renewed 1991 Coretta Scott King.

Published with assistance from the Kingsley Trust Association Publication Fund
established by the Scroll and Key Society of Yale College.

Published with assistance from the Louis Stern Memorial Fund.

Yale University Press books may be purchased in quantity for
educational, business, or promotional use. For information, please
e-mail sales.press@yale.edu (U.S. office) or sales@yaleup.co.uk
(U.K. office).

Designed by Sonia L. Shannon.
Set in Minion type by Integrated Publishing Solutions.
Printed in Great Britain by TJ International Ltd, Padstow, Cornwall

ISBN: 978-0-300-18141-8 (hardback; alk. paper)

Library of Congress Control Number: 2015935963

A catalogue record for this book is available from the British Library.

This paper meets the requirements of ANSI/NISO Z39.48–1992
(Permanence of Paper).

10 9 8 7 6 5 4 3 2 1

For W.E.G., M.H.L., M.B.S., C.L.H., and B.DeL.,
who have shared the walk through Elysian fields

Contents

Maps

Making History

HOW DO YOU MAKE HISTORY? Most of us think in terms of someone changing the course of events by performing deeds that will endure in human memory. That's making history by living it.

I'm someone who makes history another way: I write it. As a historian, it's my job to discover the details of the past and make sense of them.

Making history by living it seems exciting, vital, even dangerous. The greatest of those who do are often honored, sometimes denounced, always remembered. The people who *write* history, on the other hand, are mostly invisible. They inhabit a world of libraries filled with old books, fading photographs, and dog-eared records. Indeed, writing history and living it seem to belong to two different worlds. Yet those worlds are tied together more closely than might first appear.

Consider two men who grew up in the early part of the twentieth century. Michael King was born in 1929 in Atlanta, Georgia, during the hard times of the Great Depression. His father, a preacher, nicknamed him Little Mike (the father, of course, being Big Mike). Mike was a boy of strong emotions. When his grandmother died of a heart attack, he was filled with such grief that he threw himself out the second-story window of his home. (Fortunately, he was not badly hurt.) But he grew up with high spirits, too. Entering college, he had a reputation for liking parties, flashy sport coats, and two-toned shoes. It is probably safe to say that history was not his first love.

Yet there was another side to him. For all the parties, he did read about the past. One library book that set him thinking was Henry David Thoreau's *On Civil Disobedience*, written in 1849. Thoreau talked about whether an American citizen could ever be justified in disobeying the laws of his nation. Even when Michael King was only five years old, his father exposed him to history in a very personal way. Big Mike decided that he would rename both himself and his son after one of his own heroes, the German religious reformer Martin Luther. From then on, Michael King, Jr., became Martin Luther King, Jr.—and went on to make history as the most famous leader of the civil rights movement. In fact, he became one of the most famous people in American history.

Halfway around the world from King, Valentine Untalan grew up in the Philippines. During World War II he joined the army to defend his nation from a Japanese invasion, fighting side by side with American forces. On the Bataan Peninsula Untalan was captured and then herded along with thousands of other Filipinos and Americans onto a huge field. There Japanese guards announced that the prisoners were going to march to the city of Manila, where they would be housed temporarily in hotels.

The last thing on Val Untalan's mind was whether he was making history. He merely wanted to stay alive and knew he had to escape. The prisoners' grueling journey later became known as the Bataan Death March; thousands of soldiers died. It took Untalan four tries, but he finally evaded the Japanese, reached his village, and returned to the fight. After the war he moved to the United States, became an American citizen, made a career in the army, and raised a family. I know his story because years later I married one of his daughters.

Martin Luther King, Jr., you have heard of; Valentine Untalan most likely not. Yet both men made history by living it, in large ways and small. Neither could have imagined, when they were young, how reading history would change their lives. But it did. When Val Untalan's Japanese captors announced the march to Manila, he recalled, "I had read a history of World War I, with all its horrible scenes and acts of cruelty; and I said to myself, they are not taking us to any hotel!" When Martin Luther King thought about ending the injustice of segregation, he was struck by how Thoreau had chosen jail "rather than support a war that would spread slavery's territory into Mexico."

Is it possible to say that because Valentine Untalan read history, he saved his own life? That would be too simple. Ingenuity, determination, and sheer endurance all played a part. Is it possible to say that because Martin Luther King read history, he lost his life to an assassin's bullet, even though he brought greater freedom to millions of Americans? That, too, oversimplifies. King did not decide to risk death for a noble cause just because he read a book.

But both men used their knowledge of history to make history. And when you think about it, history shapes our lives in a thousand different ways. Our very identity—who we say we are—is really nothing more than a history of ourselves. This personal history is made up of what we have done and where we have been and what we have read. We construct it—we make our own history—out of vivid personal memories and from the stories passed along by parents and relatives. We make history out of the lore of the sports teams we join, out of the Internet pages we link to—and yes, we even get it from history books describing the life of a nation.

This book is a history of how the United States came to be. The tale is remarkable, spanning over five hundred years. It describes how one nation spread across a continent filled with an enormous variety of peoples. And it explains how they came to unite under a banner of freedom and equality. The motto of the United States is the Latin phrase *E pluribus unum:* Out of many, one. The Founders who declared the nation's independence insisted that its citizens—in fact, all humankind—had been *created equal* and possessed the right to *Life, Liberty and the pursuit of Happiness.*

On the face of it, these ideals of freedom, equality, and unity seem almost like fairy tales, far too distant from the real world. How could a nation proclaim freedom when hundreds of thousands of its inhabitants had been kidnapped and brought to America as slaves? How could the Founders praise equality when half the people living in the United States—women—were not given rights equal to men's? How could a nation that was truly united be made up of so many different sorts of people? Some were devout folk who worshiped in simple meeting houses, some in soaring cathedrals; others were members of no church at all. Some were newcomers looking to get rich by growing tobacco or cotton; others were workers sweating beside white-hot furnaces that turned out steel for skyscrapers and railroads. There were rabble-rousers who dumped tea in the harbor rather than pay taxes placed on them without their consent, farmworkers who started a union to gain a fair wage and decent living conditions, inventors who worked to create a lightbulb, a better oilcan, or a machine to project moving pictures onto a screen. Thinkers tinkered with ideas, like how to sell a newspaper to millions or how to make a large city livable.

So many different people. So different that surely they have nothing to do with you! Or do they? Whether you realize it or not, all these people are a part of your history. It's not easy to say which stories you may need one day.

We all wish to make history by living it. But never forget that the more you read, write, and remember history, the better your chances of living it in such a way that your deeds are remembered, too.

1

Where the Birds Led

THE TALL, RED-FACED captain on the ship's deck stared into the heavens, his eyes as pale blue as the sky above. A large flock of birds was passing overhead. These were not the usual gulls that follow seafarers everywhere across the oceans, nor the little petrels that seek shelter by a ship's rudder when a storm threatens. These were land birds. Because they came from the north, the man decided, perhaps they were migrating—"flying from the winter" that was coming in some distant land. The birds were a sign—one that he badly needed—for surely they, too, were bound for land.

The other sailors gazed at the sky, but they also stole glances at their captain. "Admiral of the Ocean Sea," he called himself, but they didn't completely trust him. Although the ships and the crews were Spanish, Admiral Cristoforo Columbo came from the Italian port of Genoa. For five weeks in the late summer and autumn of 1492 the *Niña, Pinta,* and *Santa Maria* had sailed west across the Atlantic. No one on board had ever been out of sight of land for so many days. And they had seen nothing of the strange countries and grand riches this foreigner had promised. Maybe it was time to rise up and throw the admiral overboard rather than let him sail them all to their deaths.

Columbo was uneasy, too, though he refused to show it. He ordered the ship to change course. If the birds were going southwest, he would follow.

It had been a long journey for Cristoforo Columbo, or Christopher Columbus, as English speakers translate his name. The son of a weaver, Columbus had chosen the life of the sea instead of following his father's trade. For years Genoa had been a prosperous port whose vessels sailed the broad Mediterranean that Europeans knew so well, picking up silks, spices, and other luxuries at ports on its eastern shores. Those goods came from distant kingdoms in Asia, transported along a series of roads and trails thousands of miles long known as the Silk Road. Columbus eagerly devoured tales of an Italian trader named Marco Polo who had traveled those paths two hundred years earlier, all the way to Cathay (now called China), where Polo met its leader, the Great Khan, and wrote of fabulous marvels and riches beyond counting.

Columbus had traveled south along the coast of Africa, where the Portuguese were finding gold, ivory, and slaves to buy and sell. He had traveled north in the Atlantic almost to the Arctic. Visiting Ireland, he saw a rude boat drift into a harbor from out of the wide western waters. In the boat lay two dead people—"a man and a woman of extraordinary appearance." Some folk guessed the people looked so strange because they had been blown all the way from Cathay. Certainly they had not. But still, stories about the Atlantic fed Columbus's imagination.

Most scholars of the day understood that the world was round. For centuries, ancient books had recounted tales of islands far to the west where unknown peoples lived. Other writers guessed that a large continent might exist there, too, while still others insisted that the Atlantic stretched all the way to Asia, a distance far too great to sail. Columbus became convinced that the world was smaller than most geographers thought. To him, it seemed quite possible that someone from Europe could sail west to Cathay.

Columbus asked King John of Portugal to bankroll an expedition. Portugal faced the Atlantic, and its captains ventured regularly down the African coast. In 1488 Bartolomeu Dias had sailed around Africa's southern tip into the Indian Ocean. His path became one water route that Europeans sailed to reach the treasures of India and Cathay. But Columbus's notion of a western route left King John distinctly unimpressed. "A big talker and boastful . . . full of fancy and imagination," the king complained. And perhaps John was right. Columbus was stubborn, a little vain, and too sure of himself. In truth, the world was bigger than he thought. The distance from Portugal to China, heading west, is closer to twelve thousand miles than the twenty-five hundred Columbus guessed it might be.

But even wrong-headed men can accomplish much when they are stubborn. Columbus next took his ideas to Spain, ruled by King Ferdinand and Queen Isabella. They paid him little attention at first, being engaged in a war with Arab rulers from Africa, who for centuries had controlled much of Spain. Only after Ferdinand and Isabella drove out the last Arab armies did they agree to finance Columbus's voyage.

In August 1492 the *Niña, Pinta,* and *Santa Maria* set out with Columbus in command. He sailed south first, to the Canary Islands off the coast of Africa. The winds in that part of the world made it easier to sail west. At night the sailors slept in their clothes wherever they could find a spot on deck. When daylight came a boy would sing a prayer: "Blessed be the light of day/ And the Holy Cross, we say." As the sun rose, the dew on deck would dry and the men would begin their chores. Flying fish leaped through the waters, even "coming on the deck in numbers." In calm seas, sailors swam alongside.

But such pleasures could not banish deeper worries. Where was the end of this vast ocean? At night, the silhouettes of migrating land birds still showed black against an almost full moon. Finally, at about 2:00 a.m. on October 12, the lookout on the *Pinta* cried out, "Tierra! Tierra!"—Land! Land! As the sun rose, the white sands of an island loomed up.

Where on earth were they? Off the coast of Cathay? Columbus burst with questions as one of the ship's boats rowed him toward shore. Marco Polo had spoken of a prosperous island named Cipangu (we call it Japan). This small spot surely could not be that. But was Cipangu nearby? Or was this some land no European had ever visited?

He spied a flash of movement on shore—then another. It seemed as if several people had run into the forest beyond the beach.

Who were they? Where was he? The waves pushed the boat up onto the beach, and Columbus stepped out.

2

A Continent in Space and Time

COLUMBUS WAS NOT THE first European to find North America. Five hundred years earlier, around AD 1000, Leif Erikson led a band of Norse men and women to the northern tip of what is today Newfoundland, Canada. From there, these Vikings explored a region they named Vinland. But the Norse settlements died out, and Europeans forgot about them. So Columbus's voyage was truly a landmark event. After 1492 the eastern half of the world would no longer be isolated from the western half.

If the island that Columbus first glimpsed was the one we now call San Salvador, as many think, it was a tiny piece of the continent: only about 63 square miles. The remaining 9,539,937 square miles of North America were still unknown to Columbus.

Today, the United States stretches from the Atlantic to the Pacific. To understand how it became a nation of such great size, we must understand how the continent shaped history from the start. We must sense the space of North America as well as its place in time.

First, consider space. Starting at the top of a piece of blank paper,

5

draw two broad vertical strokes, each sweeping down in a gentle inward curve until they almost meet at the bottom. The shape is a funnel, with a bit of a hook; and that is North America's basic outline. With the Atlantic Ocean bordering the east coast and the Pacific Ocean to the west, the land narrows down to the Isthmus of Panama. Panama's thin land bridge connects North and South America.

Next, draw a second set of lines inside the first, running roughly parallel. These are the continent's major mountain ranges. The eastern line represents the Appalachians, which run from Maine to Georgia. In the west, the procession of high peaks splits and rejoins, with the Cascade and the Sierra Nevada mountains running closest to the Pacific and the Rocky Mountains farther east. Between these western mountains lie the dry lands of the Great Basin and the Great Salt Lake.

Mountains act as barriers. The Appalachians will make it difficult for people to travel from the level plains and rolling hills along the Atlantic coast west into the open prairies beyond. On the Pacific side, the Cascade and Sierra mountains will discourage people from moving west to east.

The mountains act as a barrier to weather, too. Rain clouds sweeping in from the Pacific rise as they cross the mountains. The warm air condenses as it moves into the colder mountaintops and falls as rain, usually west of the mountains. The Great Basin and the Great Plains to the east remain much drier. On the other hand, no mountain range stretches across the northern lands that make up present-day Canada. During the winter, frigid Arctic air can spill south, deep into the continent. The mountain ranges help funnel that cold air. In contrast, many of Europe and Asia's mountain ranges run east-west, such as the Alps, the Caucasus, and the Himalaya, and thus those mountains block Arctic air. The climate to the south remains milder.

During the summer, North America's funnel works the opposite way. Waves of heat flow north across the Plains and into Canada,

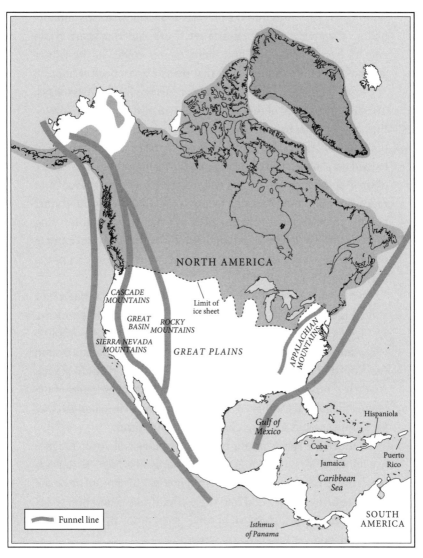

The shape of North America.

sending temperatures into the nineties or sparking storms and tor-nados. These extremes of climate set North America apart. New-comers from Europe will find temperatures colder in the winter and hotter in the summer than what many experienced at home.

North America's climate will affect history in countless ways. The dry open spaces of the Great Plains will push Indians to master the horse in order to hunt buffalo. With little wood on the prairies to build fences, American farmers will eagerly take up the invention of barbed wire, which will change life on the Plains forever. The barrier of the Appalachian Mountains will make it easier for the French to reach the middle of America from Canada, following the funnel and the rivers that drain it. Blizzards will trap wagon trains trying to cross the Sierra Nevada Mountains. The warm southern climate will make it possible for slavery to spread—but only in part of the nation, not through all of it.

One more space on the map is worth noticing: the Caribbean Sea and its islands. The region is large. Cuba, Hispaniola, Puerto Rico, and Jamaica are the biggest islands, known as the Greater Antilles. Cuba alone stretches 740 miles from end to end. If you laid it atop the United States, with one tip at New York City, it would stretch nearly to Chicago. Although these lands will not become part of the United States, the Caribbean Sea will act as the first major gateway for Europeans and Africans coming to the Americas.

So much for space. As for time, this history will cover roughly five hundred years. To a single person, that span is huge. Historians speak of a generation, the time from someone's birth until he or she is able to bring a new child into the world. If one generation spans about twenty years, then twenty-five generations of families will come and go over the course of our story.

On the other hand, five hundred years is a snap of the fingers compared to the time people have lived in North America. The first humans reached the continent about fourteen thousand years ago. At that time, a sheet of ice covered most of present-day Canada. In many places the ice was over two miles thick. (The map's dotted line shows how far south the ice sheet reached.) With so much water frozen, the ocean levels sank, opening up a broad stretch of land in the northwest, where the Bering Strait is now located. This land bridge allowed the first humans to make their way into an American continent utterly new to them.

Stretch your arm out to one side and sight down it. Imagine that the fourteen thousand years that humans have lived in North America begin at your shoulder and extend to the tips of your fingers. The last five hundred years of that history, which this book covers, begin only around the last inch of your fingers. In fact, the United States came into existence only in the last *half* of those five hundred years. That time span almost fits onto one fingernail.

Thinking of time in this way should humble us. Five hundred years may seem like a huge canvas upon which we paint our story. But looking down your outstretched arm, a fingernail looks pretty small. Then take those fourteen thousand years that fit along one arm and measure them against the previous 65 million years of North America's existence. That's the amount of time that passed between the end of the age of dinosaurs and the present. The dinosaurs died after a meteorite at least six miles wide came crashing down in what is now the Gulf of Mexico. The explosion was equal to setting off 100 million megatons of explosives. That big bang quite literally "fried America," as one scientist put it. In doing so, it wiped out thousands of plant and animal species and began the age of mammals. To include those years in our scale of time, keep your arm stretched out; then line up a friend behind you, with her arm extended for another fourteen thousand years; then another friend behind her, then another and another . . . until forty-five hundred people snake out the door and into the street, arms stretched shoulder to shoulder, for two and a half miles. And remember that the history we're covering—everything you'll read in the next three hundred pages—takes place on the tip of your finger.

3

OUT OF ONE, MANY

ON A FINE AUTUMN DAY, sunlight heats the slopes of the Appalachian Mountains. As warm air rises, it creates an upward current that a hawk uses to soar above the land looking for prey. A sparrow hawk's eyesight is remarkably keen. Perched atop a sixty-foot tree, it can spy an insect on the ground the size of this *i*.

Imagine what you would see if you joined these birds on their journey south. Most people think of North America in 1492 as a vast, unspoiled wilderness teeming with wildlife. Indians, they imagine, can be glimpsed now and then: paddling a birch-bark canoe across a lake or pursuing buffalo on horseback. But such a picture would be highly misleading. To correct one detail immediately, remove the Indians on horseback. In 1492, no horses had been seen in North America for thirteen thousand years. In fact, some archaeologists believe that the earliest humans in North America killed off the horses as well as many gigantic mammals that roamed the land, including wooly mammoths and mastodons, giant sloths taller than a giraffe, and eight-foot lions.

Still, later European settlers reported immense numbers of wild animals in America. Virginia rivers were so full of fish that the hooves of horses killed them as English colonists trotted in the shallows. New York fishermen hauled in foot-long lobsters, which they preferred for "serving at table" because they were more convenient to eat than the five- and six-foot lobsters they also caught. Bison not only roamed the Great Plains but were also seen as far east as Pennsylvania and Virginia. So many passenger pigeons darkened the skies that when they landed to sleep, tree branches broke under their weight. In 1492, then, we certainly will see plenty of wildlife. Even so, such tales of plenty may be misleading. As we will see in chapter 5, the large numbers of animals may have been in part created by the *arrival* of Europeans in North America, strange as that may seem.

In 1492 around 8 million Indians lived in North America. That number is not large, especially for an entire continent. More than 8 million people live today in the city of New York. Still, the number is significant. To compare, the British Isles held 2 to 3 million inhabitants in 1492. France, Europe's most populous nation, had about 15 million people. And in Asia, over 100 million lived in China alone. So, thinking of 8 million Indians spread across North America, let's join the soaring hawks. What we see below is a continent that is less of a wilderness than we expected. No matter where we glide, almost everywhere we see plumes of smoke.

Where there's smoke there's fire, the saying goes. And Indians used fire for more than cooking and keeping warm. High above the Mississippi, smoke swirls upward from fires used to build dugout canoes. The fires were allowed to burn until the boat's insides had been hollowed out. On the river, dozens of dugouts glint in the sun, forty to sixty men in each one. No small birch-bark canoe, this! On a day of ceremony or war, the boatmen's faces are painted reddish-brown and many heads sport white feather plumes. Some Indians kneel as they paddle, others stand behind them, shields ready to ward off an attack. A canopy at the stern shades each ca-noe's commander.

Across the Plains, Indians set fires to stampede buffalo and in the Great Basin burn grasslands to flush lizards from the ground. Some peoples burn fields to encourage wild blueberries or sun-flowers to grow; others set fires to drive off hordes of devilish mos-quitos. In the Rockies, Indians even use fire to celebrate. Entire fir trees are set aflame, their branches blazing sparks into the night like fireworks. Humans from one end of the continent to the other all use fire as a tool for shaping the land to their liking.

In other ways, Indian peoples differed greatly. In fact, we might say that the motto of North America in 1492 was the opposite of *E pluribus unum.* Not *Out of many people, one,* but *Out of one con-tinent, many peoples.* Depending on which birds you follow, you'll see large differences in the ways Indians adapted to the world around them. Some lived in simple bands, hunting and gathering food. Other civilizations boasted farm fields, monuments, temples, cities, astronomers, high priests, and rulers.

A flock of geese setting out from the western Arctic will spy Inuit bands chasing whales in *umiaks*—open boats made from walrus skins stretched over driftwood. The Inuit (also known as Eskimos) possess harpoons strong enough to pierce the tough skin of whales, a valuable source of food. (Whale blubber also burns nicely in oil lamps.) Inuit women have developed the skill of sew-ing seal gut and fish skin to make clothing that fits the body more closely and is thus warmer for those living in such wintry lands.

Two thousand miles to the south, in present-day Oregon, the same geese fly through the Willamette River Valley. Below, Indians mend a fish trap—a line of sticks pounded into the river bottom along a rapids. Salmon swimming upstream can make their way through only a few openings, and there they are caught in woven baskets. The climate is milder, and there are many seals and otters, clams and mussels, large porpoises and thousands of small candle-fish, a creature so fatty it can be dried and burned in a torch.

Farther south, birds crossing the Sonoran Desert in present-day Arizona can see lines carved in the land. These are not the branches of rivers, for their lines run too straight. They're man-made. In the centuries after AD 300, the Hohokam people dug six hundred miles of canals, some over sixty feet wide, to bring water to the beans, squash, and corn they grew. The birds in 1492 can still see the remains of the canals, but the Hohokam are nowhere to be found. As to the reason why, we'll return to that question in a moment.

In short, the Indian peoples of North America differ greatly from one another partly because the environment has forced them to invent different ways of surviving. In the mild and wet Pacific Northwest, who would think about making canals to irrigate crops? On the other hand, no desert Indian would invent dugout canoes in a land where large trees are unknown.

The environment is not the only reason that the Indians of 1492 differ among themselves. Even in similar climates, different humans will think of different solutions to the same problems. By 1492 people had been living in North America for thousands of years—long enough to develop different beliefs, customs, and cultures. In the dry lands of the Great Basin, where survival was difficult, small bands were each led by a hunter who had proved himself. Indian societies of the southeast had much larger settlements and more complex political systems. The Natchez, for example, divided themselves into different ranks, ruled by a king (known as the Great Sun) and his relatives (Little Suns). Below them came nobles, known as Honored People, and, lowest of all, a larger class called Stinkards. As the name of Great Sun suggests, sun worship played an important part in the religious life of the southeastern Indians.

In 1492 the most complex civilization in North America was found in the Valley of Mexico. This people called themselves the Mexica, though in later years the Spanish referred to them as Aztecs. Their capital city, Tenochtitlán, was built on an island on Lake

Texcoco and was larger than any city in Europe. Canoes glided everywhere along canals. Merchants brought goods to market from thousands of miles away. There were parrots for sale, cotton cloaks and steaming hot chocolate, tortillas, turkeys, rabbits, animal skins, beautiful feathers of all sorts, and gold dust, packaged carefully inside the quills of geese. Tenochtitlán boasted zoos and special museum gardens filled with exotic plants. Aqueducts brought drinking water to the city from the mountains miles away. Aztec religion and culture were as advanced and unique as those of any civilization in Asia or Europe.

Behind the culture of any group, there is a history—that is, a story of how any custom got its start. In modern America, for example, many people wear blue jeans, pants held together by rivets. That's a custom; and it has a history. Actually, two Americans, Levi Strauss and David Jacobs, thought of the idea in 1873. In similar fashion, someone, or perhaps a group of Indians, must have figured out how to make better skin clothing or a sharper spear—or had the idea to set up a political system in which "Honored People" received special recognition. But none of the early peoples of North America invented writing. So we have no histories telling how individuals contributed to the way people lived, or about the villages they built or the wars they fought.

Archaeologists have made it their business to discover what happened before there was any written history. Their detective work has been truly astonishing, with new knowledge gained every year. Even so, many puzzles remain. What happened to the Hohokam people, who built canals? Before 1492, that desert region of Arizona probably supported more Indians than any other spot north of the Mexica empire. Why were the canals abandoned? Did the climate become hotter and drier, making survival too difficult? Did there get to be too many people living in too small an area? Did Indian newcomers from the north attack these peoples? We don't have that history.

A similar puzzle surrounds the only city to be built in the present-day United States before 1492. Cahokia grew up along the Mississippi River where St. Louis stands today. Around 1050, a central plaza bigger than ten football fields was fashioned, built in the shadow of a human-made mound standing 130 feet high. Thousands of people lived there and erected over 120 similar mounds. Some archaeologists think that the city was built partly out of religious wonder after a blazing light lit up the night sky. This was a supernova, the explosion of a dying star, which was seen by Chinese astronomers in 1054. But that is only a theory. Nor do we understand why the city's inhabitants moved away, leaving it deserted by the time Columbus reached North America. There were no written records.

After October 1492, written records did come to North America. Birds flying near the island of San Salvador looked down and saw something never seen before. Yes, smoke rose to the sky as usual and men in dugout canoes chased fish. But now three bigger boats appeared on the vast blue ocean, their weather-beaten canvases stretched high on poles. Strange boats with even stranger humans on board. The people watching Columbus and his sailors from beneath the island's trees must have been astonished. What odd clothes they wore! Tight stockings and puffy knee britches. Hot, heavy quilted jackets. Who were they? What did their arrival mean?

History was coming to North America—written history, scrawled in journals, printed in books, stored in stout chests, or tucked into pockets. Nothing would ever be quite the same again.

4

A Golden Age and the Age of Gold

TODAY THE STORY OF COLUMBUS is so familiar that few stop to wonder what the world would have been like if events had turned out a little differently. Instead of celebrating Columbus's birthday on October 12, we might honor the day Admiral Zheng He dropped anchor along the California coast in 1429 . . . the first Asian in modern times to reach America.

Preposterous? During the 1400s China stood at the center of civilization, and all of Asia and Europe wanted Chinese goods. Even as traders made their way along the Silk Road, China launched a great fleet of trading ships that took seven voyages across the Indian Ocean, as far as Madagascar and the coast of East Africa.

To compare, Columbus had three ships whose crews numbered ninety men. Admiral Zheng He's treasure fleet numbered anywhere from two hundred to three hundred ships. Columbus's largest vessel was eighty-five feet long; Zheng He's four hundred feet, with nine masts and silk sails. Each ship could carry more than five hundred people, and the fleet included separate ships carrying horses and fresh water for drinking. If the Ming emperors had continued to support such voyages, the history you are reading now might be written in Chinese. But Mongol peoples from the north of Asia were attacking China, drawing the emperors' attention elsewhere. After 1433 the treasure fleet was destroyed and no more large ships built.

Europe, on the other hand, was not the center of the civilized world. Seafarers along the Atlantic coast were anxious to get ahead, full of energy and—*hungry*, it might be said: hungry for fame, riches, power, and glory. If Columbus hadn't reached America in 1492, someone else from Europe would have.

But Columbus did get there. As he splashed up onto the beach, the small island before him seemed like paradise. Ancient writers had told tales of a golden age before history, where "men lived simply and innocently"—no laws, no quarrels. The people on this island seemed to be folk from such a time. "They go as naked as when their mothers bore them," Columbus reported, and were so meek and friendly, they were "ready to give the Christians all that they possess." Columbus called the new people Indians because he thought he was somewhere near Asia—what Europeans called the "Indies" of the Far East. He gave out red caps and glass beads, "that we might form great friendships," and he hoped to convert the Indians "to our holy faith by love [rather] than by force." He wrote that the people he met were "also fitted to be ruled and to be set to work" and should be taught "to go clothed and adopt our customs."

Columbus's words hinted at what was to come in the years ahead. First, the devout admiral was eager to turn these "Indians" into Christians. But he also wanted to set them to work. In return, Indians would learn Spanish customs, wear Spanish clothes, and be "ruled" by Spain—whether they wanted to or not. Columbus thought he could get his way because the islanders had few weapons and seemed afraid of fighting.

Then, too, there was the matter of gold. Putting Indians to work seemed to Columbus one way to profit from his discoveries. Finding gold struck him as an even better method, especially when the island people readily gave him the few bits and pieces of gold they possessed. Columbus looked for more on Hispaniola, a much larger island nearby, which today has become Haiti and the Dominican Republic. There, the Taino peoples lived in larger villages and possessed more gold ornaments, many representing the Taino's spirit-god Cemi. When Columbus returned to Europe with tales of precious metal, good farmland, and peaceful natives, several thousand Spaniards sailed to Hispaniola, seeking their fortune.

In truth, Columbus wasn't terribly interested in setting up colonies. He quarreled all too often and made enemies easily. So he left Hispaniola behind and sailed off to explore more of the Caribbean. Along one coast the ocean currents began to toss his ship strangely as night was coming on. Peering through the gloom, to his alarm he saw the sea rise "like a broad hill as high as the ship . . . and on it came, roaring with a mighty crash. . . . To this day I can feel the fear in my body." The twisty currents turned out to be coming from a huge river entering the ocean—the Orinoco, one of the largest in South America. A river that size could hardly come from an island, Columbus realized. In his journal he wrote, "I believe this is a very large continent which until now has remained unknown." That observation is why Columbus deserves credit not only for reaching the Americas but also for understanding what his discoveries meant. Furthermore, he pioneered a reliable sailing route to the Americas that was used by the Europeans who followed him.

But back in Hispaniola, Columbus discovered nothing but trouble. His colonists had come expecting to gather gold and spices "by the shovelful," and when they didn't, they complained bitterly. The admiral allowed them to make money by catching Indians and sending them to Spain to be sold as slaves. The peaceful Tainos were also given to the new settlers as workers—slaves in practice if not in name. Every colonist had "two or three Indians to serve him and dogs to hunt for him," Columbus wrote.

Hearing of the many complaints from his enemies, King Ferdinand and Queen Isabella had Columbus arrested and sent home in chains. He managed to regain their trust and make one final voyage, but it proved a disaster. Storms tossed his ships, hostile Indians attacked his men, disease left him half delirious, termites ate through the hulls of his ships. He returned home a beaten man.

Columbus had called himself admiral: his sailing skills were what brought him fame. The Spanish who followed became known by a different title: *conquistadors,* or conquerors. Grand as that name sounds, the first of this new breed began his rise to power on the run, in the dark, shut up in a barrel. It was supposed to be packed with supplies, but instead it was filled to the brim with Vasco Núñez de Balboa. Balboa had tried farming on Hispaniola, but he owed money and decided to leave town on the quiet. Somehow, he not only got himself loaded onto a ship in a barrel, he also smuggled aboard his most valuable possession, a stout dog with reddish fur and a black nose named Leoncico—"Little Lion." When the captain discovered Balboa, he threatened to maroon him on the nearest desert island. But the stowaway was a friendly fellow and the crewmen liked him better than they liked their captain. They demanded that he stay.

The episode says much about Balboa's character. During the early years of Spanish settlement, the islands of the Caribbean became a harsh, cruel world. Hundreds of thousands of Taino Indians died from war, slavery, overwork, and disease. Only a few Spanish officials were on hand to keep order and colonists often ignored them, enslaving Indians (against the king's orders) or killing Indians when they refused to work or provide gold. For his part, Balboa could be ruthless. More than once he set Leoncico on his enemies, to tear them limb from limb. (Like many peoples, including the Egyptians and Romans, the Spanish used dogs in war.) But Balboa understood that he needed friends to succeed—not only Spanish but Indian allies. Exploring the Isthmus of Panama, he conquered one Indian kingdom after another, but he didn't just sell his captives for slaves. He encouraged the leaders of these defeated peoples to join him as he conquered new territory for Spain.

More than a few agreed. After all, better to help these strange Europeans conquer some rival kingdom than have them causing trouble at home! One Indian, Panquiaco, watched one day as several of Balboa's lieutenants quarreled over gold they were weighing. Panquiaco angrily knocked over the scales and said, "If you are so hungry for gold that you leave your lands to cause strife in those of others, I will show you a province where you can quell this hunger." There was a kingdom along the coast of "the other sea," he reported, where people drank from goblets of solid gold.

Balboa's ears pricked up. What other sea, and what treasures? Hacking through thick jungle, he and his followers pushed across Panama's narrow isthmus until they reached the Pacific Ocean in 1513. At last, Europeans began to understand that America was made up of two large continents, one to the north and one to the south, connected by a narrow land bridge. Several years later, Ferdinand Magellan crossed the Pacific's wide waters. His ships became the first to circle the globe, sailing home by way of India and Africa, although Magellan himself was killed in the Philippines.

Balboa, the first conquistador, gained lands and treasure by using Indian allies to help conquer other Indian territories. So did another conquistador, Hernán Cortés. Like Balboa, Cortés heard rumors of rich empires yet undiscovered. In 1519 he and about six hundred followers marched toward the seven-thousand-foot-high plateau and the Valley of Mexico. The empire he was seeking, of course, was that of the Mexica, or Aztecs, whose capital lay on the glittering island-city of Tenochtitlán.

The march was not easy. Thousands upon thousands of Indians lived along the route and one of the nations, Tlaxcala, fought Cortés bitterly. But then Tlaxcala's rulers decided to help rather than to oppose the Spanish. They bore no love for the Mexica, who for years had forced them to send warriors to be sacrificed in religious ceremonies. The Mexica worshiped a god named Huitzilopochtli, whose job, according to sacred teachings, was nothing less than to sustain the life of the sun. Its burnishing rays brought life to all people, all animals, and all plants. Yet every day the sun was driven out of the sky by the moon and the stars. It would return again the next morning, the Mexica believed, only so long as Huitzilopochtli provided it with enough life spirit. That could be obtained only through the gift of the lifeblood of humans.

The Mexica believed this custom of human sacrifice to be their duty. They forced the peoples they conquered to send three or four thousand people a year to be sacrificed atop sacred pyramids. There, priests cut open the prisoners' chests with sharp knives of black obsidian in order to give the god these beating hearts and save the sun. Small wonder Tlaxcala decided to send its army of twenty thousand along with Cortés.

But once he reached Tenochtitlán, Cortés left behind his Indian allies. With a daring that was nearly foolhardy, he and his men marched along one of the narrow causeways that led across Lake Texcoco into the island-city. The Spaniards were astonished by the bustling markets and merchants, canals and canoes, goldsmiths, feather workers, baths and steam houses, torchlight dances, gardens, zoos . . . The city contained "all the things to be found under the heavens," Cortés marveled.

The emperor of the Mexica then was Moctezuma. With good reason he feared and distrusted these unknown people, with their swords of steel, strange horses, and ferocious dogs. But once Cortés saw "the size and strength of the city," he recognized that the Mexica had the power to surround and kill him "without any defense being possible." A more cautious man might have retreated. But Cortés doubled the stakes by making Moctezuma a hostage in his own city. The conquistadors no longer allowed the emperor to live in his palace; he must sleep in the Spanish quarters. When Moctezuma walked about town, Spanish guards kept him company. For eight months Cortés tried to find some way to convince the Mexica to surrender without a fight, but as time went on they became angrier and more rebellious because their king was led about like a puppet by these strangers. At last Moctezuma agreed to address his people and plead for cooperation. But as he stood on a roof to speak, his subjects pelted him with stones; he died the following day. Cortés and his soldiers tried to sneak out of the city in the dead of night but the Mexica discovered them and began battle. Cortés himself almost plunged into Lake Texcoco as he and his men fought their way off the city-island.

Eventually, Spanish reinforcements arrived from the coast. Cortés surrounded Tenochtitlán so that no one could get out to bring food. Then he and his Indian allies captured the city section by section. The Mexica surrendered, their once-splendid capital in ruins.

The sad truth is, the world in AD 1500 was a brutal place. When Cortés first followed Moctezuma up the 113 steep steps of a pyramid to the temple of the sun, he was horrified by the skulls and the blood-caked altar. But the European "conquerors" were ruthless and bloody, too. Soon after Balboa discovered the Pacific, a jealous Spanish governor had him beheaded. His dog Leoncico was poisoned. And the minor officer who arrested Balboa—Francisco Pizarro—went on to conquer another civilization in South America, the Inca empire. This man, too, was eventually stabbed to death by his rivals.

The new age of gold turned out to be nothing like the legends of the golden age. The Indians of the Americas were no more innocent than the Spanish were gentle. Yet despite their belief in human sacrifice, the Mexica gave the world a stunning civilization of warriors and poets, craft workers and astronomers. The Spanish, too, were destined to shape the Americas in creative ways, in spite of the conquistadors' appetite for gold.

But in the next chapter, there is one last conqueror to meet—more deadly and dangerous than Balboa, Cortés, and Pizarro combined.

5

WHEN WORLDS COLLIDE

SOMETIMES THE TINIEST events have immense consequences. Who would think it would be worth mentioning that somewhere in Hispaniola, a conquistador pulled on boots that he had stored in a sea chest? Or that a woman shook out a blanket to air that she had brought from Spain? Or that an African coughed as he sat in an Indian house near the Gulf of Mexico? Yet such small events sparked big changes.

Before 1492, each half of the world had developed largely on its own. The trees in America "were as different from ours as day from night," commented Columbus. Nowhere in Europe did eels produce electric shocks to defend themselves, as they did in South America. Nowhere did ring-tailed, mask-eyed creatures roam European forests, as raccoons did in North America. For their part, American Indians were astonished by the strange horses and dogs Europeans brought with them.

Consider the colonist shaking out her blanket. When people packed for a voyage, a few seeds sometimes got folded up in their belongings, or perhaps they stuck to the mud clinging to a pair of boots. In the Americas, some of those seeds, unnoticed, dropped off, fluttered away, then sprouted and spread. Dandelions and blue-grass are common sights today in American fields; both came from Europe after 1492. Colonists brought with them lemons, oranges, bananas, and figs from Africa; melons, radishes, and onions from Europe. Juan Garrido, a black conquistador who was with Cortés at Tenochtitlán and afterward settled there, became the first "to plant and harvest wheat in this land."

Horses had an especially hard time crossing the Atlantic since they were kept belowdecks. When a storm threatened, the Spanish slipped belly bands under the animals and hoisted them until their hooves dangled in the air to prevent frightened stallions from rear-ing and raising havoc. In the tropics, calm seas were even more dan-gerous—the fierce heat could kill the poor animals in their dark, stuffy quarters. For that reason those deadly regions of the ocean were known as the "horse latitudes." European pigs were also trans-ported as the conquistadors' insurance policy against starvation, herded along to feed men on the march. And as Leoncico showed, conquistadors brought dogs both as companions and warriors.

Just as important, American plants and animals traveled to the other half of the world. Modern Italian cooking could hardly exist without the tomato, an American fruit. Spaniards brought home the white potato that Indians grew in the highlands of the Andes Mountains. By the 1800s the Irish depended so much on the crop that peasants starved by the thousands when a plant disease ruined it. American corn spread not only across Europe but also through Asia; today, in addition to corn on the cob, corn bread, and pop-corn, a thousand different foods and beverages are sweetened by corn syrup, while cornmeal is fed to farm animals and even to fish that are farmed. The Indians who first raised the vegetable five thousand years ago called it *teosinte,* and at that time an ear grew only as big as a man's finger. Over centuries, Indian farmers gradu-ally increased the plant's size.

Plant seeds are small, but they are visible to the human eye. The unintended voyagers that journeyed with a man named Francisco de Eguía were invisible. They were microorganisms—germs. We know almost nothing of de Eguía other than that he was African and came with the conquistadors; and of course people of that day knew nothing of invisible disease-spreading germs. Soon after arriving in Central America, Francisco fell ill, wracked by a cough and burning fever. Sores appeared all over his body—*viruelas,* the Spanish called them. They were caused by smallpox, a disease that had tormented Europeans for centuries. By 1520 most Europeans were able to resist it to some degree because their bodies had been exposed to the germs for so many years. They had developed an immunity.

But smallpox was entirely new to Indians, who had built up no such immunity. Its victims were plagued by sores covering "their faces, their heads, their breasts," recalled one of the Mexica. The sick "could not move; they could not stir; they could not change position. . . . And if they stirred, much did they cry out." Fathers and mothers, sisters and brothers died in agony, lying next to one another. So many perished in Tenochtitlán that houses were sometimes just pulled down over the bodies to serve as graves. And because the sick were too weak even to find food or "go to the fountain for a gourd full of water," thousands more died from starvation.

Smallpox helps explain how Cortés managed to conquer a city of over one hundred thousand inhabitants. True, the Mexica had never fought armies that possessed cannons, war dogs, and rearing horses. But Cortés had only a limited number of such weapons and animals. It was the invisible newcomers that turned the tide in his favor. When the victorious Spanish marched into the city, they discovered that "the streets, squares, houses, and courts were filled with bodies, so that it was almost impossible to pass. Even Cortés was sick from the stench." Sadly, smallpox was only the beginning. By 1600, fourteen epidemics had spread through Central America; at least seventeen swept South America. Historians and archaeologists can make only very rough estimates of the death toll. But European diseases such as measles, typhoid fever, influenza, diphtheria, and mumps, together with the wars of the conquistadors, seem to have killed anywhere from 50 to 90 million people in Central and South America. Never in history have so many died of disease in a single century.

North America was spared these deadly epidemics at first because it proved a much harder land for the Spanish to conquer. Its Indians possessed no glittering cities and large empires, only smaller territories, each controlled by a different chief. And even friendly Indians found it hard to get along with Spaniards who marched into their towns, several hundred strong, and asked for gold and silver as well as food, staying for months on end. Juan Ponce de León led several expeditions to Florida, but he was driven away by a hail of arrows. From the Pacific Francisco Vázquez de Coronado marched into the southwest, where some of his men became the first Europeans to see the Grand Canyon. Coronado himself ventured across the Plains as far as present-day Kansas with nearly three thousand soldiers, women, slaves, and Indian allies, making war as he went. These expeditions of discovery almost always ended badly for both the Indians and the Spanish. When conquistadors suspected that the Indians had deceived them, they took hostages, set the dogs on their captives, or killed them. Ponce de León died of a wound inflicted by an Indian's poison arrow. Coronado returned to Mexico badly injured and bankrupt.

Better, perhaps, to speak instead of four very different conquistadors, ones who proved that not all newcomers to North America behaved badly. The four were part of an expedition to Florida led by Panfilo de Narváez, a conquistador of the usual stripe. His band plunged miserably from one Indian settlement to another, looking for gold, fighting, and, eventually, starving. His men ate the expedition's horses one by one as they put together makeshift rafts for a desperate journey back to Spanish settlements in Mexico. Narváez was blown into the Gulf of Mexico one night while sleeping in his raft; the remaining vessels broke apart soon after, along the coast of present-day Texas.

In the end, only four men survived: a thin fellow named Cabeza de Vaca, the expedition's treasurer; two Spaniards named Castillo and Dorantes; and a friendly African nicknamed Estevanico (or "Little Steve"—so named, perhaps, because he was really rather large). For nearly six years, the four men were slaves to the local Indians, forced to dig up roots, haul water, and tend the smoke fires used to keep off mosquitoes. Finally the men escaped and began hiking across Texas—feet blistered, hands bloody, no clothes to keep them warm. Over the years they had occasionally tended sick Indians, and now on their trek they discovered that the stories of their healing had spread. Indians from all over brought ill people to be cured by these strangers—holy medicine men and "children of the sun." Hundreds, even thousands of Indians sometimes escorted the pilgrims on their journey. For three years the four men hiked—across Texas, over the mountains, eventually nearing the Pacific Ocean. No longer were they conquerors, looking for jewels and riches. They were healing Indians, working with them, cooperating together. Cabeza de Vaca had a vision—to bring together Spaniards and Indians to farm and live peacefully. It was an unusual dream for those times. It suggested that very different sorts of people might find a way to come together without insisting that one group be the rulers, the other the ruled. It was a novel dream of creating one out of many.

One day the travelers spied Spanish men riding across the country. The soldiers were dumbfounded to see four strangers of their own nationality walking nearly naked and trailed by hundreds of Indians. Cabeza de Vaca's beard reached to his chest and the hair on his head hung to his waist. Were they truly from the Narváez expedition, lost nearly ten years ago? Surely that was impossible! But it wasn't.

Sadly, what turned out to be truly impossible was the dream of living peacefully with the Indians. For the Spaniards who found

Cabeza de Vaca were slave hunters. "We had great disputes with them," he noted, "because they wanted to enslave the Indians we had brought with us." When he returned to Spain, he asked his monarch to grant him the lands first given to Narváez. But Emperor Charles had already promised the territory to another adventurer, Hernando de Soto. He, like so many before him, set out on yet another treasure hunt filled with hardships, battles with Indians, and little else. Exhausted after three years of marching, de Soto died along the Mississippi River in 1542, thousands of miles from home. His soldiers wrapped his body with stones and sank it one night in the middle of the river, so the Indians would not know the conquistador had died.

North America had defeated Europeans, for the time being. Although the Spanish continued to nibble at the edges of the continent, no European entered its heart, as de Soto had, until 1682. In that year the French explorer La Salle canoed down much of the Mississippi River, all the way to the Gulf of Mexico. 1542 to 1682— think about those 140 years between de Soto and La Salle. It's a *huge* silence in the history books. If we knew nothing about the 140 years between 1860 and the year 2000, we would never have heard of the Civil War, World Wars I and II, the invention of skyscrapers, airplanes, computers, and a thousand other things. What happened in America between 1542 and 1682?

The two explorers had very different experiences on their trips. On the Mississippi de Soto's men were forced to fight their way past one Indian kingdom after another. Large dugout canoes packed with warriors swarmed the river. La Salle, on the other hand, saw only a dozen small settlements along many of the same stretches. Why the change? Historians now realize that European diseases did not bypass North America after all. De Soto brought hundreds of pigs along on his march, and some escaped into the forest. Indians stole others, and the pigs may have begun the spread of deadly infections in the southeast. Whether or not hogs were to blame, one way or another European diseases took their toll.

There is one final twist to this 140-year silence. As we saw in chapter 3, colonists who came to America in the 1600s wrote about the abundant wildlife: bison wandering as far east as Virginia, streams crowded with fish, huge flocks of birds. We have long considered these to be examples of what North America was like before 1492. But all these animals may point instead to the catastrophe of European disease. If thousands upon thousands of Indians died between 1542 and 1682, there would have been fewer hunters left to chase beasts, fish, and birds. Did the number of animals grow? De Soto saw plenty of Indians but not a single bison along the Mississippi River. La Salle saw few Indians but many bison.

Historians have long spoken of the Americas as the New World, contrasted with the Old World of Europe, Africa, and Asia. I have not used those terms because the Americas were certainly not new to the Indians, who had been living there for thousands of years. But two hundred years after the first contact between Europeans and Americans, much of North and South America *was* new—vastly different from the world before 1492. The Americas had *become* a new world, transformed by wars of conquest, germs of smallpox, and the seeds of dandelions, melons, onions, and oranges.

6

How Can I Be Saved?

IN 1505—THE SAME SUMMER that an old and discouraged Christopher Columbus sat down to write his last will—a twenty-one-year-old student trudged a dusty road in Saxony, one of about 150 small German states that were a part of the Holy Roman Empire. On a road like that, the young student might have passed peasants in a field cutting hay with their scythes or perhaps a couple of girls in front of a hut playing knucklebones, a game like jacks played with the bones of sheep. As the student made his way, the sky darkened and thunderclouds rolled in, letting loose a torrent of rain. Suddenly, a bolt of lightning struck so close that it knocked him to the ground. "St. Anne help me!" he cried. "I will become a monk."

Some folk might have forgotten such a vow once the storm passed, marveling at how a close call could scare a man half out of his wits. Not young Martin Luther. He abandoned his studies in the law and dedicated his life to living in poverty as a monk.

Like many Europeans at the time, Luther believed that eternal life was promised to those who followed Jesus, and that the agony of hell awaited those who were not saved. The Roman Catholic Church offered many rituals to help a believer reach for salvation. Baptism washed away a child's sins in case he or she should die young. Confessing their sins to priests helped adults mend their ways. The last rites of placing oil on the forehead pointed a dying believer toward heaven. Then, too, many churches kept relics— objects passed down over the centuries that were said to be associated with saints. At Wittenberg, where Luther came to live, the castle church proudly claimed to have four hairs from the head of Mary, mother of Christ; a wisp of straw from the cradle in which the baby Jesus once lay; and over nineteen thousand pieces of bone from various saints. A believer who paid respects to these relics (and made a contribution of money) was told that God forgave many sins for such prayers and gifts.

Joining a religious order—becoming a monk, a friar, or a nun— marked an even more dramatic path to a holy life. As a boy, Luther had looked in wonder at William of Anhalt, a prince who had given up his worldly wealth to walk the streets begging—"mere bone and skin," Luther recalled. "No one could look upon him without feeling ashamed of his own life." And that was Luther's problem. Even after giving up the comforts of the world, he felt unworthy in God's eyes. Yes, he prayed. Yes, he went to mass. He fasted. He even went on a pilgrimage to distant Rome, home of the Pope. Nothing convinced him that he led a good enough life. In contrast, Luther was shocked to meet priests in Rome who seemed unconcerned about religion. "Passa, passa!" one barked, before Luther had finished confessing his sins, "Get on with you! Move along!"

After years of anguish, Luther found comfort in the Bible passage that declared, "The just shall live by faith." No one could ever pile up enough good deeds to be saved, he decided. A Christian was saved by faith alone—the faith that Jesus had lived a perfect life and had died for the sins of all people. Equally important, Luther put the Bible at the center of his religion. He rejected many of the

Catholic Church's rituals. Did the Bible say saints' relics could get a person into heaven? If not, then relics must go. So also last rites and confessions to priests. The two principles Luther clung to were first, that believers were saved by "faith alone" and second, that the Bible—and only the Bible—provided the path to salvation.

As legend has it, in 1517 Luther nailed a paper listing his ideas to the door of the castle church. Taken together, these ninety-five theses marked the start of a reform movement that became known as the Protestant Reformation.

Next to Luther, one of the most important Reformation leaders was the French minister John Calvin. The two men couldn't have been more different. Luther was down-to-earth, friendly, and emotional. His broad face lit up when he smiled and looked thunderous when he frowned. He spoke plainly, as when he warned the "gross, ignorant fools at Rome" to "keep their distance from Germany" or else "jump into the Rhine or the nearest river, and take a cold bath." John Calvin, on the other hand, was cool and logical—a brilliant thinker whose long, angled face and pointed beard shone with the confidence that he was carrying out God's word. He gathered his followers in the city of Geneva in the Alps.

Calvin dreamed of a time when "the elect"—believers whom God had saved—would govern the world in peace. In Geneva, he and his reformers gained enough influence to set up a holy commonwealth, a government run on Protestant principles. Some of the city's laws seem petty or harsh today. You could be fined for passing tobacco to another worshipper or making a noise in church. You could not name your child after Catholic saints because Protestants didn't believe that the earthly church had the power to decide who was a saint. But Calvin's strict laws were meant to make an imperfect world better. Reformers flocked to Geneva to see how a holy commonwealth might work.

It may seem strange for a history of the United States to spend so much time in distant Europe. Why speak of Luther and his theses when Cortés was challenging the Mexica during those very same years? Why watch Calvin in Geneva instead of de Soto along the banks of the Mississippi? But ideas are a bit like dandelions. Like a tiny seed clinging to an explorer's boot, an idea can cross the Atlantic lodged in the back of someone's head. Give the dandelion a few hundred years to grow and spread and America looks different. Give an idea the same amount of time and that distant land may be truly transformed. Luther's ideas and Calvin's would transform America.

But just as plants can change over time, so can ideas. Consider Luther's belief that the Bible was the only guide to salvation. What made it revolutionary? During the Middle Ages, popes and church councils acted as the final judges of the Bible's meaning—not ordinary people. Luther, on the other hand, wanted everybody to read the Bible. "The Christian must judge for himself," he insisted. The Bible should be available in the language of ordinary folk, not just in Latin, which only educated people understood. Luther translated the Bible into German. Thousands of copies were printed. Thousands of people began reading it, now free to judge for themselves. Then there was Calvin's idea of a holy commonwealth. Many Protestants would come to America hoping to found communities in which people supported one another for the "common wealth." By that, Calvin meant not just wealth in the sense of money but also spiritual wealth—the kind gained by supporting one another as the faithful lived together.

Two big ideas: *judge for yourself* and *build a holy commonwealth*. They would have a tremendous influence on what it meant to be an American. But when the flood of newcomers actually arrived in America and began to judge for themselves, they had very different ideas of how a holy commonwealth should work.

In Europe, quarrels over the Reformation's new ideas began almost immediately. When Catholic officials demanded that Luther renounce his beliefs, he refused. "Here I stand. God help me. Amen." He insisted that he was bound "to defend the truth with my blood and death." Catholics felt just as strongly. "A single monk who goes counter to all Christianity for a thousand years must be wrong," insisted young Charles V, the Holy Roman Emperor. "I am resolved to stake my land, my friends, my body, my blood and my soul," he declared after hearing Luther speak. "I will proceed against him as a notorious heretic." In Europe, someone convicted of being a heretic—teaching false religious ideas—was burned at the stake. The punishment was fierce, excruciatingly painful, and every bit as terrifying as having one's heart cut out with an obsidian knife. Fortunately for Luther, Charles was never able to carry out his vow. But thousands of other heretics were burned in many countries, including a scholar condemned by Calvin's commonwealth in Geneva. The disputes sparked by the Reformation plunged Europe into a century and a half of religious war, as Protestants and Catholics battled each other bitterly.

If half the people in a kingdom became Protestant and half remained Catholic, could a monarch allow both groups to believe as they pleased? Few rulers in Luther's time thought so. Most monarchs allowed only one church to be established: the one that agreed with their beliefs. Subjects who disagreed either had to keep silent and attend the established church or worship secretly and risk being arrested, jailed, or burned at the stake. Some nations, including Spain, Portugal, and Italy, remained strongly Catholic. Others, including England, Scotland, and the Netherlands, became Protestant. It was not long before the wars of religion spilled into the Americas.

That meant trouble for Catholic Spain. When the gold and jewels from the Mexica ran out, a new set of adventurers discovered huge deposits of silver in the mountains of Mexico and South America. The biggest mines were at Potosí, thirteen thousand feet above sea level in the Andes, where the thin air made breathing difficult. No matter: by 1600 more than 150,000 people worked there, making Potosí the largest settlement in North or South America and bigger than any city in Spain itself. Indians were forced to toil in deep tunnels where the dust brought sickness and death from black lung disease. (The Indian name for the place meant "the mountain that eats people.") Thirty thousand tons of silver were hauled out in carts, refined in furnaces, and shipped to Spain as well as to the Philippines and China. Spain's power and prosperity increased by leaps and bounds.

The Spanish also sailed up North America's coasts, but they planted no permanent colonies. A handwritten scrawl on an old map gives a good hint why. "No hay alla de oro," it read: "There is no gold there." On the other hand, the treasure fleets that sailed from Central and South America were like magnets to Spain's rivals. French pirates raided them so often that Spain was losing almost half its silver. When several hundred French Protestants built a fort in Florida, Spain wiped out the colony and established St. Augustine, Florida.

English Protestants also chased after Spanish treasure. The men who did are sometimes called sea dogs—adventurers prowling the oceans for fame and glory. But *sea dog* is simply a polite way of saying *pirate*. One such adventurer, Francis Drake, plundered Spanish treasure in the Caribbean and, even more boldly, sailed around South America into the Pacific Ocean, which the Spanish were used to having all to themselves. Drake continued as far north as California—and then struck east across the Pacific, his ship loaded with silver, voyaging around the world to reach home. Queen Elizabeth knighted him for his service and took half of the booty he brought back.

Several years later, in 1585, Drake's friend Walter Raleigh sponsored an expedition that landed off the coast of present-day North Carolina at Roanoke Island. Very likely Raleigh hoped to use the new outpost as a way station from which to attack Spain. The Indians at Roanoke, reports said, were "most gentle, loving, and faithful . . . such as lived after the manner of the golden age." (Do these words sound familiar?) But the English at Roanoke quarreled with the Indians, just as the conquistadors had. One English commander, Sir Richard Grenville, liked to show how tough he was:

The age of gold, 1492–1600. Europeans first made contact with North America through the Caribbean Sea. From the islands of Hispaniola, Cuba, and Puerto Rico, the Spanish branched out toward the mainland, which became known as the Spanish Main. Nearly a century went by before the English began to challenge Spain's huge treasure fleets.

after drinking three or four glasses of wine, he would "take the glasses between his teeth, and crush them in pieces, and swallow them down, so that oftentimes the blood ran out of his mouth." Under such violent leaders, Roanoke nearly starved.

Then for several years nobody from England could get back to the colony with supplies and additional colonists. In 1588 Spain had sent its vast navy, the Armada, to invade England. The more nimble English defeated their foes, but by the time a relief mission returned to Roanoke, it found only ruins, a few pieces of rusting armor, and the word "Croatoan" carved on a tree.

Did the English move to another location—this "Croatoan"? No one knew and the colony was counted lost. Spain could breathe a sigh of relief, but only for a few decades. The English were not done with America.

7

SAINTS AND STRANGERS

IN 1620 FIVE OR SIX Nauset Indians were trotting down the Cape Cod beach one November day, their dog in the lead, when they saw sixteen strangers coming toward them. The Indians didn't wait for an introduction; they turned and ran, whistling for their dog to follow.

The newcomers were a scouting party of Pilgrims—so named by William Bradford, one of their leaders, who was along that day. Following the tracks of the Nausets, the men eventually crossed a stream, "of which we were heartily glad, and sat us down and drunk our first *New-England* water." As they hiked through the woods, they ran across an Indian deer trap baited with acorns spread around a hidden noose. As Bradford walked through, the trap gave "a sudden jerk up, and he was immediately caught by the leg." A "very pretty device," commented one of the men.

Of course, by 1620 when the Pilgrims arrived, Spanish, French, and English ships had been exploring the coast for a hundred years. Europeans were no longer new to the Indians. They were only foreigners and people to be wary of. The Nausets fled out of fear that this was another band of Europeans come to do battle. But the Pilgrims didn't stay on Cape Cod. They sailed west until they reached a more sheltered harbor, unloading their gear near the boulder known today as Plymouth Rock. The following spring, a Wampanoag Indian named Squanto appeared to welcome them— speaking English, much to the Pilgrims' delight.

That first winter had been a hard one. With no time to plant crops, half the Pilgrims had died. Squanto showed the newcomers how to plant Indian corn and fertilize it by placing a dead fish atop each seed. Was this more Indian craft, like the deer trap? Probably not. Squanto almost certainly learned about fish fertilizer from Europeans. Six years before the Pilgrims arrived, he had been captured by an Englishman and taken to Spain to be sold in the slave markets. Somehow he reached England, learned the language, and returned to America. Sadly, he also learned about European diseases, which swept through his homeland while he was gone. So many Indians died, Bradford recalled, that "not being able to bury one another, their skulls and bones were found in many places lying still above the ground . . . a very sad spectacle to behold."

The Pilgrims were the first of many Protestants who came into New England looking to create a holy commonwealth of their own. To these reformers, who wanted to follow the teachings of the Bible more closely, England seemed not nearly pure enough. True, the Church of England was Protestant, but its members (called Anglicans) still celebrated Christmas and saints' days. Where did the Bible mention *those* holidays? The Anglican Church was governed by archbishops who wore handsome silk vestments. True ministers, reformers insisted, should wear simple robes and hold services according to "the primitive pattern of the first churches." Anglicans mocked the reformers as "Puritans" and the name stuck.

Although Puritans thought that the Church of England strayed from biblical teachings, they were willing to remain within it and try to make it better. Other Protestants withdrew completely. These

Separatists, as they were known, included several hundred folk who lived in the town of Scrooby. It was from these people that the Pilgrims were drawn. Mocked by their neighbors for their religious beliefs, fined and harassed by the government, they departed England for the Dutch Low Countries, where the laws allowed them to worship as they saw fit. But twelve years among the Dutch made them homesick for English ways and uncertain of their future. So in 1620 the *Mayflower* set sail for the English colony of Virginia, where King James had given the Pilgrims permission to settle, so long as they behaved "peaceably." Unfortunately, the *Mayflower* was blown off course. And the Pilgrims' charter, the legal document from King James setting out what they could do, said nothing about settling elsewhere.

On board ship, the passengers made a remarkable decision: to create a government of their own, combining together "into a civil body politic" that would make "just and equal laws" for the colony's good. This agreement, the Mayflower Compact, had no authority in British law, but the king's royal officials were three thousand miles away—so how could they complain? The new colony of Plymouth Plantation began holding annual elections in which the free men chose a governor and some assistants to manage Plymouth's affairs.

The idea that people might elect representatives to govern themselves would become central to the founders of the future United States. But the belief was unusual in 1620. Kings became distinctly peevish when their subjects spoke up too much. That was one reason King James disliked Puritans and Separatists—they might judge for themselves, as Luther would say. "Then Jack and Tom and Will and Dick shall meet," complained the king, "and at their pleasures censure [criticize] me and my council and all our proceedings." In truth, the Pilgrims didn't mean to speak out against the king. James *did* rule over them, they agreed. What worried them more were the people on board ship whom Bradford called the "strangers." The fact is, fewer than half of the *Mayflower*'s 102 passengers were Pilgrims. The rest were other English folk, brought along to help pay expenses.

To these voyagers, the Pilgrims were the strangers. And when a few of these folk discovered that the *Mayflower* wasn't heading for Virginia anymore, they pointed out that the Pilgrims had no "power to command them." The strangers were in the majority, after all. Bradford called their complaints "discontented and mutinous," but at least he didn't ignore them. The Mayflower Compact allowed all free men to take part in the colony government, not just Pilgrims.

The Pilgrims were happy enough just to be left alone in America. The next holy commonwealth founded in New England aimed higher. Ten years after the Pilgrims landed, nearly a thousand settlers came to begin the Massachusetts Bay Colony, forty miles north of Plymouth. On the voyage over, their governor, John Winthrop, spoke to them. God was making an example of their commonwealth, he said. "For we must consider that we shall be as a city upon a hill. The eyes of all people are upon us." If the colony followed God's law, "men shall say of succeeding plantations, 'may the Lord make it like that of New England.'" Like John Calvin of Geneva, these Puritans were not only determined to succeed but also confident of their place in history.

Within a few years, the Massachusetts Bay Colony dwarfed Plymouth Plantation. Most who joined the Puritans' "Great Migration" traveled as families. They settled in bustling Boston and other villages around the bay. A farmer might own many acres outside town, but he walked to those lands from his village home. This custom made for tightly knit communities. And well educated ones: like Luther, Puritans wanted everyone to be able to read the Bible. Perhaps six out of ten men who came to Massachusetts could read—double the usual number in England. Fewer women could, only about three in ten. (If you wonder why—and you should— we'll learn more later.) Furthermore, almost every New England town had a public elementary school for boys; and many girls learned to read at what were called "dame schools."

From the start, the Puritans discovered how hard it was to create a holy commonwealth. How pure should their churches be? Unlike Anglicans, Puritans felt that church members should include only the saved, not everyone in the community. All colonists were required to attend services, even those who weren't Christian. But to become a full church member, a person had to explain the personal religious experience that brought him or her to be born anew in the Holy Spirit—in short, how the person had been "converted." As for keeping the colony pure, Massachusetts Bay openly favored its own religion. Unlike in the Pilgrim colony at Plymouth, only church members could vote in elections. Anyone who taught ideas leading to the "destruction of the souls of men" was banished from the colony; and if such undesirables returned to again spread false beliefs, their tongues might be bored out with a hot iron or they could be hanged. (To be fair, the laws of England listed even more crimes for which the punishment was hanging or burning.)

But even Puritans disagreed among themselves about religion. Hartford, Connecticut, was founded by Puritans who believed that the Massachusetts authorities were too strict. New Haven was begun by those who thought they were not strict enough. And some settlers wanted very little to do with religion. A rambunctious fur trader named Thomas Morton set up his own outpost, called Merrymount, near Plymouth. Morton enjoyed the company of Indians, learned their language, and complained that the Pilgrim graces before meals went on so long that "the meat was cold." Morton and his trader friends invited the Indians to dance, sing, and carouse around an eighty-foot maypole, a creation made from a tall pine tree with a pair of deer antlers nailed on top, which was then "reared up" on the highest ground of Merrymount. The Pilgrims were horrified by such irreligious celebrations and doubly angry when Morton traded guns to the Indians in return for their furs. Pilgrim leaders took him prisoner and forced him to leave

New England. A city on a hill was one thing, a monstrous maypole on a mountain quite another.

Did the Pilgrims go too far in driving out unholy traders? Both Puritans and Pilgrims discovered that making the rules to keep other people holy led to unexpected difficulties. It was a bit like that walk in the Cape Cod woods with William Bradford. One moment you're enjoying a fine morning hike; the next a snare has grabbed hold of your leg and won't let go.

It was a minister named Roger Williams who came to understand the trouble with forcing people to be pure. Williams was friendly, generous, and soft-spoken. But he sailed into Boston with a burning desire to become the holiest of the holy. When the members of one church asked him to be their minister, he refused. He was a Separatist, and this church wouldn't condemn the Church of England outright. Not pure enough! So Williams moved to Plymouth, where Separatists did condemn the Church of England. But some of the Pilgrims there returned on visits to England and there they attended Anglican services. Still not pure enough! Williams went back to Massachusetts, where he continued to speak out. True Christians should not pray in the company of unsaved people, he declared—even if they were your own wife and children. When Massachusetts Bay tried to discipline Williams for preaching his unusual ideas, he condemned the colony's ministers. The Puritans then banished Roger Williams before he could banish them. He fled in the middle of a howling, snowy gale to spend the winter with the Wampanoag Indians, who agreed to shelter this stranger.

And here Roger Williams made an astonishing turnabout. He remained as devout as ever. But he decided that in an imperfect world, it was impossible for churches to figure out who was truly pure. He decided instead that he would "pray with all comers"— the sinners, the saved, and anybody in between. Not only that, he announced that government had no business meddling in religious affairs. It was not the state's job to make people go to church if they didn't want to, or to decide who was a dangerous heretic. Forcing someone to worship in a certain way "stinks in God's nostrils," he said. The government's business should be kept separate from the church's.

So a strong line was drawn between the church and the state in Williams's settlement, which eventually became the colony of Rhode Island. Roger Williams had mastered an important truth: that a state could not make one out of many by forcing everyone to believe the same way. Better to "pray with all comers" and hope for the best.

8

Boom Country

IT WAS PROBABLY LUCKY that the Pilgrims were blown off course and never reached Virginia, where they were headed in 1620. By then that unfortunate colony had spent more than a dozen years struggling desperately just to survive. But some Virginians were beginning to discover the secret of how to prosper—and their solution would not have pleased the Pilgrims, people who wanted only to create a holy community and farm in peace. Virginia was turning itself into what we might call a rip-roaring boom country.

A number of things are needed to make a country boom. The first is something that everybody wants—yet something that's not easy to get. And when that something is discovered, people rush in, eager to control it, sell it, and make a handsome profit. Think about the gold and silver the conquistadors brought home. Potosí was the biggest settlement in the Americas by 1620 because it sat on a mountain of silver. It was prime boom country. But people run after more than silver and gold. Recall the Asian spices that came down the Silk Road—or consider a red berry in Africa that the people of Kaffa grew. When roasted, it made a drink that Europeans quickly learned to savor. The Turks called it *kahve;* the Dutch (who learned of it from the Turks) called it *koffie.* The English created special places to drink it called coffeehouses. Puritans liked it because, unlike alcoholic drinks, it made you more alert. As one Puritan poet wrote, "Coffee arrives, that grave and wholesome liquor, / That heals the stomach, makes the genius quicker."

But the food product that sparked the biggest boom was sugar, a sweetener we now take for granted. During the Middle Ages, sugar was so scarce that only wealthy lords and ladies could afford it, usually as a medicine for a sore throat or upset stomach. Spain and Portugal began growing the crop on islands off the coast of Africa; then South America and the Caribbean became prime sugar regions. Sugarcane was grown on large farms called plantations, where dozens or even hundreds of workers chopped down the tall stalks and carried them to mills, where they were crushed and boiled into molasses (mostly used to make rum) or into sugar itself. By the early 1600s, plantations in the Americas were sending thousands of tons of sugar and molasses to Europe. Gold, silver, sugar, coffee, spices, tea . . . What do you have that's scarce that everyone wants? It's not too much to say that the age of discovery, which brought together the two halves of the world, created boom countries everywhere.

A number of English merchants and gentlemen pooled their money together to form what was known as a joint stock company, with the idea of making a new colony boom. Virginia's climate was too cool to grow sugar or coffee, but the new Virginia Company sent 105 colonists to settle on Chesapeake Bay in 1607. They had high hopes. No holy "city on a hill" for them—what they sought were "gold-showing mountains." On a river flowing into Chesapeake Bay they founded Jamestown.

Alas, neither mountains nor gold was anywhere to be seen. Jamestown might have withered away like Roanoke, except for Captain John Smith, a soldier of fortune who had knocked around the far corners of Europe before joining the Virginia Company. Smith's confidence in himself was as large as his big bushy beard. However, the expedition's high-born gentlemen hated this common fellow. They had been ready to hang him from a gallows at one point, for the unlikely crime of plotting to "murder" the colony's leaders "and make himself king." But Smith talked his way out of that scrape. After several months in Virginia, with many colonists dying from "burning fevers" and almost everyone dissatisfied with the colony's original leaders, Smith took charge and set everyone to work. He wouldn't allow colonists who didn't pull their weight to eat.

Heading upriver to trade for food, Smith was taken prisoner by Indians. Some twenty thousand Native Americans lived around Chesapeake Bay, held together in a loose confederation by a chief named Powhatan. After calling a council, Powhatan ordered that Smith's brains be dashed out with a war club. It was then that one of the chief's young daughters, Pocahontas, stepped in and begged that the captain's life be spared. Or so Smith claimed years later—no one else mentioned the tale and he was *very* good at telling stories. If Powhatan did threaten Smith, it may have been merely to scare him, to make sure the newcomers understood who was in charge around Chesapeake Bay. Later, the English held the same sort of ceremony—a "coronation" at which they asked Powhatan to kneel and accept a crown as a subject king. The colonists had a "foul trouble" making him do it, succeeding only by "leaning hard on his shoulders."

If Smith had remained in Virginia, he might have leaned hard enough on everyone to make the colony work. But one night as he slept, a sack of gunpowder caught fire and exploded, badly burning him. The powder may have been lighted by his enemies in a plot to kill him. In any event, Smith returned to England and the colonists went back to quarreling and starving. Even after ten years, Jamestown was in such bad shape that when a new governor arrived from England, he found only a half dozen houses standing, the fort fence broken, "the bridge in pieces, the well of fresh water spoiled; the storehouse . . . used for a church." The town looked terrible— there were even plants growing in "the marketplace and streets."

That was the one odd detail in the middle of utter ruin. The plants in the streets had not sprung up from neglect. They had been *planted*—as a crop called tobacco, the very crop Virginians needed to set their colony booming. Settlers were so eager to make money that they planted tobacco in every open spot they could find. King James thought the custom of smoking was "loathsome to the eye, hateful to the nose, harmful to the brain, dangerous to the lungs." Centuries later, science proved him right on that last point. But many English were willing to pay a pretty penny for this new American fad.

Growing tobacco was hard, monotonous work. A man cleared an acre or two of brush (or a woman did—some women worked at tobacco, too). After breaking up the ground, you made a mound for each tobacco seedling by sticking your leg out and drawing the earth around it with a "grubbing hoe" until the mound was like "a mole hill, and nearly as high as the knee." Pull out your foot, "flatten the top of the hill by a *dab*" and stick in the seedling. Then make another mound . . . and another . . . and another . . . for about eight thousand plants. During the hot summer, weed the plants constantly and pick off the worms that eat tobacco leaves. In August pick the leaves and hang them up to dry. Finally, when the leaves are seasoned, pack them into large barrels, roll them down to the river, and ship them to England.

It was backbreaking work—but the crop brought in five to ten times as much money as working on an English farm. And that was for just one person. Suppose you brought over ten or twenty servants to work for you? That's ten or twenty times the profit. Thousands of people began to pour into Virginia. The tobacco boom was on.

Like most booms, the stakes were high and so were the risks. Virginians had a name for what newcomers faced in their first year in the colony: "the seasoning." If you survived your first twelve months, you were "seasoned"—that is, you had adjusted to the hazards and climate of the new land and had a better chance of continuing to stay alive. Newcomers died in large numbers from malaria spread by mosquitoes. They died from typhoid or dysentery spread by germs in the water. They were killed by Indians, unhappy about the land the English had taken to plant tobacco. Even in the 1630s, 1640s, and 1650s colonists died at great rates.

And because so many adults died, Virginia found itself full of young orphans. The father of Agatha Vause perished when she was two years old. Her mother remarried, so Agatha had a new stepfather, but he soon died, too. So did Agatha's mother a few years later, leaving her to live with her Uncle James. But then James died, so only Aunt Elizabeth was left to care for her. On average, the English who came to Virginia lived to be only thirty-five or forty. Someone who stayed in England, on the other hand, could expect to live to about sixty. And in New England, settlers lived to an average age of seventy.

That's not to say Virginia was only a land of death, disease, and toil. The early Virginians lived hard, but they often made interesting lives for themselves. A lucky few became masters of tobacco plantations. Fewer families came to Virginia than to New England: the colony was made up mostly of single young men taking their chances. Also in contrast to New England, fewer settlers lived in villages and towns. They spread out, setting up farms and plantations along the rivers flowing into Chesapeake Bay. And unlike the Puritans, Virginians cared little about educating everyone. "I thank God, there are no free schools, nor printing," wrote Virginia governor William Berkeley, "and I hope we shall not have these [for a] hundred years; for learning has brought disobedience and heresy." In 1632 a second colony, Maryland, was founded in the northern portions of Chesapeake Bay.

Life in the tobacco colonies was more isolated, but once a month neighbors in every county could get together for Court Day, held in the parlor of a well-to-do planter. There a judge dealt with complaints of hog stealing, quarrels over inheritances, reports on the care of orphans, and the like. In a nearby field, spectators bet on horse races. On election day, men in each county chose two men to represent them in the legislature, called the House of Burgesses. The sheriff asked each voter, "Who do you vote for?" And the voter might reply, "For John Clopton." Then Clopton would bow, thanking the man for his vote.

Gradually Virginia and Maryland became healthier places to live. And tobacco remained the biggest crop, which brings to mind one final point. Any boom country needs workers; and the more workers a planter controlled and the less he paid them, the richer he got. For those who came to Virginia, it made a big difference whether they were gentlefolk with money or poor. Most people could afford to come to Virginia only as indentured servants. A servant signed papers ("indentures") agreeing to work for a period of four to seven years for a master who in return would pay for the servant's passage to America and expenses there. Most who signed up were down on their luck. Some had been forced off English farmlands with no place to work or to stay. Orphans were swept up off the streets and out of poorhouses. In Virginia the lucky servants who didn't die before their seven years were up received "freedom dues": a new set of clothes, tools, and fifty acres of land.

There is one last twist to the story of those who worked in Virginia boom country. Consider the case of a young man who came to the colony in 1621. He survived his first year's seasoning, escaped death in a big Indian attack of 1622, and lived nearly fifty years more, to die one of Virginia's few old men. Legal documents list his name as Anthony Johnson, though he was Antonio when he arrived. And even that was not his original name, which we don't know. All we know is, he was listed as "Antonio a Negro."

A slave, you say. Perhaps. But we just don't know that much about the first African colonists. Early Virginia had no laws about slavery. Antonio and his wife, Mary, worked for a white planter, ei-

ther as servants or slaves, and eventually gained their freedom. Antonio changed his name to the English-sounding Anthony Johnson. At his death, he owned several hundred acres of land, a herd
of cattle, and several slaves. The Chesapeake Bay could be a hard
place to live, but in 1650, it was not a land full of slaves. Only about
three hundred Africans lived among the thirteen thousand settlers.
Dozens became free. "I know mine own ground and I will work
when I please and play when I please," Johnson told one neighbor.

In other words, during these early years a *system* of slavery was
not in place in Virginia or Maryland. The laws defining what a
slave could and couldn't do only grew up over the next century.
And the strange thing—perhaps the strangest thing in all of American history—was that this system of slavery was spreading during
the same years that ideas about freedom and liberty were growing.
But this is such an important part of our story that we need a separate chapter to consider it.

9

EQUAL AND UNEQUAL

ALL MEN ARE CREATED . . . what?

Almost every American can complete that sentence. But a hundred years before Thomas Jefferson wrote the Declaration of Independence, virtually no one believed this. The aristocratic Governor Berkeley of Virginia would no doubt have thanked God there were "no free schools, nor printing" presses to spread such nonsense.

Equality was an idea that had to be created. It had to be built up gradually, through decades of experience. And strange to say, to understand equality, we have to understand the history of *inequality* as well. British colonials living in North America needed only to look around to convince themselves that their world was unequal. In 1700 the small farmers, merchants, and tradespeople of New England still would have accepted what John Winthrop had said seventy years earlier: that God had created a world where some people "must be rich, some poor, some high and eminent . . . others mean and in submission." The tobacco planters, small farmers, and indentured servants of Virginia and Maryland also saw inequality all around them. Only well-born gentlemen represented their counties in the legislature. At church, plantation owners chatted outside until all the "lower sort" of people went in. Then the "better sort" paraded in together. By 1730 these original southern colonies had been joined by North and South Carolina and, a few years later, by Georgia. The swampy coast around Charles Town (later Charleston), South Carolina, proved particularly good country for growing rice, though the area was very unhealthy to live in.

In the lands between England's northern and southern colonies, inequality also held sway. Yet it was here, in the middle colonies, that some of the earliest signs of equality appeared, like the first green shoots of spring.

England paid little attention to these lands at first. That allowed two other peoples to sneak in, the Dutch and the Swedes. Several hundred settlers founded New Sweden along the Delaware River, building rough-and-ready cabins out of logs, a technique that later Americans would put to good use. But the Swedes didn't last because a hundred miles to the north the Dutch had already planted their colony of New Netherland along the Hudson River. The Dutch, determined to prove that they were certainly more equal than the Swedes, raided New Sweden. When the Swedes surrendered their fort, the Dutch forced them to march out with musket balls in their mouths—to remind the Swedes that their conquerors had the power to shoot them all if they pleased.

The Dutch were very powerful. During the 1600s their homeland, the Netherlands, grew into a great trading empire whose influence stretched across the globe. In East Asia the Dutch traded spices; in Africa they bought slaves and carried them to the Americas; in South America they refined the sugar these slaves were forced to grow and carried it back to sell in Europe. New Netherland along the Hudson was a tiny part of the Dutch empire. It contributed beaver pelts, which traders bought from the Iroquois Indians. Meanwhile, farmers spread out around the town of New Amsterdam on Manhattan Island.

Like the first Pilgrims, the Dutch were outnumbered in their own colony by "strangers." People such as Anthony van Salee lived there, a Moroccan pirate turned farmer, whom everyone called "the Turk." So did Anna van Angola, an African widow and farmer. Asser Levy and Abraham de Lucena, both Jews, set up shop—Asser from Poland and Abraham from Brazil. Norwegians, Italians, French, Walloons, Bohemians, Mohawk Indians, and Montauks all walked New Amsterdam's streets. That included Waal Straat, on the town's far end next to a dirt wall. Three hundred years later Wall Street became the center of its own empire of finance, something the Dutch merchants surely would have savored.

New Netherland had English folk, too, ranging from pious Anne Hutchinson, banished from Massachusetts for her religious beliefs, to cantankerous Simon Root, who got his ear sliced off in a tavern fight. The Dutch distrusted the English, a people "of so proud a nature that they thought everything belonged to them," as one New Netherlander complained. And sure enough, England attacked New Netherland in 1664. Then it became the turn of the Dutch to be driven from power, though the English didn't force them to chew musket balls when they surrendered. England's King Charles II gave his brother the Duke of York the newly conquered lands, which were renamed New York; and the town of New Amsterdam was called New York as well.

English immigrants also settled the neighboring colony of New Jersey, but most newcomers flocked to the lands along the Delaware River, which became Pennsylvania, Latin for Penn's Woods. These lands were another gift of King Charles, to his friend William Penn. (The king rather liked to reward friends, and it was easy to be generous when you took the lands at gunpoint from one set of Europeans and ignored the Indians who had been living there for centuries.) Penn advertised his colony in England and in Europe, printing pamphlets in French, Dutch, and German. Within twenty years, fifteen thousand settlers had moved to the lands around Philadelphia, the new "city of brotherly love."

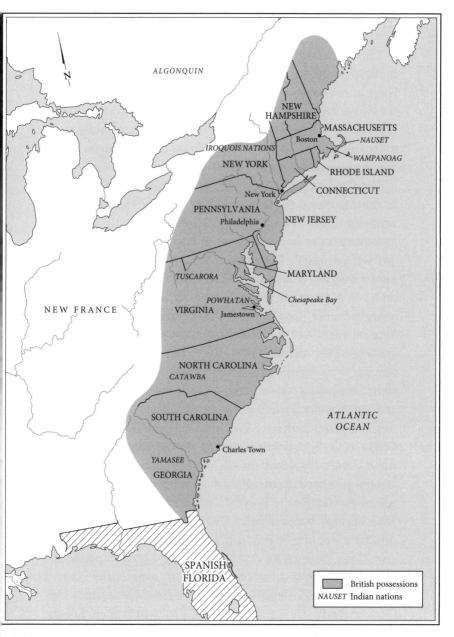

ALGONQUIN

N

NEW
HAMPSHIRE

MASSACHUSETTS

Boston
NAUSET

IROQUOIS NATIONS
WAMPANOAG

NEW YORK
RHODE ISLAND

CONNECTICUT

New York

PENNSYLVANIA
NEW JERSEY

Philadelphia

TUSCARORA
MARYLAND

POWHATAN
Chesapeake Bay

NEW FRANCE
VIRGINIA
Jamestown

NORTH CAROLINA
CATAWBA

SOUTH CAROLINA
ATLANTIC
OCEAN

Charles Town

YAMASEE
GEORGIA

SPANISH
FLORIDA

British possessions
NAUSET Indian nations

Britain's colonies in 1700. The shaded areas give only a rough idea of British settlement. Indians
continued to occupy land in these regions; only a few groups are shown here.

Unlike the king, Penn was not the sort of Englishman who thought everything belonged to him. He bought Indian land at a fairer price than most Europeans, who frequently just took what they wanted. Like the Puritans, Penn considered his colony a "holy experiment." But he behaved differently partly because he belonged to the Quakers, a religious group that most English thought were at the very least odd and at the worst dangerous.

The Quakers called their church the Society of Friends, but in worship they sometimes trembled when the Holy Spirit over-whelmed them, so opponents nicknamed them Quakers. Their movement began in the 1640s when England was torn apart by a civil war between Parliament and the king. English fought English, armies marched across the land, Charles I was beheaded. In the midst of the turmoil, groups sprang up with strange ideas and stranger names: Levellers, Ranters, Diggers, Fifth Monarchists, Muggletonians . . . The first Quakers disrupted church services, challenging the teachings of ministers and priests. But what they said was more unsettling than the way they behaved, for their ideas were talked about long after most Quakers had become peaceful and King Charles II had restored the rule of kings.

Like Luther, Quakers judged for themselves. But they put more weight on God's Holy Spirit speaking to them directly. Why should some church-appointed minister lecture believers? At Quaker "meetings" (they did not call them church services), no priest led. All people were free to speak if the "Inner Light" called them to. Their enemies beat and jailed Quakers so often that the Friends decided it was immoral to fight, and they refused to serve in any army. They chose not to wear fancy clothing or bow to nobles and kings or take off their hats for gentlemen because they believed that all people were equal in God's sight. Horrid, dangerous idea, that everybody was somehow equal! Or so most English thought. After all, inequality stared them in the face—morning, noon, and night.

How? Well, the clothes people wore depended on their station in life. In Massachusetts Bay, wearing fancy lace or silver buttons, silk scarves or big leather boots was against the law—unless you were an owner of a large estate. Ordinary folk had no right to imitate their betters, even if they scraped together the money to buy such luxury items. Where people sat at dinner also depended on their rank in society. A dish of salt lay at the center of the long table: those of higher rank sat "above the salt"; others sat below the salt. On Sunday, the more respected families sat in the better church pews. College students doffed their hats when an instructor walked toward them on the street. Their heads had to be bare at least fifty feet away for the college president, forty feet for a professor, twenty-five feet away for a tutor. At college, inequality could be measured by the foot.

Books of etiquette laid out the rules of proper behavior. In Virginia, a fourteen-year-old named George Washington copied out some of them for study:

> In speaking to men of quality do not lean nor look them full in the face, nor approach too near them at least keep a full pace from them.
>
> In company of those of higher quality than yourself speak not till you are asked a question then stand upright, put off your hat, and answer in few words.

In such a world, how strange for Quakers to keep on their hats!

If you were a woman, the world said you were unequal in even more ways. John Winthrop dearly loved his wife, Margaret, but following Bible teachings, he considered himself "her lord" and she was "to be subject to him." If Margaret wanted to sell property, the law required that John do it for her. She could not sue someone in court or sign a legal contract; only her husband had those rights. Such laws varied from colony to colony. In New Netherland women kept their maiden names when they married and could sign contracts, which made it easier to take part in business.

Spanish women could buy and sell land on their own and represent themselves in court. And some English, such as the Quakers,
insisted that women as much as men should be able to speak up in
religious services.

Slaves, of course, were in the lowest position in this world of
inequality. Yet we should remember that during the colonies' early
years, most slaves were *made,* not born. Their fall from freedom
began in distant lands where men, women, and children were kidnapped and marched on a long trek from one kingdom to another
until finally the ocean was reached. There, European ships spirited
them away to work on distant plantations. You may have read stories about slave hunters in Africa, but the same thing happened
in America. Before 1715, anywhere from thirty thousand to fifty
thousand Indians were captured and shipped south to Caribbean
islands or north to the middle colonies and New England. The
bustling settlement of Charles Town was the center of this trade,
though the French also followed it along the Gulf of Mexico. Before 1715, more Indian slaves were shipped *out* of America than
African slaves were brought in.

But as more Europeans craved tobacco from Virginia and rice
from South Carolina, the demand for slaves grew. As plantations
in North and South America clamored for workers, the number of
slaves sent from Africa skyrocketed. When we imagine immigrants
coming to America, we often think of Puritans and planters from
England, Spanish conquerors like de Soto, or even Turks like Anthony van Salee. But from 1492 until 1820, five times as many enslaved Africans came to the Americas as all European immigrants
combined. And this trade—this inequality—grew steadily in the
hundred years after 1700. Over the entire life of the slave trade,
over 12 million Africans made the difficult journey across the Atlantic and well over 1 million of those died before they reached
their destination. For those who did live, the terror came partly
from not knowing what was coming. Olaudah Equiano, one of the
few who wrote about the experience, remembered being aston-

ished at the vast Atlantic Ocean and the strange men who seemed
to live only on these huge hollowed-out wooden ships floating
on the sea. Once aboard, he saw a large copper kettle boiling and
fainted, believing he was going to be "eaten by those white men,
with horrible looks, red faces and loose hair." The journey itself
was so awful, many captives wanted to end their lives and refused
to eat, but guards pried their mouths open and forced down food.
Enslaved Africans died from the sweltering heat belowdecks, from
infections, from despair. Sharks trailed the ships across the Atlantic, waiting to devour the bodies that were regularly thrown overboard. This so-called Middle Passage, from Africa to the Americas,
was truly a horror.

Of the millions who came in chains, over nine out of ten went
to South America and the Caribbean. Less than 4 percent came
directly to North America. Even so, slavery became a growing part
of colonial life. By 1730 Africans and their children outnumbered
white colonists in South Carolina two to one. The southern colonies had the most slaves, but by 1740 one out of every four men
working in New York City was African American. New England
merchants made large profits in the slave trade. Those hard facts
guaranteed that slavery would remain the most dramatic example
of a land where almost no one could imagine that all men were
created equal.

Behold equal and unequal. Like two uneasy dance partners,
they wheel through a series of steps they weren't expecting to take
and don't completely understand. We won't be done with them for
many chapters. Perhaps never—because the world is always changing and the dance never ends.

10

ENLIGHTENED AND AWAKENED

AS SETTLERS, SERVANTS, AND SLAVES continued to pour into
Britain's colonies, two unusual movements blossomed that stamped
American life in very different ways. One, the Great Awakening,
was a religious movement that was all about finding certainty and
faith; the other, the Enlightenment, was its opposite, concerned
with questioning and doubt. To begin with doubt and the Enlightenment, let's follow a runaway apprentice hiking to Philadelphia
in 1723. A puffy loaf of bread sticks out from under each arm and
his pockets are "stuffed out with shirts and stockings." His name is
Benjamin Franklin.

Servants and slaves often ran away. In doing so they showed
themselves to be doubters, at least about inequality. Their masters
claimed, *I am above you; do as I say.* Runaways doubted that, pulled
on a pair of boots, and walked. They went in search of a life of
greater equality than the one they were living—as young Franklin did, heading toward Philadelphia with bread under his arms.
Benjamin had been working for his older brother James, a printer

in Boston. But by the age of seventeen he had tired of being cuffed and taking orders.

He was the youngest of seventeen children. Benjamin's father meant to dedicate this son to the church by training him to be a minister. But the boy didn't take to church. He skipped out as much as possible and complained about saying grace before meals just as the Pilgrims' neighbor Thomas Morton did at his rowdy settlement of Merrymount. The Franklin family would save time, Benjamin suggested, if his father blessed a whole side of beef *once* rather than saying grace over the meat every evening.

A print shop is the sort of place where all manner of ideas turn up. As Benjamin worked in his brother's shop, he borrowed books by philosophers who were part of a movement in Europe known as the Enlightenment. These thinkers believed in God—many called themselves "deists." But their God was not the sort who divided the Red Sea to help Moses escape the Egyptians or the God who sent his son Jesus to earth to walk on water and be raised from the dead. God governed the world through natural laws, deists argued. Call him the "Supreme Architect" or "Nature's God"—he had no need for miracles. Deists believed that human reason was the key to uncovering nature's laws. The famous British scientist Isaac Newton had made huge advances in human knowledge, using mathematics to plot the path of the planets through the heavens and discovering the force of gravity.

Like the deists, young Franklin adopted the methods of Socrates, the ancient Greek philosopher who was forever asking questions. And the questions Franklin asked seldom occurred to others. As a boy, he watched his friends fly kites and wondered how strong the wind might be. So he launched a kite, jumped into a nearby pond, and begged his friend to take his clothes to the other side—where he picked them up, having proved that the wind was strong enough to blow him and the kite across the pond. Years later Franklin became famous by flying a kite during a thunderstorm to prove that lightning was a form of electricity. He designed a stove that heated houses better than open fireplaces and bifocal glasses to help the nearsighted. He liked to encourage "experiments that let light into the nature of things."

Franklin's attitude is what counts here: he was intensely interested in this world, not the next. He was secular, we should say—a word that comes from the Latin *saecularis,* meaning *of the world.* "I love company, chat, a laugh, a glass, and even a song." After setting up a print shop in Philadelphia, he and some friends formed a club called the Junto, which met on Friday nights at a tavern. There, amid chat and drink, they made it a point to debate serious questions, such as whether a citizen should resist if the government took away his rights. Like the Quakers, Franklin doubted customs that most people took for granted. Why give gentlemen fancy titles like "Sir Anthony" or "Archbishop Robinson"? The great figures in the Bible were never called "the Reverend Moses" or "the Right Honorable Abraham," he commented. "No, no, they were plain men" and honest. Who needed titles?

By the time Franklin turned forty-two, he had earned enough from his printing business to devote most of his time to projects for the public good. He encouraged Philadelphia to create a "library company" for those who couldn't afford to buy books and a hospital to provide free care to the poor. He organized a volunteer fire company and, as a postmaster, improved mail service from New England to Georgia. Not least, he interested himself in the science of government. If the laws of nature could be discovered, why not also observe the natural laws of politics?

In England the Enlightenment philosopher John Locke had written about how governments came to exist. Kings and queens claimed that their authority came from God. Locke doubted that. Why did kings have any "divine right" to rule? He suggested that the first human governments had been formed centuries ago, when people in a state of nature joined together to protect themselves. If kings ruled, it was not because God blessed them with power but because people had created that form of government. Locke also spoke out against established churches. With so many religions claiming to possess the truth, it seemed absurd to suppose that governments could decide who was right. Better to tolerate all beliefs rather than engage in the religious wars that had shaken Europe for hundreds of years. Locke's ideas about the science of government would one day help Franklin and other Americans to consider how political systems came into being, how the affairs of church and the state should be separate, and why the freedom to believe in any religion or in none was important.

As for the second big movement, the Great Awakening, the man who set it going at first acted much like a student of nature, too. In 1723, the year Franklin ran away, twenty-year-old Jonathan Edwards sent an essay to the Royal Society, a scientific organization in England. In it, Edwards recorded his observations on the way spiders spun out lines of web and went "sailing in the air . . . from one tree to another." (In fact, they used their webs the same way Franklin used his kite to be pulled across the pond.) In college Edwards read the writings of John Locke and Isaac Newton. But instead of a career in science, he became a minister. Unlike Franklin, he was "by nature very unfit for secular business."

At his church in Northampton, Massachusetts, Edwards struggled to bring the town's young people to a "new birth" in Christ. He wanted them to undergo a conversion experience rather than spend their evenings in "frolics," partying and drinking. In 1735 he suddenly began making progress. Young people flocked to services and to study sessions with their pastor. Conversion was an intensely beautiful state, Edwards assured them—"all pleasant and delightful" and full of a "sweet calm." On the other hand, sinners who didn't convert faced a horrible fate. Imagine a spider, he suggested—and not one blowing pleasantly from tree to tree but a creature "thrown into the midst of a fierce fire." There could be no question of resisting the flames. "Here is a little image of what you will be in hell, except you repent and fly to Christ." Edwards preached his sermons "without much noise" and with "little motion of his head or hands," only staring at the bell rope at the back of the church. But surely such visions scared the hell out of his listeners. So to speak.

In a matter of weeks Northampton's revival of religion "became universal in all parts of the town" and spread to neighboring villages. But these awakenings were modest compared with those that broke out five years later, when an English preacher named George Whitefield arrived in America. Whitefield preached from Maine to Georgia, often outdoors, attracting thousands of listeners as families hurried along in carriages, on horseback, and on foot to get a glimpse of him. He became America's first true celebrity. Whitefield visited Edwards in Northampton, leaving "almost the whole assembly in tears." Could these awakenings be the start of an even greater movement, Edwards wondered? Bible prophecies spoke of Christ's return to earth at the time of the millennium, a thousand years when the saints would rule before the Last Judgment. The predictions were hard to understand, but countless ministers studied them. Edwards's own reading convinced him that by the year 2016, "whole nations" would be awakened.

When Whitefield visited Philadelphia, the Awakening's most famous preacher had a chance to meet the Enlightenment's leading American. Ben Franklin was not much interested in being saved, but he attended one of Whitefield's sermons and performed a scientific experiment. He had heard that the minister's voice carried over great distances. As Whitefield preached atop the steps of Philadelphia's courthouse, Franklin paced "backwards down the street" until he could hear him no longer; and then, calculating the space available, computed that Whitefield "might be heard by more than thirty thousand" people at one time. While Franklin used reason to reach his answer, Whitefield used emotion to beg his listeners for money to build an orphanage in Georgia. Franklin doubted: he thought the project was impractical. But as Whitefield continued preaching, Franklin "began to soften." He decided to donate the pennies in his pocket. As Whitefield continued, Franklin became "ashamed" of being so ungenerous and pulled out a few silver dollars as well. By the time the sermon ended, he had emptied out all his change, including some gold coins. The power of Whitefield's appeal melted even the heart of the Enlightenment doubter; and the two men parted on good terms.

The rival camps did not always get on so well. Edwards and other revivalists warned deists that they would join the poor spiders in eternal flames. Deists like Franklin—and even quite a few ministers—complained that preachers of the Awakening depended too much on emotion and not enough on reason. But both movements influenced American life in significant ways.

Supporters of the Awakening looked to perfect the world through spiritual revival. They saw John Calvin's holy commonwealth and John Winthrop's city on a hill as "forerunners of those glorious times so often prophesied of in the Scriptures," as Edwards said, when holiness would spread through the world. In years to come, the fire of faith would spark crusades against slavery and the abuse of alcohol as well as campaigns in favor of women's rights, to name only a few. But at bottom the movement wanted unbelievers to awaken and convert. The other reforms, they believed, would follow naturally.

Enlightenment supporters distrusted the Awakening's high emotions. They preferred using reason and science to decode nature's mysteries. As for the science of government, Enlightenment thinkers didn't believe that a holy commonwealth, where everyone shared the same beliefs, was the way to unite a nation. They gave more thought to how an effective political system worked—so that people of different beliefs could live together.

And so the British colonies continued to grow, whether their inhabitants were enlightened or awakened. Most were reasonably happy with their rulers. But little more than a dozen years after Whitefield's tour through the colonies, a war broke out that swept North America along a very different path—toward the creation of a new nation that few could have imagined.

11

BE CAREFUL WHAT YOU WISH FOR

THE FIRST TRUE WORLD WAR—A war in which the battles of nations spread across the entire globe—did not begin in 1914 with muddy trenches, screaming artillery shells, and millions of men at war in Europe. It began in 1754 with a few dozen soldiers huddled in a wilderness known as Ohio Country. The war was sparked by a twenty-two-year-old lieutenant colonel from Virginia. Thirty-five years later, he would become the first president of the United States, but early this May morning, George Washington crouched on a rock outcrop overlooking an encampment of French. With him were about forty soldiers and a dozen Indian warriors led by an Iroquois Indian chief. The chief, known as the Half King, had led Washington to this glen "in a heavy rain and a night as dark as pitch." The last showers were lifting as the French crawled out from under their bark lean-tos to cook breakfast.

This was truly an unlikely spot to begin a world war. But by 1754 North America was being pulled into a struggle that would reach from America to Europe, Africa, and even Asia. Known as the Seven Years' War, it brought to a climax the rivalry between European powers in their push to dominate North America. To understand the war, we must see how that competition between Spain, France, and many Indian nations was growing.

A full two and a half centuries had passed since Columbus first set foot in the Caribbean, and by now European colonies ringed much of North America. To the south, dozens of Spanish missions and a few towns had been planted from Arizona to Florida through the efforts of Franciscan friars. The friars belonged to a religious order that cared little for the gold and treasure of conquistadors. The holy men wore simple robes, rope belts, and sandals. Bible prophecies convinced them that the world would soon end and they meant to convert the Indians before Jesus returned. On that score their hopes were disappointed, but by 1754 about fifteen thousand Hispanic settlers lived in the northern borderlands of Spain's empire. In addition to Franciscan missions, there were military forts known as *presidios*. The Spanish in these northern regions found themselves raided by Apache Indians, who attacked their farms and herds of sheep. And Comanches, people new to the Plains, made life difficult for both the Apaches and the Spanish.

Spain had long ago chased the French out of Florida, but they returned to America through a northern back door. The St. Lawrence River wound deep into Canada's forests, and French explorers followed its waters, building towns at Quebec and Montreal for their colony of New France. Farther west, traders hopped from one Great Lake to another exchanging hatchets, knives, and copper for Indian beaver skins. In France these pelts were turned into fashionable felt hats, and a large valuable trade grew up for the skins of beaver. The French traders were known as *coureurs de bois*—"runners of the woods"—and they used Indian gear to travel efficiently: birch-bark canoes in warm weather and rawhide-laced snowshoes in winter. The coureurs were joined by Jesuits, who were missionaries much like the Franciscans.

Sadly, the fur trade did more than provide hats. It sparked a

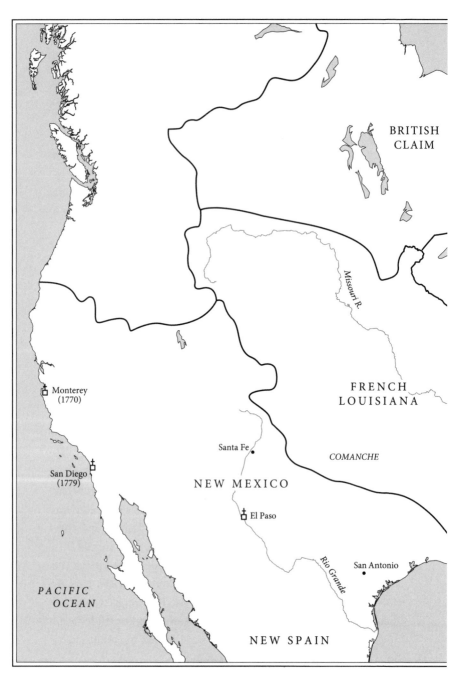

BRITISH
CLAIM

Missouri R.

Monterey
(1770)

FRENCH
LOUISIANA

Santa Fe

San Diego
(1779)

COMANCHE

NEW MEXICO

El Paso

Rio Grande

San Antonio

PACIFIC
OCEAN

NEW SPAIN

North America at the time of the Seven Years' War. France, England, and Spain all claimed
territory in North America. The Spanish anchored their lands with missions and presidios (or
military forts) that spread from Florida to New Mexico. The French used a kind of backdoor

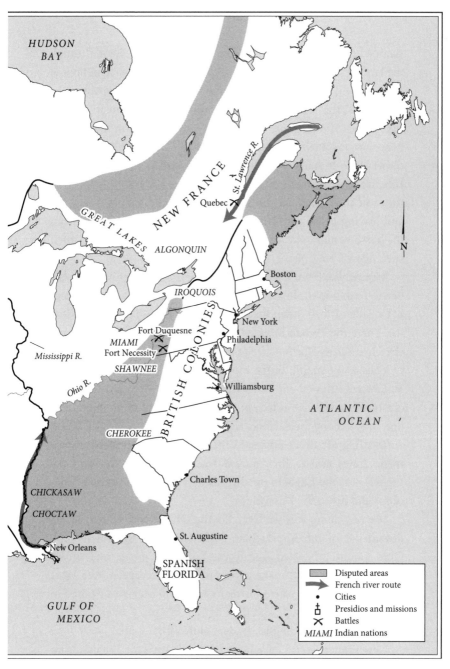

route into the continent, along the St. Lawrence, Mississippi, and Ohio rivers. Indian nations continued to control large portions of North America.

rivalry known as the Beaver Wars, which spread chaos through the land. As pelts made their way down the St. Lawrence in French canoes, the Dutch of New Netherland encouraged their own Indian allies, the Iroquois, to bring furs to the Hudson River. For many years the Iroquois had formed a confederation to keep the peace among their five nations. But this League of the Iroquois didn't spare Indians living farther west. Armed with Dutch muskets, Iroquois warriors attacked the Hurons and other peoples. At the same time smallpox spread through the land, killing thousands and leaving those who survived to face starvation or death from the harsh winter cold. The Beaver Wars eased only after the Dutch surrendered New Netherland to England.

Meanwhile, French traders, missionaries, and explorers continued to push into the heart of the continent and, as we saw in chapter 5, La Salle canoed down the Mississippi River to the Gulf of Mexico. There the French founded Louisiana. By 1754 French outposts stretched across North America like beads on a necklace, from New Orleans at the mouth of the Mississippi to Nova Scotia, where the St. Lawrence flowed out to the sea. The eighty-five thousand French colonials seemed like a drop in the bucket next to more than 1 million British along the Atlantic. No matter: whoever controlled North America's great rivers possessed the keys to the continent. Rivers made travel easier. They moved trade goods quickly. And the French, not the English, paddled as they pleased up the St. Lawrence and down the Mississippi.

Midway along this necklace lay the Ohio River, whose waters flowed out of the Appalachian Mountains into the Mississippi. Ohio Country boasted fine forests, plentiful game, and grassy meadows that would make good farms. The savage Beaver Wars had turned the area into a no-man's-land, but everyone desired it: the Indians, the French, and the English. At a place where two rivers joined the Ohio, English traders built a fort.

New France would have none of this. "Drive the English from our lands," ordered the colony's governor-general. A thousand soldiers sent the English packing, and in place of the old post, the French began building Fort Duquesne. As that stronghold went up, Lieutenant Colonel Washington and his Virginia soldiers were already trudging toward it, on the order of Virginia's governor. When the French got wind of Washington's force, they dispatched a few dozen men to warn the English to turn back. It was this party that the Iroquois Half King had discovered encamped in the ravine. He had willingly led Washington there, for the Iroquois hoped to gain from trade with the British.

Victory for Washington took no more than fifteen minutes of musket fire. In the glen fourteen French lay wounded, including their commander, Ensign Jumonville. Jumonville cried out that he came in peace, bearing a letter from his commander. Washington, who spoke no French, found the message difficult to understand and turned to fetch his translator.

Meanwhile, the Half King, whose real name was Tanaghrisson, stepped up to the wounded Jumonville. The Iroquois had their own interests in this high-stakes game. They most definitely did not want to see the French keep their influence in the Ohio Country, for the French had never supported the Iroquois. What was this talk of coming in peace on the part of the ensign? "You're not dead yet, my father," the Half King told Jumonville. With quick, hard blows, his hatchet split open the officer's forehead. Then Tanaghrisson reached down—in a kind of ritual gesture—and took some of the Frenchman's brains, washing his hands with them. *Now* the Indian enemies of the Iroquois would think twice about trusting French power.

Young Washington was surely shocked, even stunned by these acts, for he did nothing as the Half King's men set to work killing the rest of the wounded French. Then the Virginians retreated seven miles to their encampment, dubbed Fort Necessity. But this stockade, hastily thrown together, was no defense against the seven hundred French and their Indian allies who arrived to exact revenge. The Virginians were penned up in the fort, shot at by their enemies during a day of pouring rain. Their muskets wet and use-less, they were unable to defend their position; Washington had no choice but to surrender. The French allowed him to lead his exhausted men away on July 4, 1754, "almost naked . . . scarcely a man" with "either shoes, stockings or hat." War had begun—with a great embarrassment for Great Britain.

The following summer General Edward Braddock tried to re-take Fort Duquesne from the French, but he was too confident that his European-trained soldiers—"regulars"—could outfight anyone. As his force approached the settlement, the French and Indians hid in the woods, "creeping near and hunting us as they would do a herd of buffaloes or deer," reported one bitter American. Braddock rode up and down, rallying his men through withering fire. But a bullet finally felled him and, with many other officers also dead, the British fled back down the trail. (Washington had two horses shot from under him during the ambush.) As the war continued, the French conquered British forts in northern New York, on Lake George and Lake Champlain.

The tide of battle turned only after a remarkable politician named William Pitt took charge of the war for Great Britain. Nick-named the Great Commoner because he had refused to become a lord when given the chance, Pitt was strong willed and eloquent, though moody. For months on end he was laid low by splitting headaches or spiking pain in his joints caused by gout. Still, his confidence was unbounded. "I know that I can save this country, and no one else can," he declared. France had to be thrashed—not just driven out of North America but attacked everywhere. British forces were sent to Europe, to the Caribbean, and to West Africa to attack French outposts. Pitt refused to count the cost. Was the British navy stretched thin, trying to do all he asked? Build more ships, recruit more men! Were American colonials angry about not being paid for supplies and troops they provided? Pay them gener-ously, no questions asked! Parliament passed the largest budget in English history.

In 1759 the British general James Wolfe led an assault on the French fortress at Quebec, which stood high on bluffs above the St. Lawrence River. Wolfe was deathly ill, not only from fevers but also from being bled by his doctors, a remedy of the day that did more harm than good. Better a glorious death, Wolfe decided, than scorn for doing nothing. A British sailor who had spent time in Quebec knew of a rough path zigzagging up the bluffs to the flat ground that spread out before Quebec's fortress walls. It would never occur to anybody that the British would come that way. In the dark of night Wolfe led his men up the narrow path, two by two. By daybreak over four thousand redcoats were spread across the plains, astonishing the French general, Louis-Joseph, Marquis de Montcalm. As Montcalm marched his men out on that showery day, Wolfe made his troops lie flat to avoid giving the enemy much of a target. It took nerve to lie there as French cannonballs came thundering by or bouncing along, ripping apart anything in their way. But when the French got close enough, the British stood up, fired calmly, and scattered the enemy. In the heat of battle both Wolfe and Montcalm were wounded and later died of their injuries.

North America was as good as won for Britain. But Pitt wanted more. The British had already attacked French trading posts in India, and he ordered a new force to speed toward Spain's colony at Manila in the Philippines. Young King George III, who had just taken the throne, protested. Britain was too much in debt and wasn't even at war with Spain! In a huff, Pitt resigned. Then Spain declared war anyway and the British promptly captured not only Manila but also Spanish Havana in the Caribbean.

By then the European powers, exhausted by so much war, were eager to sign a peace treaty. France gave up all its territory in North America, although Britain allowed it to keep its rich sugar islands, its African slave ports, and its trading posts in India. Pitt would not have been so generous, but he was no longer part of the government. Crippled by gout, his aching legs bundled in felt, he was carried by servants into Parliament, where he crawled to his seat with the help of a crutch, and for three and a half hours protested loudly—in vain—against the treaty. Even so, Britain had won a magnificent victory.

Or had it? American colonials lit bonfires, rang church bells, and fired off cannon. Fort Duquesne was renamed Fort Pitt; eventually it became the city of Pittsburgh. But the war, like so many in history, had nearly bankrupted the victor. How would Britain ever pay its massive debts? How could it manage its new North American lands, full of French and Indians not used to taking orders from the British? Already American colonials were crossing the Appalachian Mountains in a rush to settle Ohio Country.

Glorious victory! But, as the proverb warns: Be careful what you wish for.

12

More Than a Quarrel

THE HOUSE OF LORDS WAS silent and empty, save for a sentry who stood watch. Its lead-cased windows were placed high, and a dark tapestry illustrating England's defeat of the Spanish Armada did little to brighten the shadows. But there was no mistaking the throne, reserved for King George III. Benjamin Rush, a young doctor from Pennsylvania, stared: he felt as if he "walked on sacred ground." Gazing at the splendid chair, on an impulse he asked to sit in it. The sentry hesitated, but Rush wouldn't take no for an answer and at last settled himself on the throne "for a considerable time . . . as a crowd of ideas poured in upon my mind." Here he was in London, the center of the British empire, and in Parliament, the center of the empire's power. Behold: House of Lords, House of Commons, and a majestic throne for a king to preside over all.

At the end of the Seven Years' War most colonials felt as Rush did about their king. Yet in the dozen short years that followed, so many changes swept the colonies that a great many Americans, including Rush himself, wanted nothing to do with Parliament or king. The changes were so far-reaching that we call them a revolution—a kind of turning, as the word suggests, that takes the old ways of doing things and stands them on their head. What happened by 1776 to turn so many loyal subjects upside down?

To begin with, the bills for the Seven Years' War came due. William Pitt's adventure had doubled Britain's debt and more than doubled the number of troops in America. Some redcoats went home, but others were needed to put down an uprising led by an Ottawa chief named Pontiac. During the Seven Years' War, Indian towns and cornfields had been burned, smallpox had spread terror, and British settlers began rushing in to take Indian lands. With the war over, Indians all across the backcountry attacked settlements on their lands. Officials in England tried to calm matters by issuing the Proclamation of 1763, which forbade colonials from settling west of the Appalachians. But troops remained. And settlers generally ignored the proclamation.

Parliament, led by Britain's new prime minister, George Grenville, thought it only fair that Americans help pay for their own security. "If America looks to Great Britain for protection, she must enable [us] to protect her," insisted one member of Parliament. To another member, however, these words rang false. Isaac Barré was an Irish veteran who had actually fought at the battle of Quebec, where a bullet took his sight from one eye. Now, he jumped to his feet. It was Parliament, he thought, that was blind.

[The colonials] protected by your care? No! your oppressions planted them in America. They fled from your tyranny to a then uncultivated and unhospitable country. . . .

They nourished up by *your* indulgence? They grew by your neglect of them: as soon as you began to care about them, that care was exercised in sending persons to rule over them. . . .

They protected by *your* arms? They have nobly taken up arms in your defense. . . . And believe me, remember I this day told you so, that same spirit of freedom which actuated

that people at first, will accompany them still. . . . [They] are
as truly loyal as any subjects the King has, but a people jealous of their liberties.

Around Barré "the whole House sat awhile as amazed, intently
looking and without answering a word."

But George Grenville was determined to raise money. For decades, a law had required colonial merchants to pay a customs duty,
or tax, on molasses they imported. (New England distillers turned
the molasses into rum and sold it at a profit.) The duties did Britain
little good, however, because most merchants smuggled in their
molasses, bribing customs officials to look the other way. With the
Sugar Act, Grenville tightened up the system. Now merchants had
to fill out papers for every cargo they imported. Parliament also
passed the Stamp Act, which required Americans to purchase special stamped paper for all sorts of business. If you made a will, it
had to be written on stamped paper. Newspapers, almanacs, and
even playing cards needed stamped paper. The English already
paid stamp taxes; Grenville thought it only fair that Americans
share the burden.

But colonial legislatures howled in protest. In Virginia's House
of Burgesses, a fiery young lawmaker named Patrick Henry led the
way—using "very indecent language," sniffed Virginia's royal governor. Opponents of the new taxes called themselves Sons of Liberty, a
phrase that Isaac Barré had used in his speech. The Sons organized
parades, urged Americans to boycott goods from England, and
threatened anyone who favored Grenville's taxes. Mobs in Boston
and Newport hanged likenesses of the official stamp distributors
on gallows, while rioters broke into the homes of prominent supporters of the tax, including a merchant in Newport, "destroying
and demolishing all his furniture, instantly dashing into pieces all
his china, looking glasses &c.," and then breaking into his cellars,
where they "drank, wasted and carried away all his wines and other
liquors."

Why did colonial Britons—so proud of king and country—react so angrily? Well, *because* they were Britons. They claimed the same "rights and liberties" as the people of England. The English elected representatives to the House of Commons, so the English had a voice in whether they should be taxed. Not everyone had the right to vote, to be sure, but at least some property owners in every county did. Americans, on the other hand, elected no representatives to Parliament. As Patrick Henry put it, "The distinguishing characteristic of *British* freedom" was the right of the people to be taxed "by persons chosen by themselves to represent them, who can only know what taxes the people are able to bear."

Americans didn't entirely reject Parliament's authority. In 1765 a Stamp Act Congress met in New York, where delegates from nine states agreed that Parliament had the right to regulate trade between different parts of the empire. But not laws meant to raise money. The power to tax belonged to American legislatures, the delegates insisted. Then the crisis passed, because Parliament repealed the Stamp Act. Peace seemed to return; but in fact, the Stamp Act quarrel set the pattern for what was to come. Parliament never doubted it had the right to tax and soon came up with another tactic. Americans said Parliament could regulate their trade? Very well, Parliament would place new taxes on paint, lead, glass, paper, and tea—the Townshend Acts, they were called. These taxes were all on imported goods. They were regulating trade! The laws also gave customs officials the power to confiscate the ships and cargoes of any merchants accused of breaking the law. Dishonest customs collectors made fortunes by arresting merchants on trumped-up charges.

Again came the protests against taxation without representation. Again came the boycotts organized by the Sons of Liberty and now Daughters of Liberty, too, who produced homespun cloth on their spinning wheels rather than buy British woolens. After three years of arguing, Parliament gave in once again and repealed the Townshend Acts. But this time, it left one fee in place to mark its authority: the tax on tea. Americans didn't like paying it, but they did like their tea. For several years relations between the colonies and Britain became less troubled.

But in the end, even tea brought trouble. In 1773 Parliament decided to help out the ailing East India Company, Britain's biggest importer of tea. Under the new Tea Act, the company for the first time was allowed to sell directly to colonial merchants, instead of through middlemen. The new system actually meant that the price of tea dropped, though the tea tax continued.

But by now everyone's guard was up. If a small tax was accepted, what was to stop Parliament from passing larger ones? When the first ships carrying East India tea sailed into Boston, the Sons of Liberty were ready, organized by a tough local politician named Samuel Adams. Adams was a round-faced man, blue-eyed, pale-skinned, and utterly determined. "Put your adversary in the wrong and keep him there," he liked to say. When the royal governor of Massachusetts insisted the tea must be unloaded, Adams stood before a candlelit crowd in Boston's Old South Church and spoke words meant to be a secret signal: "This meeting can do nothing more to save the country." Immediately, a Boston mob dressed as Indians swarmed down to the harbor, chopped open the tea chests, and dumped the leaves into the icy waters.

This time Parliament didn't back down. As punishment, it closed Boston's port to all trade and forbade town meetings from assembling to plan and protest. These Coercive Acts, along with other harsh measures, convinced colonials that they needed to gather again to speak in unison. In 1774 the first Continental Congress met in Philadelphia.

To this point, the story about stamps, taxes, and tea sounds a lot like a quarrel that turns into a fight, and a fight that turns into an uprising. You *shall* pay taxes. We shan't—*make us.* Redcoats had already been sent to Boston and New York to keep watch on unruly Americans, which led to fights between "lobsterbacks" (British soldiers with their red coats) and angry locals. In the old days the militia, or local armed forces, would meet from time to time to march, then eat and drink at pleasant gatherings. Now they began training as "Minutemen," bands ready to assemble and fight at a moment's notice. They gathered ammunition and stored it in places safely away from British troops.

One such depot was in Concord, Massachusetts, twenty-one miles outside Boston. In the middle of the night, British regulars marched out to confiscate the powder and shot. But the countryside was warned of their coming by several men, including a silversmith named Paul Revere, who galloped on horseback to spread the alarm from village to village. At dawn on April 19, 1775, about seventy Minutemen stood on Lexington green blocking the British troops. Shooting erupted, though no one could say for sure who fired first. Eight Americans fell dead and the British moved on. But at Concord hours later, hundreds of militia attacked. By afternoon thousands more had swarmed into the area, firing from behind trees and stone fences as the British beat a hasty retreat to Boston. A quarrel that turned into an uprising had spiraled into a full-fledged rebellion.

But not a revolution—not quite. You can fight your way to a rebellion. You have to think your way to a revolution. The quarrel forced Americans to consider ideas they had long taken for granted. In 1765, most Americans agreed that Parliament could regulate them, even if it couldn't tax. But then Parliament passed "quartering acts" that required Americans to shelter British troops in empty farm buildings and houses, and provide them with bedding and food if needed. These laws at first seemed like regulations, but they certainly felt like taxes to the Americans forced to provide supplies! The Coercive Acts were not taxes, but they were unjust and tyrannical. Delegates to the Continental Congress began to argue that Parliament should have *no* authority over Americans.

If so, then what tied Americans to the British empire? Only the king, wrote John Adams, a lawyer from Massachusetts. Adams was a delegate to the Congress and a cousin of that rabble-rouser

Sam Adams. John pointed out that there were many provinces or realms in the British empire. "Massachusetts is a realm, New York is a realm"—just as Ireland, England, and Scotland were. And "the king of Great Britain is the sovereign of all these realms." If His Majesty would only see matters properly, he would stop Parliament from acting without authority. Unfortunately, the king agreed with Parliament. The rebellion was led by "wicked and desperate persons," King George declared, and he intended "to bring the traitors to justice."

In the summer of 1775, with fighting under way, a second Continental Congress met. Benjamin Rush, the doctor who once had sat on the king's throne, was a delegate. Like other Americans thinking their way to a revolution, he had begun to imagine the unthinkable. Could America do without a king? "I had been taught to consider [kings] nearly as essential to political order as the sun is to the order of our solar system," Rush admitted. He thought about writing an essay but "shuddered" to think what others might say if he suggested Americans could do without a monarch.

But Rush had a fearless friend who was up to the task. Thomas Paine had moved to Philadelphia from England only the year before. The son of a Quaker, Paine had tried everything from schoolteaching to corset making before becoming an editor and writer. A freethinker who considered the teachings of Christianity mostly superstition, Paine jumped at Rush's suggestion to write a pamphlet. He called his essay *Plain Truth,* and read parts of it aloud to Rush as he wrote it. Rush liked the message but suggested another title: *Common Sense.* The pamphlet came out in January 1776.

Paine didn't mince words. He was ready to fling this king—and all kings—out of the political solar system. Any nation ruled by a monarch was "poisoned" by that form of government, and George III in particular he called "the royal brute of Great Britain." Paine insisted that "one honest man" was worth more "in the sight of God, than all the crowned ruffians that ever lived." When *Common Sense* appeared, Americans bought an amazing one hundred thousand copies in six months. The pamphlet convinced many readers that Americans should throw off their monarch and cut all ties with Britain.

But that thought only raised a bigger question. For years colonials had proudly claimed their rights and liberties *because they were British.* If Americans were British no longer, how could they justify the rights they held so dear?

While Congress debated the question of independence, another writer came forward: a quiet young delegate to the second Continental Congress from Virginia. Sitting in his Philadelphia lodgings at the corner of Market and Seventh streets, a writing desk in his lap, he thought his way to a revolution. His name was Thomas Jefferson.

He dipped his pen into the inkwell and began to write . . .

13

EQUAL AND INDEPENDENT

When in the Course of human events, it becomes necessary for one people to dissolve the political bands, which have connected them with another, and to assume among the powers of the earth, the separate and equal station to which the Laws of Nature and of Nature's God entitle them, a decent respect to the opinions of mankind requires that they should declare the causes which impel them to the separation.

We hold these truths to be self-evident, that all men are created equal, that they are endowed by their Creator with certain unalienable Rights, that among these are Life, Liberty and the pursuit of Happiness.

WHEN THE YOUNGEST delegate to the second Continental Congress wrote these words, he was thirty-three and possessed of sandy red hair and a jutting jaw. Born in the foothills of the Blue Ridge Mountains, Thomas Jefferson loved his home country; and when he came to build his own plantation, Monticello, he set it on a mountaintop. It was an impractical spot, but as he put it, "I can ride above the storms and look down into the workhouse of nature, to see her clouds, hail, snow, rain, thunder, all fabricated at our feet!" For Jefferson, here was Nature's God at work, following Nature's Law.

Like Franklin and Paine, Jefferson was an Enlightenment man and a deist. "Fix reason firmly in her seat," he advised his nephew. He agreed with John Locke that humans in their natural state were born "equal and independent" and he even used Locke's phrase in his first draft of the Declaration of Independence. Locke had also argued that "no one ought to harm another in his life, health, liberty or possessions." Jefferson omitted health and, instead of "possessions," spoke of the right to "Life, Liberty and the pursuit of Happiness."

These were words that turned rebellion into revolution. The people of "these United States" were not claiming rights the king *gave* them as Britons. Or even that their Congress gave them because they were Americans. *All* people had these rights from birth: they were natural rights. The rest of the Declaration explained the quarrel with Great Britain, listing Americans' complaints, but the document's first sentences set forth an ideal that would inspire people for centuries to come. Eighty years later, Abraham Lincoln realized how astonishing it had been that Jefferson, under the "pressure of a struggle for national independence by a single people," should place a truth about *all* people in the Declaration. The nation's Founders meant to set up equality as a "standard," Lincoln explained, "which should be familiar to all, and revered by all . . . constantly labored for, and even though never perfectly attained . . . constantly spreading and deepening its influence."

Of course, the evidence was everywhere that not all people were being treated equally. Abigail Adams wrote her husband, John, about the new "code of laws" that she knew the delegates would be drawing up. "Remember the ladies," she insisted. "If particular care and attention is not paid to the ladies we are determined to foment a rebellion, and will not hold ourselves bound by any laws in which we have no voice, or representation." She was joking, but at the same time entirely serious about her feelings. As for Jefferson, he arrived in Philadelphia riding in a horse-drawn carriage attended by three slaves. Did Jefferson believe that Richard, Jesse, and Jupiter were created equal?

The nation's Founders were two-faced, some have said. They preached up equality while keeping down slaves. They assured their wives that women were the real masters in life while confiding (to other men, as John Adams did) that a woman's "delicacy" made her unfit to vote or to manage the great "cares of state." Others have suggested that even great individuals are products of their times, that only later generations could fully appreciate that equality should extend to black Americans and to women.

Surely, our understanding of equality has grown over the years. But deep down, it is likely John Adams only joked with Abigail because he didn't quite have the nerve to order her to be subject to her husband, as John Winthrop might have done. As for slavery, Jefferson admitted in the first draft of the Declaration that anyone who enslaved Africans had stolen their "sacred rights of life and liberty." But he said so only to blame King George for encouraging the slave trade. Congress dropped that passage from the final Declaration, no doubt because it did seem rather foolish to hear slaveholders blame the king for encouraging slavery.

Lincoln was right: saying something and achieving it are two different matters. Jefferson was uneasy about slavery his entire life, though never uneasy enough actually to free his slaves. As we will see later, he even began to backtrack in his commitment to freedom and his hope that slavery would gradually wither away. But for all his considerable failings, Jefferson did place the idea of equality at the center of the Declaration. And in so doing, he turned rebellion into a revolution, which has continued to work its changes to the present day.

By the time Congress published the Declaration on July 4,

1776, its army had been battling the British for more than a year. George Washington was in command—the logical man to lead, in everyone's eyes. Six feet tall, erect and dignified, a sword at his side and silver spurs on his boots, he was the only American officer with experience in the Seven Years' War who was still relatively young. A general of that era had to be comfortable on horseback, and Washington was bold, "leaping the highest fences and going extremely quickly" without "letting his horse run wild." He *led* his men into battle rather than followed them, rarely lost his self-control, and pushed on against long odds. Unfortunately, the army he commanded was at best a ragtag lot. The militias at first seemed impressive. A month after Lexington and Concord, they made a daring midnight march up a hill that overlooked the British forces in Boston. (They planned to take Bunker but actually reached Breed's Hill.) The redcoats retook it the next day, but only after suffering heavy casualties, as the rebels fired from behind breastworks thrown up the night before. "Don't shoot until you see the whites of their eyes!" yelled General Israel Putnam.

Great bravery—but also great weakness. Putnam shouted because too many of his men were trigger-happy and lacked training. (Remember how the British held their fire at the battle of Quebec?) True, the militia always swarmed out when redcoats marched into their villages. But once the enemy moved on, they went back to their farms and shops. "Here today, gone tomorrow," Washington complained. He knew he would never win without organizing a truly effective force (which came to be called the Continental army), one that was willing to train and fight for more than six months at a time. As a Virginia gentleman, he expected ordinary folk to be led by their betters, and the New England soldiers at first struck him as "exceedingly dirty and nasty." Why, the troops *elected* their own officers, joked with them, and sometimes even received shaves from them! How could anyone succeed with such an undisciplined mob?

For most of a year Washington somehow managed to keep the

British army bottled up in Boston as he drilled his troops, all the while hiding one huge and frightening fact from the enemy. His army had virtually no gunpowder and little artillery. Gradually the gunpowder began to trickle in; and after Ethan Allen and Benedict Arnold captured the British fort at distant Ticonderoga, they loaded 120,000 pounds of mortars and cannon onto forty-two massive sleds and sent them to Boston in the dead of winter. Soldiers dragged the big guns to the top of Dorchester Heights during one long and moonlit night. General William Howe, commanding the British, could hardly believe his eyes the next morning. "My God, these fellows have done more work in one night than I could make my army do in three months!" He loaded his troops onto ships and sailed away.

Why waste time with the stubborn rebels of Boston, Howe decided, when farther south many more New Yorkers remained loyal to the king? Howe landed thirty-two thousand troops on Long Island, including eight thousand Hessians—German soldiers the king had hired to fight for the British. Washington and his ten thousand raw recruits were utterly outgunned and outmaneuvered. Through the autumn of 1776 each desperate retreat seemed to lead to another. The British captured New York, then drove Washington and his Continentals south through New Jersey and across the Delaware River into Pennsylvania, where they came ashore exhausted. One member of the Pennsylvania militia watched them land: "A man staggered out of line and came toward me. He had lost all his clothes. He was in an old dirty blanket jacket, his beard long and his face full of sores. . . . Only when he spoke did I recognize my brother James."

Washington was as desperate as his army. He needed a bold stroke to show the British that American soldiers could do more than retreat. He needed to buck up civilians, who might turn into "Loyalists"—those faithful to the king—if the rebellion seemed about to fail. Most of all, he needed to show his own men that they could win. On Christmas Eve he led them back across the

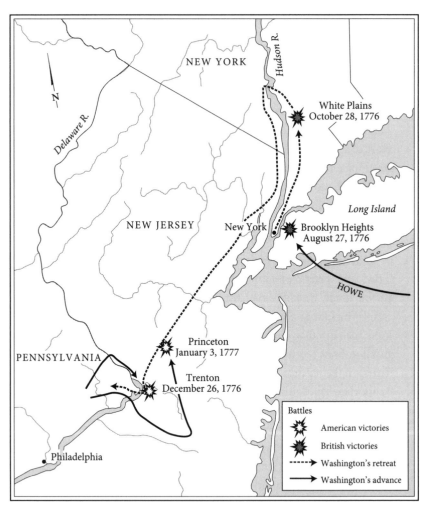

Washington's retreat and advance. In the fall of 1776, General William Howe chased Washington's army out of Long Island and New York City, across the Hudson River, and down through New Jersey. In Pennsylvania, Washington regrouped and crossed the Delaware River twice to achieve victories at Trenton and Princeton.

Delaware—in the teeth of hail, sleet, and rain, through ice floes spinning downstream—to surprise a garrison of Hessians at Trenton, New Jersey. After that victory, he marched forward to capture more British at Princeton rather than retreat into the hands of the astonished redcoats who chased him.

It would be pleasant to say that the tide of battle now turned. But nearly five years of fighting remained. General Howe captured Philadelphia the following summer, where the Continental Congress was meeting. The members scattered "like a covey of partridges," groused John Adams. Washington was discouraged, but he came to realize that even if he could not win, neither could the British—never mind how many cities they conquered. "The possession of our towns, while we have an army in the field, will avail them little," he noted. The point was to keep the American army from being beaten and captured, which meant avoiding large battles unless the Americans truly had the British army trapped.

Meanwhile, Britain launched a plan to cut off New England from the rest of the rebellion by taking control of the Hudson River from New York City to Albany and beyond. General John Burgoyne led an army south from Canada to meet General Howe's forces coming up from New York. "Gentleman Johnny" was confident. He had bet 50 guineas with members of his social club in London that he would "return from America victorious." But as the gentleman general struggled through thick wilderness forests, he discovered that his army was overworked, his baggage overstuffed, and his abilities overrated. A disastrous battle at Saratoga forced him to surrender his entire army. Learning the news, King George "fell into agonies," for this victory changed the war dramatically—not only in America but also in Europe. Benjamin Franklin had already been sent to Paris to beg aid for the Americans from Britain's old rival, France. The French had hung back, trying to decide whether these upstart Americans could truly challenge Britain's might. The victory at Saratoga convinced them to join the United

States in its war. That, more than any other event, turned the tide of battle.

France's large navy forced Britain to send a third of its troops in America to protect its valuable sugar islands in the Caribbean. The remaining forces now focused on the southern colonies. There, redcoats captured Savannah and Charleston, just as they had taken northern cities. But the real conflict played out in the countryside, where many Loyalists still supported the king. Rebel and Loyalist bands raided each other's farms, burning homes and viciously murdering men, women, and children. Unfortunately for Britain, its own troops carried out some of the most brutal raids. "Great Britain now has a hundred enemies, where it had one before," reported one Loyalist sadly.

The British didn't pursue one other possible source of soldiers. A third of all people between Delaware and Georgia were African American, virtually all enslaved. From time to time British officials promised freedom to any slave who fought for Britain, and perhaps one hundred thousand slaves tried to become free in one way or another. But most British didn't like the idea of using slaves to fight their white masters, and neither did white Loyalists. Many slaves who ran to British lines found themselves neglected or even sold into slavery again in the Caribbean. As for the Continental army, Congress didn't recruit African Americans until it grew desperate for soldiers. Then northern states sent five thousand black volunteers, who served in hopes of winning their freedom.

Meanwhile, in the Carolinas, American forces outran and outwitted General Charles Cornwallis, fighting only when they thought they had an advantage. Cornwallis tired of the chase and took his army north to Virginia, where he encamped on Yorktown Peninsula. He was only a few dozen miles from where the first English colonists had landed at Jamestown in 1607. Washington, still outside New York City, leapt at the chance to trap Cornwallis when he learned that the French navy was sailing north from the Caribbean under the command of Admiral François Joseph de Grasse. If de Grasse reached Yorktown in time, he could prevent Cornwallis from escaping by sea. As Washington hurried his army south along the Delaware River, another American officer was astonished to see the usually solemn general call from afar, waving a handkerchief in one hand and his hat in the other, grinning and shouting, *de Grasse!* with "the greatest joy." The French had arrived in Chesapeake Bay. Victory was within reach.

Surrounded by land and by sea, Cornwallis surrendered his entire army on October 19, 1781. As British soldiers laid down their arms, their band played a tune called "The World Turned Upside Down."

Victory came thanks to the Continental army, which had turned the British upside down. Washington had once considered these soldiers "dirty and nasty." But for seven years he led them through the turmoil of battle and then begged them to reenlist—"in the most affectionate manner," one sergeant recalled. When a few Virginians still complained about New England recruits, Washington set them straight. "I do not believe that any of the states produce better men, or persons capable of making better soldiers," he said.

The Continental army was where the United States first experienced a sense of real unity. Out of many, one. They were "old men of 60, boys of 14, and blacks of all ages, and ragged for the most part," reported one British officer, turning up his nose. "Their army is the strangest that was ever collected." But these Continentals had come to think themselves anyone's equal. And they had fought long and hard enough to make themselves, and their new nation, thoroughly independent.

14

MORE PERFECT UNION

AMERICANS THOUGHT THEIR WAY TO a revolution and fought their way to independence. But could they stay united? At war's end, Congress issued an official Great Seal of the United States featuring an eagle with the motto: *E pluribus unum.* Out of many, one. But how could this possibly be managed?

It already *had* been managed, suggested Patrick Henry at the first Continental Congress. "We are in a state of nature," he told the delegates. "Where are your landmarks, your boundaries of colonies? . . . The distinctions between Virginians, Pennsylvanians, New Yorkers, and New Englanders are no more. I am not a Virginian, but an American."

In truth, the colonies were hardly so united. Notice how the Declaration of Independence put it: "These United Colonies are, and of Right ought to be Free and Independent States." United, yes,—but as a confederation of independent states. John Adams continued to think of Massachusetts as his "country," just as Jefferson called Virginia his. At one point, when General Washington asked some of his New Jersey recruits to swear allegiance to the United States, they refused. "New Jersey is our country!" they protested. In fact, "these United States" were a confederation much like the present-day United Nations. Each state sent a delegation to Congress, just as nations today send delegations to the UN General Assembly. In both cases, each delegation cast a single vote.

The rules of the new government were set out in the Articles of Confederation. In creating the Articles, Congress wanted to avoid the kinds of problems that had led to war in the first place. Obviously, the United States would crown no king—Tom Paine and *Common Sense* had made short work of that. The Articles also forbade giving out titles of nobility. There would be no Lord Washington or Baron Adams, nor even a president of the United States to enforce the laws. This confederation would be managed by a legislature with thirteen votes. Congress did have the right to declare war and sign treaties. It could appoint military officers, as it did Washington. It could issue coins and paper money. It reserved the power to make agreements with Indian nations.

But those were rather limited powers. Congress could appoint army officers, but couldn't create the army that its officers commanded. It could only *ask* states to send soldiers. Congress couldn't tax Americans to pay for its expenses; it could only *request* money from the states. It had no power to regulate trade between the thirteen states and the rest of the world. These limits made sense to a people already at war with a distant Parliament that had taxed them, regulated their trade, and stationed troops in their backyards. Why would any state want another legislature in far-off Philadelphia lording it over them? The Articles of Confederation never once referred to the United States as a nation, only as a "league of friendship."

Unfortunately, these "friendly" states began quarreling. To begin with, the larger and the smaller states didn't trust each other. When Patrick Henry announced that he was an American, not a Virginian, it was because he thought smaller states like Maryland and

Delaware had too much power. Each had one vote in the Congress, like Virginia. But Virginia had many more people. "It is known in my province that some other colonies are not so numerous or rich," he pointed out. Shouldn't Virginians have the right to send more representatives to Congress? Smaller states like Maryland, on the other hand, worried about large states gaining too much influence from their size. Virginia claimed lands stretching all the way to the Mississippi River, where the United States ended in 1783. It could raise money by selling those lands to settlers, which would keep Virginia taxes low; while Maryland, which had no western lands to sell, would have to raise taxes.

After much arguing, the larger states agreed to give up their western lands. As these lands were settled over time, they would be divided into "territories" and eventually become states that would be the equals of the original thirteen states. That was one dispute solved, but many states continued to go their own way, showing little respect for the national government. Sometimes states didn't even bother to send a delegation to Congress. Looking on, Europeans suspected that the confederation might just fall apart.

And the state governments themselves seemed ineffective. In Massachusetts, a thousand desperate farmers rose up in protest when the Massachusetts legislature ignored their petitions for help in the midst of hard times. Led by Daniel Shays, a veteran of Lexington and Concord, mobs closed the local courts for a time. Shays' Rebellion was put down, but many Americans were shocked by the violence. James Wilson of Pennsylvania sadly recalled Patrick Henry's words from 1774, "that Virginia is no more, that Massachusetts is no more, that Pennsylvania is no more . . . " But instead of the states joining in a strong union, they had become "frittered down" and powerless. Convinced that the Articles of Confederation needed to be revised, delegates from twelve states gathered in Philadelphia during the summer of 1787.

No one was more concerned about a weak confederation than James Madison, a Virginia planter. Five feet four inches tall, slender, with dark eyes and thinning hair, Madison lacked the stature of a Washington, and he was a bit shy. "A gloomy, stiff creature," judged one woman who met him. But Madison was a sharp listener and a sharper thinker. An Enlightenment man, he was fascinated by the science of government. What caused nations to succeed or fail? How could governments give leaders enough power to be effective, but not so much that they became tyrants? Madison not only devoured books about such questions, he practiced politics day in, day out as a member of Virginia's legislature and later in the Confederation Congress. Knowing that most Americans would accept a stronger government only if respected leaders got behind the project, he visited George Washington more than once. The general hated to leave his Mount Vernon home, but the confederacy was like "a house on fire," he agreed, and in danger of being "reduced to ashes." So Washington came, as did Benjamin Franklin. By then he was eighty-two years old, "a short, fat, trunched old man," reported one visitor, though he still exercised daily with a barbell.

After choosing Washington to preside over the convention, the fifty-five delegates made a bold decision. Instead of just revising the Articles of Confederation, they began work on an entirely new constitution. Madison and the Virginia delegation had already put together a plan. It proposed a national legislature; but unlike the Confederation Congress, this legislature would have two houses. Representatives to the lower house would be chosen by voters, their number in proportion to a state's population: the greater the population, the more representatives. Members of the upper house would be chosen by the lower house from a list of candidates provided by each state legislature. Under the Virginia Plan, the new Congress was much stronger. It could not only tax citizens but also veto any state laws that conflicted with the powers of the national government. A second branch of government, the executive, would carry out the laws. And a third, the judiciary, would settle any disputes over federal law through a system of courts.

The smaller states didn't like Madison's plan, especially the idea of proportional representation. They wanted each state to have a single vote, as before. New Jersey presented a plan based on this arrangement, but most delegates agreed that it didn't give the national government enough power. Everyone turned to making the Virginia Plan acceptable to more delegates.

Creating a system of government from the bottom up meant deciding on dozens, even hundreds, of details. Most delegates agreed that an executive was needed to carry out the laws, but what sort? A president with a four-year term seems obvious now—because that's what the delegates chose. Why not have three "co-presidents" to represent different regions of the nation? That was one proposal. Why not limit the president to a single six-year term in office? That would allow enough time to get something done and remove the temptation to spend a lot of energy on getting reelected. Should the president be able to veto any law Congress passed? The delegates debated these issues and many more.

With so many choices to be made and so many different opinions, compromise was essential. The makeup of the legislature sparked the most debate, not only between large and small states but also between the northern and southern regions. In 1787 the populations of the North and South were about equal, but the South was growing more quickly. So southern delegates (including Madison) wanted the number of representatives to be based on population. The North, on the other hand, was divided into a greater number of smaller states. If each state had one vote, northern states could more easily outvote southern states, even if more people lived in the South.

Slavery complicated the argument even more. If each state was given representatives according to its population, should slaves be counted as part of that number? No, argued the northern states, which had many fewer slaves than the South. Slaves can't vote, you southerners consider them your property, and the number of representatives shouldn't be determined by how much property you own. We northerners wouldn't ask for more representatives just because we have a lot of cattle and horses! Southern delegates replied that slaves should be counted because people with more property have a greater stake in society and would be paying more taxes. "Money is power," argued South Carolina. States "ought to have weight in the government in proportion to their wealth."

Finally a committee led by Benjamin Franklin proposed a series of compromises. The number of members in the House of Representatives (the lower house) would be determined by population, as Virginia suggested—a victory for the large states. Small states were pleased that the Senate (the upper house) would have two senators from each state, no matter what their population. Senators would not be elected by the people but chosen by their state legislatures. Slaves would be counted as part of a state's population (without being able to vote)—a win for the southern states. But each slave would count only as three-fifths of a person. The "Three-fifths Compromise" did not please northerners, but the southern delegates would go no further.

Perhaps the biggest hurdle to creating the Constitution was finding a way that thirteen independent states could think of themselves as one. People who studied government were used to thinking of *sovereignty*—the ultimate power in a state—as existing in one place. Was the new national government sovereign? Did all power flow from it? Or was each state sovereign, with the right to say no to the federal government? The delegates came to realize that sovereignty could be divided. Under the system of federalism they created, the national government had ultimate power in some areas, but the states reserved ultimate power in others. And the national government divided its own powers among three separate branches: executive, legislative, and judicial. Each branch had ways to check the power of the other branches, a safeguard if one branch should seem to go astray.

By September the Constitution was ready to be presented to the states for their approval. Its supporters, called Federalists, countered attacks by the Anti-Federalist opponents. Sam Adams of Boston opposed, as did Patrick Henry, who hadn't attended the convention because he "smelled a rat." The Anti-Federalists' strongest argument was that the Constitution had no bill of rights, including such guarantees as the freedom of speech, freedom of religion, and the right to a trial by jury. Some states voted in favor of the new union only after being assured that a bill of rights would be added later—as it was. By June of 1788 nine states had ratified, enough to put the Constitution into effect. Rhode Island, the last holdout, joined the Union in 1790.

"Well, Doctor, what have we got—a republic or a monarchy?" asked one woman as Franklin left the convention. "A republic, if you can keep it," he replied. His answer mixed caution with hope. The Constitution's opening words are *We the People of the United States, in Order to form a more perfect Union . . .* That Union was surely *more* perfect than the Articles of Confederation, but not *most* perfect. How could it be, when so many compromises were made? Franklin, who had only a few years left to live, knew that compromise was the only way to succeed. "I confess that there are several parts of this constitution which I do not at present approve," he told the delegates. After all, "when you assemble a number of men to have the advantage of their joint wisdom, you inevitably assemble with those men, all their prejudices, their passions, their errors of opinion, their local interests, and their selfish views. From such an assembly can a perfect production be expected?" Even so, Franklin supported the Constitution "because I expect no better, and because I am not sure, that it is not the best."

Over time the new frame of government would need to change. And it has, because the delegates provided a way for the Constitution to be amended. But 1789 marked a momentous new start. A confederation among thirteen "free and independent" states had been replaced by a stronger, more perfect Union, whose ultimate power—its sovereignty—lay in three key words: not *We the states*, but *We the people.*

15

WASHINGTON'S FEAR

THERE WERE TWO LINES OF soldiers waiting as George Washington stepped out of his carriage and walked between them up to New York City's newly painted Federal Hall. On the second floor where the new Senate met, John Adams, the vice president–elect, led the general onto a balcony to take the oath of office. As the crowd in the street gazed up on this April afternoon in 1789, Washington pledged to "faithfully execute the office of President" and to "preserve, protect, and defend the Constitution." Then he returned inside and spoke briefly to the Congress. He did not look happy. "This great man was agitated and embarrassed more than ever he was by the leveled cannon or pointed musket," one observer noticed. "He trembled and several times could scarce make out to read" his speech.

Washington's fear would have seemed strange to most Americans, if they had known of it. As the president-elect traveled from his plantation in Virginia to the temporary federal capital of New York, he was treated nearly as a god. Church bells pealed; cannons fired; maidens scattered flowers in his path. Philadelphia even dangled a boy above him, to lower a crown of laurel onto his head. Washington was so mortified by the attention that he snuck out of town the next morning an hour before a cavalry guard arrived to escort him. But there was no escape: a forty-foot barge rowed him into New York City as thousands of spectators on shore crowded in "as thick as ears of corn before a harvest."

"My countrymen will expect too much from me," Washington worried. And he was not just being modest: he had read his history. He knew very well how difficult it was for republics to survive. The generals of ancient Rome had quarreled, murdered their rivals, and turned their republic into a dictatorship of Caesars. The leaders of the English civil war had chopped off King Charles's head to create a Puritan commonwealth that lasted less than five years. Today we don't take Washington's fears seriously. We know how the story turned out. Yet ten years after his inauguration, Washington went to his grave still unsure whether the United States would survive.

His election had been unanimous, although he was not chosen directly by the people. The framers of the Constitution hadn't trusted the people with that power. How could a farmer in Massachusetts judge whether a candidate from South Carolina was fit to serve? In a land without radio, television, or the Internet, the Constitution instead required that each state choose a group of electors—people with broader experience—who were more likely to know the candidates personally. Meeting as the Electoral College, these electors would choose a president and vice president.

To assist Washington in his duties, Congress created several executive departments and the president chose leaders to head them. These officers became known collectively as the cabinet, a word that originally referred to a small, private room used as a study or retreat. Indeed, to begin with, the cabinet met at Washington's home. Each member paid particular attention to one part of government. The two most important cabinet members were Thomas Jefferson, secretary of state, and Alexander Hamilton, secretary of the treasury.

The Constitution said nothing about a cabinet; and it breathed not a word about political parties. Everyone agreed that parties had no place in the new system because the nation's leaders were all expected to pursue the "true interest of the country," as Madison put it. In England, parties were mainly groups of people who schemed together in Parliament to pass laws favoring themselves and their friends. "Factions," they were called, and the term was an insult. Jefferson said that if he were told he had to join a party in order to get into heaven, he wouldn't go.

Of course, people have always dreamed of a time when disagreements would melt away and everyone live in peace—a "golden age," Columbus might have said. Or a holy commonwealth, as John Winthrop hoped. Or a millennium of peace, as Jonathan Edwards expected. The leaders of the new Republic had high hopes for unity, too, which is why they condemned political parties. But such feelings began to break down almost immediately. In any nation there will be a wide variety of people and interests. Merchants who sell clothing have different needs from farmers who raise wheat. People who lend money see things differently from those who borrow it. English, Africans, Germans, Scots, Irish, Dutch—these peoples and many more brought differing customs, religions, and habits to America. If "the many" in this new nation were to unite as one, their government would have to deal with such differences, not expect them to disappear by magic in a new golden age. Well should Washington fear what lay ahead!

Not surprisingly, the first quarrel was over money: how to pay the debts run up during the Revolution. The new secretary of the treasury, Alexander Hamilton, wanted to act immediately. Dashing, dapper, and determined, Hamilton had served during the war as an aide to Washington. Now he proposed that the United States stand behind its debts in full, and also take over any debts that individual states still owed. Many investors who held the debts were influential. "All communities divide themselves into the few and the many," Hamilton pointed out. "The first are the rich and well-born." He wanted these people to have "a distinct, permanent share in the government." As for the many, they were "turbulent and changing" and never fully to be trusted.

But the situation was more complicated. Many ordinary folk had loaned the government money, not just the rich and well-born. A farmer supplied food to the troops and was paid with an IOU. A cabinetmaker joined the army and received some of his wages the same way. By 1789, these loans had gone unpaid for so many years that, during hard times, people in need of cash had sold their notes to investors for a fraction of what they were worth. They decided it was better to get a few cents on every dollar than nothing. Jefferson and Madison argued that it was unfair to pay the new investors the full value of the loan when the original holders of the IOUs had gotten only pennies. After much arguing, they reluctantly backed Hamilton's proposal to pay the full face value of the notes, but only after Hamilton supported their wish to build a permanent capital for the nation in a settlement to be located between Virginia and Maryland.

News from abroad sparked a second dispute. The year Washington took office, a French mob stormed a dungeon called the Bastille to free prisoners kept there by King Louis XVI. French reformers also demanded that the king allow the government to become more democratic. Americans rejoiced at this news: after all, the French had been an ally in their own fight for freedom. Within a few years, though, this French Revolution turned violent. The king, queen, and thousands of nobles were executed; and France went to war with Great Britain and other European nations, whose leaders worried that if French citizens were allowed to kill kings and nobles, their own people might try the same thing. Many Americans, including Hamilton and John Adams, felt closer to Great Britain than to the French revolutionaries. Other Americans supported France. Equality had begun to spread throughout Europe, Jefferson rejoiced. Yes, there had been violence; but that was a small price to be paid for democracy after centuries of harsh rule by kings.

Washington tried to thread his way through these quarrels. He announced that the United States would remain neutral in the war between France and England. But the disagreements within his cabinet continued, with Hamilton and Adams usually persuading Washington to take their side. Jefferson and Madison decided that if they wanted to make any progress, they would have to find ways to elect to Congress more people who shared their views. One spring the two men took a vacation in New York and New England, supposedly to fish and collect unusual plants. "Botanizing," they called it. But they were equally interested in collecting political allies and fishing for votes. They took the first steps toward creating that strange beast Jefferson said he would never go to heaven with: a political party. The supporters of Jefferson and Madison became known as Democratic Republicans, or Republicans for short. (They were unrelated to today's Republican Party, which was created half a century later.) Hamilton's followers called themselves Federalists, claiming the honor of those who supported the Constitution.

Federalists found the most support in New England, where commerce was important and ties to Great Britain were strongest. The United States would become prosperous and powerful, Federalists believed, if the government encouraged industry and business to flourish. They approved Hamilton's financial programs and favored having a national bank, which Hamilton persuaded Congress to create. And, like Hamilton, Federalists believed that the "better sort of people" should be supported, while ordinary folk should be regulated for their own good. Republicans, on the other hand, worried that the national government was becoming too powerful. They didn't fully trust merchants and bankers, instead viewing farmers and planters as the pillars of a democratic nation. The future of the country lay not in the East, with its "rich and well-born," but with small farmers in the more democratic West.

Washington was elected to a second term, but in 1796 he refused to run for a third, wearied of the quarreling. Both the Republican

Jefferson and the Federalist Adams became candidates for president; when the electors met, Adams received the most votes. But the Constitution said nothing about the electors taking a separate vote to choose a vice president. Since Jefferson came in second in the voting for president, he became the Republican vice president for his Federalist rival.

As John Adams took office, France and Britain continued their war. Each tried to stop Americans from trading with their opponents by capturing American ships on the high seas. Federalists were eager for a war against France, convinced that it would build support for their party. But Adams refused to support such a war, enraging Hamilton and many of his fellow Federalists. The president's stand took courage: with war fever running high, Adams knew he was probably ruining his chances to be reelected in 1800.

Once again, he squared off against Jefferson. But by now both Federalists and Republicans were organizing their supporters, and the battle between the two parties often became violent. Party newspapers attacked their opponents and rival editors even got into fistfights. On the floor of Congress, one Republican, angry at being insulted, spit in his opponent's face: the Federalist grabbed a cane, the Republican snatched a pair of tongs from the fire pit, and they went after each other, thrashing about on the floor.

The tension increased when Federalists, the party in power, passed laws meant to silence Republicans. The Sedition Act called for the arrest of anyone who criticized the government in "a false, scandalous and malicious" way. Twenty-five Republicans were arrested for such "crimes," even though the Bill of Rights included the freedom of speech. The quarrels became so violent because both sides feared that their opponents would destroy the Republic. Republicans were convinced that Federalists wanted to set up a monarchy. Federalists feared that Republicans would riot like the French revolutionaries.

When the election of 1800 was held, the Electoral College met, and Adams and his Federalist running mate lost. But Jefferson re-

ceived exactly the same number of votes as the Republican candidate for vice president, Aaron Burr. So who had been elected
president? Seeing the tie, Burr didn't immediately step aside; he
rather liked the idea of becoming president. So the election had
to be settled in the House of Representatives. The House took vote
after vote—thirty-five in all—and each came up a tie. Some Federalists spoke of throwing over the Constitution and taking "the risk
of civil war" rather than vote for Jefferson. Hamilton disagreed.
"If there be a man in the world I ought to hate, it is Jefferson." But
Aaron Burr was shiftier, he argued, a politician who truly could not
be trusted. Finally the Federalists gave Jefferson the extra vote he
needed.

Washington had been right to fear for the Republic, though he
died a year before this crisis. In the end, a Democratic Republican became president, with the aid of a determined political party.
And—life went on. The Republic did not collapse or spiral into
ruin, as many had feared. Fortunately, the Republicans had the
good sense to repeal the Sedition Act rather than use it to keep
themselves in office.

The election of 1800 provided an important lesson. The end of
one administration did not signal the end of the nation. *E pluribus
unum* did not mean that everyone had to think the same way and
hold the same beliefs. The nation could survive—even with differences.

16

EMPIRE OF LIBERTY

THOMAS JEFFERSON WAS AN OPTIMIST. "I steer my bark with Hope in the head," he wrote, "leaving Fear astern." He saw America differently from the Federalists and wanted to show it, even in his inauguration.

There would be no cream-colored carriage for the president, pulled by six horses, as in 1789. Jefferson simply walked to the ceremony, dressed as "a plain citizen." His swearing-in was the first held in Washington, the new capital, and Jefferson, never a good speaker, read his address in a low voice. Even if he had spoken up, few could have heard his words in the drafty, unfinished Senate chamber. Afterward the new president walked back to Conrad and McMunn's, the boardinghouse where he was living, to have dinner. Many lodgers were already eating and no one bothered to stand as he entered, which was as Jefferson wished. Even as vice president he had regularly sat at the bottom of the large table, which is to say, in the coldest spot, farthest from the fireplace. Republican society was all about equality, and Jefferson wanted to demonstrate that.

His address to Congress looked to heal the wounds caused by the hard-fought election. John Adams left town before dawn on inaugural morning—unhappy, discouraged, still angry over his defeat in such a close and bitterly fought election. In contrast, Jefferson assured his rivals that he harbored no hard feelings. "We are all Republicans, we are all Federalists," he insisted, for he truly hoped that political parties would fade away. But the differences persisted. Federalists thought the president *should* drive in a splendid carriage so ordinary Americans would experience the dignity and power of their national government. Unlike Jefferson, Alexander Hamilton wanted that government to act and be seen; it should not "operate at a distance and out of sight." Federalists pushed for a strong army and navy, eager to have their nation rival the powerful countries of Europe.

Jefferson, on the other hand, preferred a small government more like that of the old confederation. Once in office, he cut the army in half and kept only a small fleet of gunboats. The District of Columbia had been hacked out of the woods north of Virginia, and the president did govern at a distance and out of sight—of almost everything. New York and Philadelphia, where Congress had met under the Federalists, were bustling cities with churches, theaters, restaurants, and other public places. Washington claimed little more than a racetrack, where rowdies met to drink and fight, and a theater so rickety that young folk snuck in by crawling underneath and pushing up the loose floorboards. In the balcony of the Senate, a sign warned visitors not to put their shoes up on the railing, "as the dirt from them falls upon Senators' heads." The French architect Pierre L'Enfant had laid out a network of grand streets and avenues, which the town would gradually construct. But for the time being these remained muddy paths with stumps still sticking up in the streets. The President's House was half finished, with heaps of garbage outside. Inside, no stairs had yet been built to reach the second floor.

Jefferson was happy to govern in this countrified capital, where a forest of tulip poplar trees spread across Capitol Hill. The job of the government, he believed, was merely to keep its citizens "from injuring one another." Otherwise it should leave them alone, "free to regulate their own pursuits of industry and improvement."

Federalists could not share Jefferson's optimism. They distrusted ordinary folk too much to campaign enthusiastically for votes. "There must be rulers and subjects, masters and servants, rich and poor," insisted one Federalist, much as John Winthrop had said two centuries earlier. "Every day proves to me more and more that this American world was not meant for me," Hamilton wrote sadly. Within three years he had been shot dead in a pistol duel with Vice President Aaron Burr, his archrival from New York, over insults Hamilton had supposedly directed against Burr. The Federalist Party dwindled and never again regained control of Congress. In 1804 Jefferson was reelected to a second term; then James Madison followed him as president for eight years. The Federalists survived as long as they did only because Americans were divided again over a new war in Europe. France and Great Britain, which had been fighting each other on and off for more than a hundred years, joined battle again in one final struggle to become the dominant power in Europe.

In France the leaders of the Revolution had been replaced by an ambitious general named Napoleon Bonaparte. During the previous wars, Napoleon forced his way into Italy, Austria, and Egypt at the head of the French army. Then he returned to Paris and, within a short time, made himself emperor of the French people. As Great Britain and France resumed their war, both countries again began capturing American ships that traded with their opponents. New England merchants were hard hit by these raids—over eight hundred ships were taken. But so were ordinary sailors, because British captains often stopped American vessels and hauled sailors off, claiming they were British seamen who had fled the navy. Thousands had indeed fled, but many other impressed sailors were Americans, swept up by a foreign navy that was desperate to man its fighting ships.

Jefferson thought he had a peaceful way to stop these attacks. He persuaded Congress to forbid all trade with France and Britain. This embargo, as it was called, was meant to punish the nations that were taking American goods. But it ended up hurting Americans more than the British or French. So after a year Congress repealed the embargo and trade resumed. Trying a different strategy, the new president, Madison, announced that if either France or Britain stopped raiding American ships, the United States would suspend trade with the other side. Napoleon pledged a halt—and Madison promptly forbade trade with Britain. But Napoleon outfoxed the president by letting French ships go on capturing American ships anyway. And Britain, even more angry with the United States, stepped up its raids.

It would be natural to think that New England merchants would clamor for war with Britain, since it was their trade that was being hurt. But the merchants knew war would only make matters worse. The call to battle came instead from a new generation of Republicans in the South and West. Called "War Hawks," these young members of Congress complained that Britain didn't respect the independence of the United States. They pushed Madison and kept pushing until finally he declared war in June 1812. From the sidelines at Monticello, Jefferson predicted that British Canada was America's for the taking. It was "a mere matter of marching," he wrote.

But war is always more costly and deadly than the War Hawks of the world predict. Puny Republican gunboats proved no match for Britain's navy. As for invading Canada, one American general surrendered his army before even firing a shot; other militiamen simply refused to cross the border. American ships on the Great Lakes did win several hard-fought battles, but those victories were countered by a British raid on Baltimore and Washington, which forced President Madison and his wife, Dolley, to flee the President's House just as they were about to sit down to dinner. The British not only had themselves a good meal but also set fire to the mansion before leaving.

This embarrassment was countered by a stunning American victory at New Orleans in January 1815. Although the British had finally defeated Napoleon in Europe, they now faced an equally tough general from the backwoods of Tennessee, Andrew Jackson. Jackson had already beaten Britain's Indian allies in the west and then fought his way into Spanish Florida (against President Madison's orders). At New Orleans he held off the British with an army that included Kentucky and Tennessee frontiersmen, several companies of free African Americans from New Orleans, a band of Choctaw Indians, and a passel of pirates rounded up by their wily leader, Jean Lafitte.

News of Jackson's victory reached Washington just as a delegation of Federalists arrived to protest "Mr. Madison's War." For the Federalists, the timing could not have been worse. They had regained some of their power in New England, where the war was unpopular. But Jackson's victory thrilled most Americans, and in any case, British and American diplomats in Europe had signed a treaty even before the battle of New Orleans. News of the peace arrived in Louisiana only after Jackson's victory. With Britain no longer fighting the United States and Napoleon defeated, Europe entered a century of relative calm. For years to come the United States would not be dragged into European affairs. It could turn its attentions to the vast North American continent, where there was already much to consider.

Americans gained no territory from the War of 1812, but a decade earlier, Jefferson had managed to double the size of the United States without firing a shot. He accomplished this because Napoleon, then distracted by war in Europe, had offered to sell French Louisiana to the Americans for $15 million. Even before the deal was done, the president organized an exploring expedition across the region, to be led by his personal secretary, Captain Meriwether Lewis, and another army officer, William Clark.

In 1803 these were turbulent lands to cross. Since 1775 much of North America had been thrown into turmoil by a smallpox epidemic that killed some 130,000 French, British, Spanish, and Indians. (Compare that number to the 8,000 troops who died fighting in the Revolution during the same years.) In addition, the fighting during the Seven Years' War and the American Revolution had uprooted many native peoples and forced them to move.

For three years Lewis and Clark led their "Corps of Discovery" up the Missouri River in boats, across the Rocky Mountains, down the Columbia River to the Pacific Ocean—and then back home. Along the way they drew 140 maps and met with two dozen Indian nations. Lewis collected specimens of everything, from wood rats and horned toads to bull snakes, prairie dogs, and pelicans, sending many back to Jefferson. The expedition lost only one member along the way, to appendicitis. It avoided being drawn into battles with hostile Indians and had the sense to seek advice from friendly peoples. A Shoshone woman, Sacagawea, proved especially helpful when she joined the expedition along with her French fur-trading husband, Toussaint Charbonneau.

For a president who preferred a modest republic and a capital that was out of sight, buying Louisiana was perhaps one of the oddest things Jefferson might have done. To see why, stand a moment with Lewis and Clark in present-day Idaho, as Clark gave a speech to the Tushepaw Indians. His words were translated first into French, which Toussaint Charbonneau spoke, and then Charbonneau turned the speech into Minataree, a language he had learned living along the Missouri River. Sacagawea understood Minataree, for she had been taken prisoner by that people; but she had grown up farther west, so she could translate Minataree into Shoshone. Then a Tushepaw boy, who understood Shoshone, translated Clark's speech into his own people's tongue. English to French to Minataree to Shoshone to Tushepaw. The track of that speech gives a small idea of the patchwork of languages and cultures that had become part of the United States. And to these tongues and many more, add the Dutch still being spoken along the Hudson River, the Welsh and German heard among the farmers of Pennsylva-

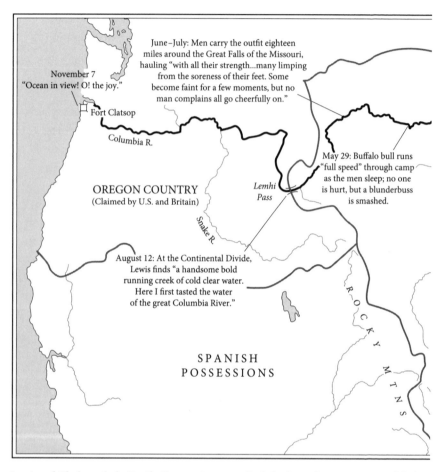

June–July: Men carry the outfit eighteen miles around the Great Falls of the Missouri, hauling "with all their strength...many limping from the soreness of their feet. Some become faint for a few moments, but no man complains all go cheerfully on."

November 7 "Ocean in view! O! the joy."

Fort Clatsop

Columbia R.

OREGON COUNTRY
(Claimed by U.S. and Britain)

Lemhi Pass

May 29: Buffalo bull runs "full speed" through camp as the men sleep; no one is hurt, but a blunderbuss is smashed.

Snake R.

August 12: At the Continental Divide, Lewis finds "a handsome bold running creek of cold clear water. Here I first tasted the water of the great Columbia River."

SPANISH POSSESSIONS

ROCKY MTNS

Lewis and Clark reach the Pacific Ocean, 1804–1805. Each day brought new surprises, delights, toil, and suspense.

nia, the Swedish in Delaware, the Gaelic spoken by Scots scattered along the Appalachians, and the Gullah dialect used by African Americans along the Carolina coast. If Republicans and Federalists found it hard to get along, how would a nation that was full of so many peoples and languages and opinions manage to settle its differences?

1804–1805: Winter with Mandan Indians.

Fort Mandan

Missouri R.

INDIANA
TERRITORY
(U.S.)

LOUISIANA
PURCHASE

August 1: Hunt for two lost horses;
William Clark celebrates his birthday
with a meal of venison,
beaver tail, and a dessert of
cherries, plums, raspberries,
currants and grapes.

August 20: Sergeant Charles Floyd
dies from appendicitis.
"We came to make a warm bath for
[him] hoping it would brace him
a little, before we could get him
in to this bath he expired."

Mississippi R.

July 4: "A snake bit Joseph Fields
on the side of his foot which
swelled much,
apply barks to the wound."

St. Louis

Jefferson briefly played with the idea that the United States
might split into two "Atlantic and Mississippi confederacies." But
in truth he wanted the Union to hold, for he had long dreamed that
the United States would become an "empire of liberty," the likes of
which had not been seen "since the creation." Jefferson believed
that the Union's democratic ideals would keep it together. True

freedom would give every voice an equal say at the table—just the way he dined at his old boardinghouse. "I am persuaded no constitution was ever before so well calculated as ours for extensive empire & self government," he told Madison.

But adding the Louisiana Purchase made it harder, not easier, for democracy to work and for everyone to find a seat at the table. Looking east from the Rocky Mountains, seeing all those languages and lands, Indians and immigrants, settlers and slaves, it was not easy to decide whether Jefferson was right to be an optimist.

17

MAN OF THE PEOPLE

JOHN ADAMS AND THOMAS JEFFERSON both died on July 4, 1826, fifty years to the day after the Declaration of Independence was proclaimed. By then an older generation had passed away and Americans were living in a changed world. The Federalist Party was gone. And strangely enough, so was the dream shared by all the Founders, that political parties would fade away. Instead, Americans fell head over heels for parties, and built a new style of democracy based on them.

The last of the old order was James Monroe of Virginia, who followed Madison as president (and died on July 4, too, in 1831). As an eighteen-year-old, Monroe had crossed the Delaware with Washington and been wounded in the battle afterward. Tall and angular, he was the last president to powder his hair and tie it back, the last to pull on knee britches, high white stockings, and buckled shoes. But more was changing than the fashions of the day. People behaved differently, with a more democratic air—even if the changes came so gradually that many Americans didn't notice.

Visitors from Europe did. They were astonished that a complete stranger might come up, shake hands, and begin asking personal questions, such as "what my business is here, and whether I carry a pistol about me; also whether I believe that it isn't lucky to play cards on Sundays." European common folk spoke to their "betters" only if their betters spoke to them. Worse, Europeans found it hard to tell who in America *was* rich or poor. A simple oyster seller along the streets of Philadelphia might wear a sleek coat, glossy hat, and doeskin gloves. Even if his outfit was not as well made as a gentleman's, it was tailored in the same style. Climbing aboard one of the new steamboats that chugged up and down rivers, Europeans were surprised to find no first-class cabins. "The rich and the poor, the educated and the ignorant, the polite and the vulgar, all herd on the cabin floor, feed at the same table, sit in each others laps," complained one gentleman. At the dining table, Americans rushed in, loaded up their plates, and "pitchforked down" huge quantities of food within a matter of minutes. At theaters they slouched in chairs, put their feet up on the bench in front of them, and didn't bother to take off their hats. Men chewed tobacco constantly and spit, indoors and out. "A perfect shower of saliva," groused a visiting Englishwoman.

Politics were just as free and easy. In Jefferson's day, most office seekers were gentlemen who expected ordinary folk to choose them to lead. By the 1830s, if a gentleman did run for office, he took care to act humble. "If a candidate be dressed farmlike," confided one congressman, "he is well received and kindly remembered." On the campaign trail, frontiersman Davy Crockett didn't give formal addresses. Instead he confessed to his audience that "there had been a little bit of speech in me a while ago, but I believed I couldn't get it out"—which made everyone roar out "in a mighty laugh." After a few more jokes, Davy admitted he "was as dry as a powder horn" and invited everyone "to wet our whistles a little" at the liquor stand. His poor opponent was left behind to speak to only a handful of remaining listeners.

During the early years of the Republic, only men who owned property could run for office—or even vote. But one by one states dropped these requirements, allowing more ordinary Americans to make a career of public service. Martin Van Buren of New York followed this path. The son of innkeepers in the Dutch-speaking town of Kinderhook, young Martin learned English as a second language. He got ahead in politics by listening politely, calculating carefully, and setting up a political network, the Bucktails, whose members were stoutly loyal to him. Van Buren was so successful at getting bills passed that he was nicknamed "the Little Magician."

And he saw what the Founders, for all their wisdom, had missed. Political parties would never fade away, and should not. Parties were "highly useful to the country," he insisted. As they competed fiercely against each other, they defended the interests of ordinary citizens. They kept their rivals honest by watching them like hawks, and they became expert at rousing supporters with rallies and torchlight parades, challenging opponents in newspapers and public debates, holding barbecues, promoting campaign songs, and wetting whistles. Their efforts stirred up thousands of citizens. In 1824, only one out of four eligible men bothered to vote in the presidential election. By 1840, three out of four did.

In the early days, party leaders chose candidates by holding a private meeting called a caucus. But many people began to condemn "King Caucus" as a backroom meeting that kept out ordinary citizens. Instead, parties held political conventions to make nominations, which allowed more people to get involved. But the new system came too late for the 1824 election, when no fewer than four candidates—all of them Republicans—ran for president. None gained more than half the votes in the Electoral College, so Congress had to choose a winner from among the top three, as the Constitution specified. John Quincy Adams, son of the second president, emerged as the winner, even though Adams had come in second in both the popular vote and in the Electoral College. He won because Henry Clay of Kentucky, the candidate with the least votes, convinced his followers in Congress to support Adams.

That left the man who *had* come in first—General Andrew Jackson—distinctly annoyed. During the War of 1812 Jackson's soldiers had nicknamed him Old Hickory because he was as tough and unyielding as the tree itself. In 1824, most political leaders had not taken him seriously. "One of the most unfit men I know of" to become president, commented old Thomas Jefferson. Jackson became convinced that the election had been stolen through a "corrupt bargain" between Adams and Henry Clay, especially after Adams turned around and appointed Clay to be his secretary of state. Four years later, Jackson's supporters stuck up hickory poles on steeples, gave away hickory canes and brooms, and voted for their man in greater numbers than ever. Jackson swept into office at the head of a new party, the Democrats. Adams and Clay eventually reorganized and renamed their party the Whigs.

Jackson's followers called him "the Hero" and "Old Hickory" and many more nicknames, most with *the people* in them. The new president was "a man of the people"; he championed the "will of the people." He was the people's idol, the people's servant. And he behaved very much like one of the people, in a larger-than-life sort of way. Jackson's parents had traveled Pennsylvania's Great Wagon Road from Philadelphia west to the Appalachians and then south, to settle in the Carolina backcountry. There, young Andrew studied law by day and partied by night. Brawling in barrooms, sporting with young ladies, moving outhouses in the wee hours as a prank, he was a "roaring, game-cocking" fellow, one neighbor recalled. Moving to Nashville, Tennessee, Jackson served as a prosecutor and later as a member of Congress. Meanwhile, he bought a cotton plantation and built it up, until eventually it used the labor of a hundred slaves. In March 1829 thousands of people flocked to Jackson's inauguration, clogging the roads and crowding into the presidential mansion, now known as the White House. Barrels of punch were spilled, glasses and china broken, and satin-covered chairs stained by muddy boots, as "the people" clambered onto every spare inch of space to see their man. He had become a symbol of America's new politics of equality.

What did equality mean to these Americans? Not that all people were equally talented, equally educated, or equally rich. Not even that they *should* be equal in those ways. What mattered most was that every citizen have an equal chance to get ahead. Or, as one American put it, "Every man shall be free to become as unequal as he can." The people wanted not equality, but equality of opportunity.

In trying to give everyone that chance, Jackson became especially suspicious of banks. The largest corporation in the country was the Bank of the United States, which Alexander Hamilton had promoted as necessary to help the economy run smoothly. The bank held all the deposits of the federal government. It issued paper money and made loans. All this gave it a great deal of power over ordinary people's lives. It had angered many during a financial crash known as the Panic of 1819, when businesses failed and people were thrown out of work or even out of their homes, if they couldn't pay their mortgages. The bank had taken away so many houses with bad mortgages, it seemed sometimes as if it owned entire towns. Jackson took such experiences personally. He had once nearly gone bankrupt himself. When Congress extended the life of the bank for another fifteen years, against his wishes, Old Hickory declared war on the "monster," as he called it. "The Bank is trying to kill me," he told his ally Martin Van Buren, "but I will kill it." And he did, vetoing the bill and then ordering that federal deposits be taken out of the bank and put in state banks.

For a while good times continued without the bank. But it had performed important services, even though it sometimes acted in a high-handed way. Without its guidance, the economy finally crashed: the Panic of 1819 seemed mild compared to the Panic of 1837. By then Jackson was no longer president. Martin Van Buren had succeeded him and, sadly for the Little Magician, the people gave him a new nickname: Martin Van Ruin.

A strange lesson can be learned here. In defeating the Monster Bank, Jackson had carried out the will of the people. And he and the people, it turned out, didn't understand the bank's importance. But a democracy doesn't succeed because the people are always right. Any government is sure to be wrong sometimes. The difference is, kings or tyrants can ignore their mistakes because they answer to no one. A democracy succeeds because, when mistakes are made, the people feel them and have the power to correct their errors. This they did in the election of 1840, when the Whig candidate for president, William Henry Harrison, soundly thumped the Democrat, poor Van Ruin. In that sense, the system worked. The people had corrected their own mistakes at the ballot box.

But America's new style of democracy contained a deeper flaw, one that could not be mended so easily. Although every American was supposed to have an equal opportunity to succeed, in truth, large chunks of the people had been left out of the system. Women could not vote. Neither could most African Americans, whether slave or free. As for Indians, their rights and wishes were ignored almost completely.

Native Americans still controlled much of North America in 1820. Even east of the Mississippi River, well over one hundred thousand lived on their own lands. Of these, many still hunted, fished, and planted corn, but others had thoroughly adopted white ways. Traveling through Georgia, you might meet a Creek Indian chief named—not Little Turtle or Wingina—but William McIntosh. His father was a Scottish trader, his mother a Creek. Although McIntosh dressed in Indian leggings and moccasins, he wore a ruffled shirt and black tie, as a white gentleman would. He owned a plantation and slaves to work it. He fought alongside Andrew Jackson during the War of 1812, against other Indians.

None of these Indians, no matter what their names or customs, were given an equal chance in the new democracy. Andrew Jackson's own plantation was carved out of Indian lands and Jackson himself led the way in taking those lands during the War of 1812. By

the time he finished forcing Indians to sign treaties, he was personally responsible for adding one-third of Tennessee, three-quarters
of Florida and Alabama, and one-fifth of Georgia and Mississippi
to the United States. As president, he proposed that the remaining
Indians living east of the Mississippi should move across the river
to lands in present-day Oklahoma. Some Indians took up arms to
resist; they were put down by military force. The Cherokee nation, which had its own written constitution, tried to protect itself
using American law. It took the state of Georgia to court when
Georgia took away its Cherokee laws and rights; and the Supreme
Court sided with the Cherokees. But Jackson simply ignored the
court's decision. About fifteen thousand Indians were forced off
their lands, some at bayonet point, and made to march hundreds of
miles along a "Trail of Tears" to their new "reservations"—land set
aside for them. Often robbed of their horses, bedding, and cooking
gear, and marching barefoot in winter weather with only summer
clothes, over three thousand Indians died along the way.

In his boldest battle as president, Jackson faced off against the
state of South Carolina. There, wealthy planters protested the tariffs that Congress had placed on manufactured goods imported
into the United States. The tariffs drove up the price that planters
paid for such items. Northern manufacturers, on the other hand,
liked the tariffs because they made it possible for them to sell similar American-made goods at a cheaper price. South Carolina was
angry enough to hold a special convention, proclaiming that any
state in the Union could nullify a law it believed was unconstitutional. South Carolina not only declared that the tariff would not
be collected in the state, it also insisted that if Congress didn't repeal the law, South Carolina had a perfect right to secede, or withdraw, from the Union.

Jackson was a southerner and a plantation owner, so he might
have been expected to support South Carolina. But he took the
threat as a personal insult. He had been elected by the people to
enforce federal laws, and South Carolina couldn't pick and choose

the ones it wanted to obey! Nor could it secede without the permission of the other states. The Union was "perpetual," Old Hickory warned, and if South Carolina tried to resist his authority with force, he would "*hang the first man of them I can get my hands on to the first tree I can find.*"

In this face-off, South Carolina blinked. It gave up the idea of nullification, although in years to come it continued to consider secession. Jackson had a hunch that South Carolina really wanted "disunion," he told a friend. It wanted to start its own "southern confederacy." The fight over the tariff was only an excuse. "The next pretext will be the negro, or slavery question," he predicted. If northerners could convince Congress to pass tariffs, what was to stop them from interfering with slavery?

In an earlier chapter I spoke about the twin histories of equality and inequality—how these forces seemed to be uneasy partners. As the belief in equality and freedom spread during the eighteenth century, so, too, did slavery. The same could be said about the new politics during the age of Jackson. Most white Americans expected to be treated equal in ways that astonished Europeans. Yet the equal rights of Indians were ignored. And African Americans—whether free or enslaved—found themselves being treated more harshly. White Americans in both the North and South were claiming that the African race was naturally inferior and could never be equal.

The dance between slavery and freedom was hardly done; it was only becoming more frantic. There was a reason for this—as the next chapter will show.

18

COTTON KINGDOMS

THE MOVEMENT OF Puritans who sailed to Massachusetts Bay
came to be known as the Great Migration, while at the same time
thousands more colonists chased tobacco in Virginia. Yet each of
those migrations was not a tenth the size of the land rush after the
War of 1812. You could glimpse the flood of settlers along the Natchez
Trace, an Indian trail that wound south from Nashville through
Tennessee, Alabama, and Mississippi. The migrants walked, rode
horseback, or drove carts through deep forests, around cypress
swamps, and in and out of canebreaks (American-style bamboo
thickets). Some were Virginians whose tobacco fields had worn
out; more were Scotch-Irish from the hills of the Appalachian
Mountains. Tens of thousands of slaves were yoked together with
wooden collars, guarded by men with guns and whips: "a wretched
cavalcade," reported one traveler, "marching half naked women and
men loaded with chains." At night, the prisoners were herded into
outdoor pens beside rough-and-tumble inns known as "stands."
Their masters and any other travelers slept inside, crowding as

many as fifty men to a room for the night. A single word explained this onrush of rich and poor, planters and farmers, speculators and slaves: *cotton.*

For centuries humans had spun the plant's white fibers into threads and woven the threads into cloth. But picking out the sticky seeds was tedious work. By the 1770s a simple machine had been invented that cleaned as much as forty pounds of cotton a day. That figure jumped to over two thousand pounds a day after 1793, thanks to newer "cotton 'gins," (short for "engines") made by Connecticut's Eli Whitney and other inventors. Suddenly two laborers could clean fifty times more cotton than before.

Now consider: farmers in South Carolina harvested about three hundred pounds of cotton for every acre they planted. But several hundred miles down the Natchez Trace, conditions were entirely different. The millions of acres Andrew Jackson forced the Indians to give up included soil so dark and rich, the region became known as the Black Belt. That land yielded eight hundred, even one thousand pounds of cotton per acre. It was boom time all over again. Mississippi and Louisiana doubled their population between 1810 and 1820; Alabama grew twelvefold.

And the South kept growing: people "pouring in with a ceaseless tide" in the 1830s; houses going up "as if by magic"; fields being cleared and crops planted. Not all were cotton. Rice plantations continued to flourish along the swampy coasts of South Carolina, Georgia, and Louisiana; Louisiana grew sugarcane as well. In the Upper South, tobacco was still planted, along with wheat and hemp. But cotton was the coming thing. By 1860 so many fields had been cleared that three-quarters of the entire world's supply of cotton came from the South. Steamboats stopped to load the heavy bales at nearly every river bend—and piled them so high that water often lapped over a ship's guardrails. "Cotton is king!" boasted Senator James Hammond of South Carolina. Indeed: cotton was king and the South was its kingdom.

It was a region filled with sharp contrasts. Speak the words "Old

South" and immediately a planter like Colonel Daniel Jordan springs to mind. Jordan was master of 261 slaves at his South Carolina estate, Laurel Hill. On fine days, the colonel could stroll down his oak-lined lawn and take a boat to dine along the Waccamaw River at the Hot and Hot Fish Club. Trout, bream, and perch were served up along with mint julep drinks—or perhaps a beverage even more remarkable in that day, a glass of water shimmering with ice. (Refrigerators had not yet been invented, but New England Yankees sawed frozen blocks from their winter ponds, packed the ice in sawdust, and shipped it south, where it was stored in underground coolers.)

Yet out of 8 million southern whites, only two thousand were rich enough to own more than a hundred slaves. (Andrew Jackson, man of the people, was one of the uncommon few.) In contrast to the mansions with Greek columns owned by such "nabobs," as the rich planters were called, many newer plantations were only unpainted wooden houses, one story high. Sometimes they even lacked window glass, which meant that the mosquitoes, fleas, and other assorted bugs could make sleeping a true nightmare. And though the cotton boom brought hundreds of thousands of slaves to the new country, three-quarters of southern white families owned none of them. Such smaller farmers were more like Ferdinand Steel of Granada, Mississippi, who planted mostly corn and only enough cotton to sell so that his family could buy a bit of sugar and coffee, gunpowder and bullets, and quinine—medicine to treat the malaria so common in those parts.

Even though only one out of four white families owned slaves, slavery lay at the heart of southern life and its economy. During the Revolution, northern states had begun to abolish the institution. Vermont led the way in 1777. A few years later, a Massachusetts slave named Mum Bett (Mother Betty) sued for her freedom in court after she discovered that the state constitution proclaimed, "All men are born free and equal." She won her case and it led to the freedom of all African Americans in Massachusetts. As slavery dwindled in the North, it grew by leaps and bounds in the South, becoming known as "the peculiar institution"—because now it was something that set the region apart.

How much did slavery shape the South? That was easy to answer for one-third of its people, the slaves themselves. Slavery forced them to make hard decisions from dawn to dusk. When the plantation bell clanged at 3:30 in the morning, long before sunrise, did you get up for work, knowing you wouldn't return to your quarters until 9:00 that night? Or were you so exhausted that you slept late and received twenty lashes with the whip? Perhaps you ran away, even knowing that the hound master would let the dogs loose to hunt you. Octave Johnson did—deep into the Louisiana swamps, to survive for more than a year with another sixty runaways. Perhaps, like Susan Hamlin, you awoke one morning to see your friends' children sold to a new master who lived hundreds of miles away. "You could hear men an' women screamin' to the tip of their voices as either ma, pa, sister, or brother was taken without any warnin'." Are you clever enough that your master makes you an overseer, one who directs the work of other slaves? If so, do you do your job faithfully? Or do you decide to take pity on your fellow slaves and sometimes look the other way when they ease up on their exhausting work? Perhaps you even decide that slavery is so evil God has called you to overthrow it. Nat Turner of Virginia had religious visions that convinced him to take matters into his own hands. In 1831 he led a band of seventy slaves who killed fifty-seven white men, women, and children before he was caught and hanged. Day in, day out, people in bondage had to decide what they thought of slavery: how far to accept it and how much to resist.

Planters made their own daily decisions. How hard do you work your human "property"? Do you avoid the harshest punishments, hoping your slaves will be more loyal? Or do you hire a hard-eyed overseer who is quick with a whip? If you're a Christian, do you let slaves go to church? If a couple wants to marry, do you allow a wedding service? (Most planters did not.) Do you let your slaves learn to read? Slave states made that illegal. After all, "there would be no keeping" a slave who could read, as one master pointed out. "It would forever unfit him to be a slave." That particular master was proved right, for one of his brightest slaves learned to read despite his orders and escaped to the North, where he became a well-known crusader against slavery. That man was Frederick Douglass.

As these questions show, even a master who wanted to treat his slaves kindly could never fully trust them, just as slaves could never trust their masters to "do right" by them. Consider the case of one plantation owner whose will provided that his slaves would be freed after his death and that of his elderly wife. A workable compromise? Not for the wife. After her husband died, she became terrified that one of the slaves would kill her, for then all his fellow slaves would go free. So she freed them then and there. Her name was Martha Washington—for it was the first president who had tried to do right by his wife and by his slaves, in writing a will that freed them.

Even southerners who didn't own slaves had to make decisions. If you saw a runaway, should you report him or her? If you thought slavery was wrong, did you dare speak out? In fact, most poor white southerners did believe slavery should continue. "Now suppose they was free," one poor farmer explained. "You see, they'd all think themselves as good as we." A poor white southerner might resent rich planters like Colonel Jordan. But even the lowliest could comfort himself that at least he was free.

The North, of course, was too cold a land to grow cotton. It had rid itself of slavery. Its people spoke out boldly for equality. It was not at all like the South. Well—how pleasant if northerners thought so! And how utterly mistaken a notion. For there grew up in the United States not one kingdom of cotton but two. The South's kingdom stretched for miles and miles along the Black Belt. The North's kingdom lay indoors, where the only black belts in sight whirred as they powered weaving machines that spun white threads. Neither kingdom could survive without the other. As the South harvested cotton, the North spun and wove it.

Northerners had to step lively to grow this kingdom. Yankees had always scrambled for a living, with their rocky fields and cold winters. Who but a Yankee would think to harvest useless ice—and then fetch worthless sawdust from the lumberyard to pack it and speed it south? In James Madison's day, Yankees watched southern planters ship their cotton bales to Britain's cloth makers. If only New Englanders could build the same clever machines that turned those bales into cloth and turned cloth makers into rich folk! But the British knew the value of their machines. Parliament passed laws forbidding anyone from taking plans of them out of the country. All across Britain, a host of inventions was changing the way people worked—so much so that we refer to the changes as the Industrial Revolution. Instead of one person spinning cotton or wool threads on a wheel at home, "spinning jennies" turned out a hundred threads at once, tended by workers in a large building called a factory. ("Jenny" was probably another nickname for "engine.") British "power looms" wove the cotton threads into cloth.

Then in 1810 a Boston merchant named Francis Lowell began a two-year visit to England and Scotland, touring factories and studying the machines closely to see how they worked. When he left, suspicious British officials searched his luggage—twice—for plans, but all the information Lowell needed was in his head. He soon erected a factory along Boston's Charles River. After Lowell died, his business partners created an entirely new factory village named after him, along the Merrimac River north of Boston. There waterwheels powered the machines of the new Lowell Mills.

Each of the new factories brought the many steps of cloth making under a single roof: from carding and combing the cotton (which made it easier to spin) to spinning the threads and weaving the cloth. The noise could be deafening: "thousands of spindles and wheels revolving, the shuttles flying, the looms clattering, and hundreds of girls overseeing the buzzing and rattling machinery," recalled one worker. The owners hired these "mill girls" from the nearby countryside. Young and unmarried, they were usually tired of the isolated, "countrified" life on farms. The mills paid a reasonable wage and housed their workers in dormitories where an older woman watched over them. In bustling Lowell, the girls could attend lectures, use the local library, and even help publish their own newspaper, the *Lowell Offering*. When Sally Rice's parents asked her to return to the farm, she replied, "I must have something of my own. . . . And where is that something coming from if I go home and earn nothing?"

Although many mill girls found factory work challenging at first or even fun, "when you do the same thing twenty times—a hundred times a day, it is so dull!" complained one. Another confessed that in cold weather, "many's the time when I couldn't feel the yarn, my fingers were so icy." The short winter daylight also meant that work began and ended in the dark. Then each factory would light several hundred whale-oil lamps. From the outside, the glowing windows made a cozy scene, but inside, the smoke fouled the air and left the workplace grimy from cotton lint, oil, and dust.

Just as the southern cotton boom most directly shaped the lives of slaves, the Industrial Revolution most directly affected northern factory workers. But cotton also transformed life for millions of Americans: through the clothes they wore. An ordinary worker could afford a decent jacket and pants now that manufactured suits came in ready-to-wear sizes at lower prices. No need to pay an expensive tailor to fit him, as gentlemen did. "All sorts of cotton fabrics are now so cheap that there is no excuse of any person's not being well provided," explained one magazine. Patchwork quilts became popular, which today we remember as quaint, old-fashioned creations. In fact, they were a sign of the modern reign of cotton. To piece together a quilt with bright patches and patterns, you needed old shirts, dresses, and other cloth to cut up. Only when factories began making so many cotton goods could mothers and daughters assemble such quilts.

So in both North and South, the kingdoms of cotton grew. Thousands of people pushed west, factories multiplied, and slavery flourished. The world had changed much since George Washington penned his will; and he would have been uneasy if he had seen the changes. In 1798, a year before his death, Washington confessed one of his greatest fears for the Republic. "I can clearly foresee that nothing but the rooting out of slavery can perpetuate the existence of our union, by consolidating it in a common bond of principle." King Cotton made that future much more difficult to imagine—in the North as well as the South. For though most northerners disliked slavery, they were unwilling to treat African Americans as equals. Mum Bett and other northern blacks might have struck blows by fighting for their rights as citizens, but they had not managed to win full respect or full equality. They lived segregated lives apart from whites to a greater degree than in the South.

Not all Americans were blind to these problems. In the same decades that cotton fields and textile factories continued to spread, some citizens dreamed of ways to make the United States a freer and more perfect union.

19

BURNED OVER

THE MILL GIRL WAS AT work in the weaving room when she saw the man; and immediately her heart began to race. She knew who he was. So did most of the girls in the room, though they had never laid eyes on him until the night before. A handsome man in his thirties, well over six feet, he had a face most solemn and eyes that missed nothing. The mill owner himself, Mr. Walcott, was his escort. The girl tried to pay attention to her work, for one of the threads at the loom had broken, but her hands trembled uselessly. When the man was within ten feet, instead of looking at the machinery, he fixed his gaze squarely on *her*, holding her eyes in such a holy and awful manner that she sank down and burst into tears, unable to stop herself. Suddenly the hush of voices in the room was more deafening than the clatter of machinery. Another girl broke down, then another and another. The first sobs had been like a match set to gunpowder.

Walcott Mills, in New York State, was one of many cotton factories springing up across the Northeast. At the same time that southerners were pushing west along the Natchez Trace, New Englanders streamed across New York and Pennsylvania into Ohio and beyond. The new Erie Canal, which passed near Walcott Mills, made travel and trade easier. Before the Erie was dug, the longest canal in the United States ran only 28 miles. By 1826 Erie's waters extended 360 miles, from Albany on the Hudson River to Buffalo on Lake Erie. Meanwhile, the steam engine—another invention of the Industrial Revolution—improved transportation on rivers. The new wide-bottomed steamboats held well over a hundred people and a hundred tons of cargo. Too big for canals, whose boats were towed by horses, steamboats moved goods not only downstream but upstream as well, against the current. Textile factories began using steam engines to run their machines, too.

On this morning in 1826, most of the workers at Walcott Mills were so shaken that the owner stopped the machines and let the visitor speak. His name was Charles Grandison Finney and he was there on a crusade to revive religion. Like George Whitefield during the Great Awakening, Finney preached from one town to the next. (The night before at the village schoolhouse, many mill girls had heard him warn that they needed to change their lives.) Like Jonathan Edwards before him, Finney hoped these religious awakenings would spread across America, bringing on the thousand-year "millennium" of peace and prosperity predicted in the Bible. But he wasn't content to follow old paths. "What do the politicians do?" Finney asked. "They get up meetings, circulate handbills and pamphlets, blaze away in the newspapers . . . all to gain attention to their cause." Finney was determined to spread the word of God by blazing away just as loudly.

His biggest revival came in Rochester, New York, the first boom town along the canal. Farmers brought their wheat to Rochester, where it was loaded into ingenious elevators that hoisted it to the mills' top floors in large buckets, then cleaned, separated, and ground it into flour as it moved down chutes. Back at the bottom of the mill, it was put in barrels and shipped down the canal toward

New York City. The workers were not quite as orderly as the machinery. At the end of long, hard days, many flocked to the theater, played in the streets, or drank in taverns, as the night echoed with "peals of *hooting, howling, shouting, shrieking,* and almost every other unseemly noise, that it is possible for the human gullet to send forth," one resident complained.

Merchants hoped that Finney would bring not only holiness but also a little order to the city, and during one entire winter he preached constantly. Women went door-to-door praying for their neighbors; businesses shut down; schools let out. Finney told listeners not to sit, meek as sheep, waiting for God's spirit—it was in *their* power to believe. "Just do it," he proclaimed. "If the church would do her duty, the millennium may come in this country in three years." Finney believed that perfection was within reach, and sometimes it seemed that half of America was burning with notions of how to make things better and how to achieve perfection.

So many revivalists and reformers traveled the roads of western New York that the area was nicknamed the Burned-Over District because of all the spiritual fires that had started there. What a time to live along the Erie Canal! Just south of Rochester, a young man named Joseph Smith published the *Book of Mormon.* Joseph had translated a set of golden tablets, he said, shown him by the angel Moroni. He used a pair of magic spectacles to read the "reformed Egyptian" characters. (The spectacles were crystals that looked like "two smooth three-cornered diamonds," his mother reported.) Smith and his fellow Mormons soon moved west, like so many other New Englanders, but fourteen years later more faithful souls flocked to Rochester, excited by William Miller, a preacher who predicted that Jesus himself would arrive on October 22, 1844, to gather up the saints for the millennium. Believers dressed in white "ascension robes" waited for Jesus all night atop the city's highest spot, Cobbs Hill. In the light of dawn, they had to walk back down, disappointed.

When the Bible said, "Be ye perfect," what did that mean? If the millennium arrived—with or without Jesus on Cobbs Hill—America would become Christian, there would be no need for political parties, and the nation's many peoples would be united as one. But by now, John Calvin's dream of a holy commonwealth had splintered into a hundred different visions, kindling a thousand different fires. In Massachusetts, minister Ralph Waldo Emerson proclaimed that every individual was "an infinite soul" who could and should rise above, or *transcend,* the "lifeless preaching" found in so many churches. Emerson's "transcendentalist" ideas urged people to seek out nature for inspiration, where "the buds burst and the meadow is spotted with fire and gold in the tint of flowers." Some prophets founded utopian communities—settlements of believers who set themselves apart to try new ways of living. (The Greek word *utopia* means "no place," which is to say, these communities could be found nowhere in the ordinary world, at least.) Emerson did not start one, but other transcendentalists founded Brook Farm and Fruitlands, communities where they shared food and the profits from working together. Joseph Smith and his Latter-day Saints started their own utopian town at Nauvoo, Illinois. Smith suggested that men might take more than one wife. He called this "plural marriage," and the teaching, along with other new ideas that his neighbors found strange, led a mob to murder him. Still other utopian reformers rejected religion entirely. Robert Owen designed factory villages where people held property as a group, not privately, and shared work equally. Called socialism, this system was meant to improve on the hard factory life that treated workers, as one mill girl put it, "just as though we are so many living machines."

No doubt some of these reforming ideas seemed impractical or even crack-brained. It is easy to mock such visions. But then, it is even easier to plod along day after day, convinced that the world should work the way it does because . . . well, it always has. The seekers of perfection dreamed boldly enough to recognize that the world could be transformed, if they supplied enough energy and elbow grease. The fires of reform spread.

When Dorothea Dix volunteered to teach Sunday school at a Massachusetts county prison, she was horror-struck to discover that mentally ill people were jailed right along with criminals. In some states, she reported, they were confined in cages, locked up in dark basements, "*chained, naked, beaten with rods,* and *lashed* into obedience!" Dix campaigned to improve the way the mentally ill were cared for. As for criminals, in Connecticut for many years an old copper mine was used as a prison. After working all day, inmates descended in handcuffs and chains down a fifty-foot iron ladder to huddle in dark, dank caverns from 4:00 in the afternoon until 4:00 in the morning, when they climbed out again. Reformers succeeded in improving many such abuses.

Other crusaders warned of the dangers of alcohol. During the colonial era, Americans consumed liquor regularly and often. But drinking rose sharply during the Industrial Revolution, especially among men. In fact, between 1790 and 1820, Americans drank more alcohol than at any time before or since. Unlike in the colonial period, when rum was popular, whiskey seemed to be spreading everywhere. It could be made in the poorest farmhouses and didn't depend on molasses from the Caribbean, as rum did. But too often the new habits of drinking produced tragic results: crimes committed, wives beaten or abandoned, children neglected. During one revival meeting in Rochester, ministers spoke out so strongly against alcohol that some merchants rolled barrels of whiskey into the streets and smashed them open. In a matter of a few years, Americans were drinking less alcohol than ever before.

Other reformers focused on slavery as the supreme evil of the day. David Walker, a free black from Boston, published a pamphlet calling freedom a "*natural right.*" Slaves should rise up and resist their owners, he said, for they were "cruel oppressors and murderers." Such views horrified most whites, northern or southern, so Walker sewed his pamphlets into the lining of coats that he sold to black sailors. They, in turn, smuggled them into southern ports, where the pamphlet was often banned. Walker might have become

more influential had he not died suddenly—poisoned by his enemies, some said.

The campaign to abolish slavery was taken to a new level by another Massachusetts firebrand, William Lloyd Garrison. Garrison
rejected the moderate solutions that many northerners were willing to consider, such as gradually ending slavery or encouraging
freed slaves to return to Africa. No, said Garrison, slavery should
be abolished immediately. His newspaper, the *Liberator,* pulled no
punches. "On this subject, I do not wish to think, or speak, or write,
with moderation. No! no! Tell a man whose house is on fire to give
a moderate alarm . . . but urge me not to use moderation in a cause
like the present. I am in earnest—I will not equivocate—I will not
excuse—I will not retreat a single inch—and I WILL BE HEARD."

Garrison was perhaps the most passionate abolitionist, but there
were many others. The escaped slave Frederick Douglass became a
talented speaker and eventually moved—where else?—to Rochester in the Burned-Over District, where he published his antislavery
newsletter, the *North Star.* Such acts took courage, because many
white Americans thought the idea of abolition was radical and
dangerous. A mob in Illinois hanged one reformer; another mob
dragged William Lloyd Garrison through the streets of Boston and
might have lynched him, too, if the mayor hadn't spirited him off
to jail—supposedly for "disturbing the peace" but really to protect
him. Garrison wrote on his prison wall that he had been confined
there "for preaching the abominable and dangerous doctrine, that
'all men are created equal.'"

Garrison encouraged women to join his campaign, but he
was unusual in doing so. Many male abolitionists frowned when
women asked to participate. But women played an important part
in the revivals and reforms of the era. Lucretia Mott traveled to
London in 1840 as a delegate to the World Anti-slavery Convention. She was a Quaker, and Quakers had been among the first to
condemn slavery. Mott refused to wear cotton clothing, eat sugar
or rice, or use any other product produced by slave labor. The an-

tislavery men in London told her that women were "unfit" to take part and would "bring ridicule" on the meeting. Female delegates were forced to watch the proceedings from a special roped-off section.

There Mott made friends with a young woman from America, Elizabeth Cady Stanton. Stanton had fallen in love with an antislavery reformer, and when her father disapproved of the match, she ran off and married him anyway. A woman of independent mind, she was delighted to hear Lucretia Mott tell her "that I had the same right to think for myself that Luther and Calvin had." The two women returned to America "resolved to hold a convention" of another kind—this time not against slavery but for women's rights.

It took time, but at last the convention was called to order in 1848 at Seneca Falls, another village in the Burned-Over District. One hundred women and men signed a "Declaration of Sentiments" that echoed Jefferson's original Declaration. "We hold these truths to be self-evident," it proclaimed: "that all men and women are created equal . . . " Just as the first Declaration listed unjust acts that led Americans to take up arms, the Declaration of Sentiments set out the "repeated injuries" of men toward women. Women had to obey laws that they had no voice in making. They were not allowed to become ministers or doctors or enter many other professions. Laws gave husbands the power to control their wives' property. The Declaration of Sentiments demanded that women be given "all the rights and privileges which belong to them as citizens of these United States," including the right to vote.

A few newspapers praised the Declaration of Sentiments, including Frederick Douglass's *North Star;* many others mocked the "spicy resolutions." Elizabeth Stanton's own abolitionist husband was so "thunderstruck" at the idea of letting women vote that he left town until the convention controversies died down.

All men and women are created equal. What an "abominable and dangerous" doctrine! But the fires of perfection and reform continued to burn. The ideals of 1776 had not yet finished their work.

20

FRONTIERS

WE COME NOW TO A BIG gulp of a chapter. In the space of a very few years, the nation expands across the continent until it reaches from the Atlantic to the Pacific. If that seems sudden, consider the energy we've already seen shimmering through the United States. Politicians parading, revivalists preaching, reformers protesting. Power looms whirring, Americans pulling up stakes and moving, steamboats racing along western rivers. (Yes, racing. To beat rival boats, crews flung log after log onto the fires that boiled steam, often causing the boats to explode and burn to the water. Over four thousand people died in such accidents.) The two kingdoms of cotton continued to flourish, harnessing energy from the millions of men and women forced to toil on cotton, rice, and tobacco plantations. The system of slavery was expanding, not contracting.

In these same years Americans pushed beyond the Mississippi River, driving covered wagons out of wooded country onto open prairies where the wild grasses grew taller than a man or woman. On horseback you sat high enough to see the grass wave in the breeze, the narrow prairie trail "winding off like a serpent . . . disappearing and reappearing." Best to travel by night during green fly season because "on a hot summer day horses would be literally stung and worried to death." Farther south, a young man named Stephen Austin rode into the part of Spanish Mexico known as Texas, where he had received permission to found a colony. Here, stands of oak, hickory, and pecan trees gave way to scrubby mesquite bush. There were buffalo to hunt as well as deer. Austin founded his colony in 1821, just as Mexico won its own war for independence from Spain.

Fur trappers known as mountain men pushed even farther, crossing the long-grass prairies of the Midwest and then the short-grass country of the Great Plains, until the land sloped up into the Rocky Mountains. These men sported fringed buckskins, deerskin moccasins, bushy beards, and greasy slouch hats. They hung powder horns from their shoulders, carried long rifles, and pulled pack mules along behind. Alongside rushing streams they caught beaver, in fat times feasting on bison and in the lean months roasting crickets. Or worse. "I have held my hands in an ant-hill until they were covered with ants, then greedily licked them off," recalled Joe Meek. In midsummer, the trappers gathered at a large "rendezvous" to sell their beaver pelts to traders who brought wagons across the Plains. Then they drank and gambled and cavorted—and sometimes bargained for Indian wives. For one thing, the men were lonely; and for another, staying on good terms with Indian nations was important if you trapped in their hunting grounds. As many as five hundred men hunted beaver—until the animals virtually disappeared from every stream. And when the mountain men returned east, they brought knowledge of the trails to the west, which hordes of other Americans followed.

Now, this tale has been told so often that two simple words—*western frontier*—make us imagine the story in a certain way. The words are a bit like Joseph Smith's magic spectacles which, when pulled on, made strange things seem clear. A *frontier,* we know, is the line between one region and another. *Western,* we know, is the direction in which that frontier was moving. Look at the Natchez Trace, the Erie Canal, or the prairie trails—all roads heading west. But that way of seeing is too simple. Take off the spectacles and view the entire continent of North America. The frontier is not a single wave moving east to west but many waves, crisscrossing each other from different directions. Not only people but also animals and even *things* move along these frontiers.

Consider horses, which the conquistadors brought to America. Some ran wild or were stolen by Indians. From out of Mexico, wild horses spread along a frontier moving north and east, not west. Indians at first were astonished to see humans ride these "big dogs." For thousands of years, native bands had hunted bison on foot by stampeding herds over cliffs. This was a huge waste of food because the Indians couldn't eat all the bison meat before it spoiled. Once Indians learned to ride, they became skilled at shooting bison with arrows. The horse made their lives easier and their hunting less wasteful.

Consider the frontier of *things.* Trade goods often travel ahead of people, so that some Indians owned metal pots and pans before they ever met a white man. The French traded guns to the Indians, too, though the Spanish would not. So a "gun frontier" began moving west and south from Canada. Guns provided a great advantage both for hunting animals and making war. And of course we've already seen the frontier of disease at work. Germs traveled north from Spanish New Mexico clinging to trade blankets; and the new steamboats brought smallpox up the Missouri River along with white men.

To officials in Washington, Stephen Austin's Texas colony was on the western frontier—sixteen hundred miles away. But for officials in Mexico City, those same lands were on their northern frontier—fourteen hundred miles distant. Texas seemed a long way from the wide, civilized avenues of Mexico's capital. So did the lands of New Mexico, where well-to-do landowners put Indians and poor Mexicans to work grazing sheep on their ranches, mostly in the valley of the upper Rio Grande. (*Rio Grande* is Spanish for Big River.) California's settlements were even smaller and farther away—a three months' journey from Mexico City by land and sea. For many years, a few dozen Franciscan missions had used Indians, in near slavery, to care for huge herds of horses, sheep, and cattle. After 1833, Mexico took these lands away from the church and gave them to powerful ranchers, who behaved much as the rich planters of the South did toward their slaves.

In March 1836 the two frontiers—American and Mexican— clashed and erupted into war. Mexicans were already fighting each other over how much control the central government should have over Mexico's individual provinces. General Antonio López de Santa Anna brought the army of the central government north to subdue the unruly province of Texas. By this time over forty thousand Americans lived there, ten times the number of Mexicans. Many of these newcomers grew cotton and held slaves, whereas Mexico had outlawed slavery. Most of the American Texans were Protestant and preferred their religion to the customs of Catholic Mexico. Just as Santa Anna arrived, a group of American Texans declared their independence from Mexico. Then they scrambled to put together an army for the new Republic of Texas.

Its commander was a remarkable character named Sam Houston. Houston was a friend of Andrew Jackson and years earlier had been the governor of Tennessee. At that time he married a nineteen-year-old woman who, to his shock, rejected him after only three months. Devastated and embarrassed, Houston quit his job and crossed the Mississippi to live with the Cherokee Indians who had adopted him years earlier, when he ran away from home as a boy. They had given him a name then, Co-lo-neh, the Raven, and treated him like a son. When he returned, he was miserable enough that the Cherokee gave him a new name, Oo-tse-tee Ardee-tah-skee: the Big Drunk. Again with the Indians' help, Houston picked himself up and began a new life—this time in Texas, where he joined Stephen Austin's colony and led the Texan army. Like General Washington outside of Boston, Houston realized that he needed time to train his ragtag band of soldiers.

Texans had taken over a fortified mission just outside San Antonio, known as the Alamo. Houston wanted it abandoned because it had little military value, but other hot-headed Texans were determined to stay. "*I shall never surrender or retreat,*" announced William Travis, one of the Alamo's commanders. "VICTORY OR DEATH." Santa Anna's large force overwhelmed the mission's 187 defenders and then brutally executed the few survivors, including none other than Davy Crockett, the Tennessee woodsman and politician, who had arrived at the Alamo not long before the battle.

Fortunately for the new republic, Houston kept his main army away from Santa Anna until he could organize and launch a surprise attack from out of the woods where the San Jacinto River and Buffalo Bayou meet. (This is now the site of Houston, Texas.) By nightfall Santa Anna had fled the battle of San Jacinto to hide in the tall grass. The rebels captured him the next day and forced him to grant Texas its independence. Houston assumed that his "Lone Star" Republic would soon join the other stars on the flag of the United States, but he was mistaken. Ten years passed before the U.S. Congress agreed to annex Texas and make it a state.

Meanwhile, Americans were discovering the Pacific coast and its Mexican ranches. Eager Yankee traders sailed around the tip of South America to sell the Californians everything "from Chinese fire-works to English cart-wheels" as well as cotton cloth from Lowell. Farther north, in Oregon Country, Great Britain and the United States had agreed to rule jointly. Early white settlers sent word east of good farmland and a mild climate that allowed flowers to bloom in February. By the mid-1840s a new wagon road known as the Overland Trail was bringing thousands of people every summer to Oregon and California.

Once the spring rains passed, covered wagons set out from St. Joseph and Independence, Missouri—mostly younger families, because travel was so hard. In peak years the route seemed almost like a traffic jam in New York City. Cattle and horses ate up so much prairie grass as they traveled that good campsites grew hard to find. (As many as eleven animals for every human marched along the trail.) Women not only had to get up early to cook, care for the children, wash and mend clothing, they also found themselves caring for livestock, fixing broken wagon wheels, and driving oxen when the men fell ill. Indians suffered because these overlanders hunted the game they depended on. Frustrated raiding parties stole livestock and even collected tolls at key river crossings, but they seldom attacked wagon trains. Less than 4 percent of deaths on the trail were caused by Indians. Travelers had to push hard to cross the mountain passes before winter snows cut them off. Most made it—there were a quarter of a million people in Oregon and California by 1860 as well as forty thousand in Utah, where Joseph Smith's Mormons migrated after he was murdered.

For years Americans had thought that a nation the size of a continent could never be united as one republic. But in 1844 Samuel Morse perfected the telegraph, an instrument that sent messages down a wire using electric pulses. His "Morse code" of dots and dashes made it possible to communicate instantly over long distances. Other inventors built steam "locomotives" to pull passenger cars along iron rails. These trains worked year round, even when rivers had frozen up. Such advances persuaded more Americans that a continental republic was not only possible but desirable. God had ordered events just so, said one newspaper editor: it was the "manifest destiny" of the United States to "overspread the continent . . . for the free development of our yearly multiplying millions."

One man determined to fulfill these predictions was a Tennessee politician who followed in Andrew Jackson's footsteps. James K. Polk's supporters called him Young Hickory, for he followed Old Hickory's advice to the letter, even asking Jackson whom he should marry. "Sarah Childress," Jackson advised—so Polk married the

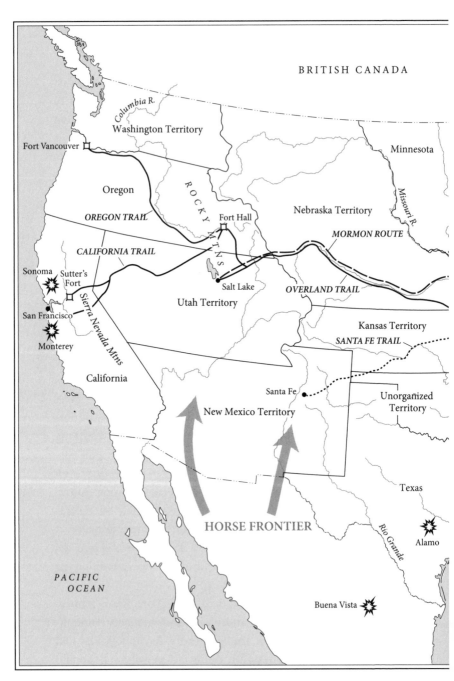

Moving frontiers. The Overland Trails were most crowded in the 1840s and 1850s. The horse and gun frontiers expanded into these lands more gradually, during the 1600s and 1700s.

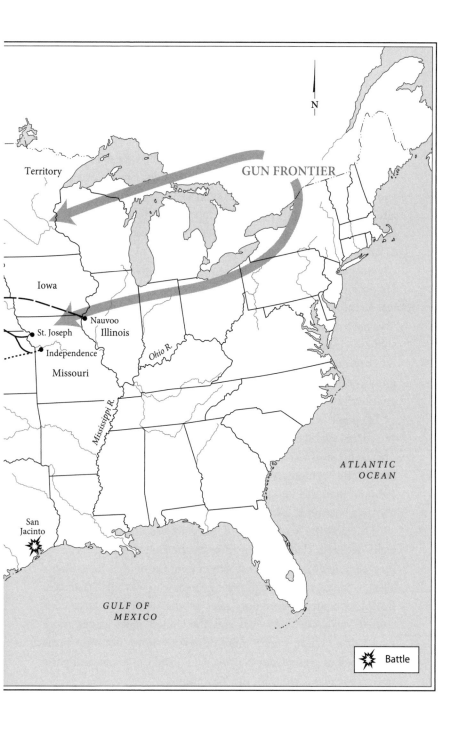

Territory

GUN FRONTIER

N

Iowa

Nauvoo
St. Joseph   Illinois
Independence
Missouri

Ohio R.

Mississippi R.

ATLANTIC
OCEAN

San
Jacinto

GULF OF
MEXICO

✸ Battle

lady. From then on husband and wife ate, drank, and plotted politics so well that Polk was elected president in 1844. By the time he took office, Congress had agreed to lasso Texas into the Union.

But Polk wanted Oregon Country, too, and told the British they must give up their claims. The two nations huffed at each other and threatened war, but the crisis ended peacefully. The United States gained control of present-day Oregon and Washington, while Britain kept the northern part of the territory. Polk was relieved, because secretly he had already decided he wanted to take not only Texas but also California from Mexico. That meant war, he was convinced, for Mexico would never agree to give up those lands. He ordered General Zachary Taylor to march U.S. troops all the way to the Rio Grande—land that both Texas and Mexico claimed. "We have not one particle of right to be here," wrote an American soldier in his diary. "It looks as if the government sent a small force on purpose to bring on a war." He was right. Polk presented Congress a declaration of war when news came that Mexican troops had attacked Taylor in April 1846. The U.S.-Mexican War had begun.

Telegraph wire hadn't been strung across the Rocky Mountains yet, so for several months no one in California knew about the war. That didn't stop a group of Americans who were already out there, led by John Frémont, from proclaiming California's independence. Frémont marched into the town of Sonoma and raised a flag with a grizzly bear on it. (At the time, thousands of golden-furred grizzlies roamed the land.) The U.S. navy arrived and, with war officially declared, claimed California for the United States. The Bear Flag went down; the Stars and Stripes went up. In Mexico, at Buena Vista, General Taylor fought Santa Anna, who was again defeated. But Mexico surrendered only after another American force conquered Mexico City. At war's end, the United States gained more than half a million square miles of new territory: not only Texas but also all of present-day Nevada, Utah, and California and parts of New Mexico, Colorado, and Wyoming.

Not since France lost the Seven Years' War had such a conquest been seen in North America. But what would become of these new territories? Would slavery be allowed within their boundaries? Many New Englanders had opposed the war out of a fear that slavery would become legal in the newly conquered lands. Henry David Thoreau, a transcendentalist, was jailed briefly for refusing to pay taxes because the United States would not "give up war and slavery." Thoreau's essay "On Civil Disobedience" argued that it was proper to oppose wars that were morally wrong.

This chapter has talked a good deal about frontiers: boundary lines. The line separating slave territory from free was also a frontier; and in the years after the U.S.-Mexican War, it became the most important dividing line in the land. Ralph Waldo Emerson, another opponent of the war, saw quite clearly the problem with an American victory. "The United States will conquer Mexico," he predicted, "but it will be as the man who swallows the arsenic which brings him down in turn. Mexico will poison us."

A victory that poisoned? But what Emerson meant must wait for the next chapter.

21

CROSSING THE LINE

"MEXICO WILL POISON US." What did Emerson mean?

When the United States took half a million square miles of land from Mexico, the newly gained territory forced Americans to deal with an issue that most politicians preferred not to speak of. Could slavery and freedom continue to exist side by side? For years most white Americans said yes. They had gone about their business, lived with slavery one way or another, and agreed to disagree. Emerson feared that slavery and freedom were such different conditions, so opposed to one another, that the argument over whether to allow slavery in the new territories would poison the Union, kill it, pull it apart. The problem of how to deal with slavery was not new. It went back all the way to the Constitutional Convention of 1787.

James Madison, the Founder who did the most to shape the Constitution, warned delegates to the Constitutional Convention that the greatest danger to the Union was not the conflict between large and small states but that "between the northern and southern . . .

principally from the effects of their having or not having slaves." Already, North and South disagreed on whether slaves should be counted in a state's population when determining how many representatives it could send to Congress. Southern delegates wanted to count them, even though slaves couldn't vote. But this *encouraged* slavery, northerners pointed out. The more slaves that lived in the South, the more representatives those states would get. Southern delegates compromised by agreeing to count only three out of every five slaves. But there they drew a line. Northerners must accept this Three-fifths Compromise or the new Union "was at an end."

Did the compromise make a difference? At times, it did—a huge one. In the bitter presidential election of 1800, Thomas Jefferson of Virginia would not have beaten John Adams of Massachusetts without the extra votes that the South gained in the Electoral College from the Three-fifths Compromise. Jefferson, complained one Federalist, "made his ride into the temple of Liberty on the shoulders of slaves." By 1819 the Three-fifths Compromise had given the South seventeen extra members of Congress.

Even so, the North's free population had grown enough to give it more votes in the House. So the Senate became the crucial battleground between North and South. With two senators for each state, and eleven free states and eleven slave, the votes between free and slave states were evenly divided.

Then, in 1819, Missouri Territory applied to become a state. Missouri's climate was not warm enough to grow cotton, but some ten thousand slaves had already been brought there, so southerners assumed it would come in as a slave state. Before that could happen, James Tallmadge, a representative from Poughkeepsie, New York, surprised the House. He proposed an amendment to the Missouri bill that the territory could enter the Union only if it gradually outlawed slavery.

At the time of the Revolution, many white southerners, including Jefferson, had hoped slavery might indeed fade away. But slavery had spread instead—and now southerners (again including Jefferson) opposed Tallmadge's amendment. "You have kindled a fire which all the waters of the ocean cannot put out, which seas of blood can only extinguish," a Georgia congressman protested. "If civil war must come," Tallmadge shot back, "I can only say, let it come!" The deadlock was broken when Maine, originally part of Massachusetts, applied to become a state. Missouri was allowed to enter as a slave state and Maine as free. At the same time, this Missouri Compromise of 1820 drew a line beginning at the state's southern boundary and running west across the Louisiana Purchase. North of that line slavery was outlawed, except for Missouri.

Draw a line. Work out a compromise. End the quarrel. For a time that approach kept the peace. But enslaved African Americans, who had no voice in the Three-fifths Compromise or the Missouri Compromise, knew that some lines were meant to be crossed. They could not vote at the ballot box, but over the next forty years they voted with their feet as tens of thousands escaped from slave states and headed north. They hiked by the light of the moon, swam rivers, and hid beneath cartloads of hay being hauled into free states. One slave, Henry Brown, secretly had himself nailed up in a wooden crate and shipped north.

The line between freedom and slavery could be crossed from north to south, too. Remember how David Walker, the free black from Boston, smuggled his abolition pamphlets south in the coats of black sailors, urging slaves to rise up? Other abolitionists slipped into slave territory to bring out runaways on what became known as the Underground Railroad. This was not really a railroad but rather a network of people who worked together and secretly sheltered slaves, guiding them as they fled north. Harriet Tubman, the railroad's most famous "conductor," had worked as a slave in lumber camps, so she was comfortable in the deep woods. Her superb acting skills got her out of more than one tight spot. Sometimes she carried a pair of chickens that she let loose and chased when she needed to distract attention from fugitives.

It had never been easy to keep slavery on one side of a line and freedom on the other, no matter how much you compromised. That was one reason Jefferson and Madison worked hard to move the nation's capital from Philadelphia to the District of Columbia. A Philadelphia law decreed that any slave living more than six months in the city would be free. That made life difficult for southern officials working in the government because they often brought slaves to Philadelphia as house servants. George Washington himself secretly arranged for his slaves to be taken back to Virginia after six months, "under pretext that may deceive both them and the public," he instructed his secretary. Washington pretended that his wife wanted the slaves to return with her. The new District of Columbia solved the problem of a capital in a city that freed slaves. Slavery was legal in Washington, and the district was surrounded by slave states.

But by the 1830s some northerners began to think it disgraceful to see slaves bought and sold in open markets in the capital of a nation dedicated to liberty. They petitioned Congress to outlaw slavery in the District of Columbia. Over a million northerners signed more than a thousand petitions. White southerners were outraged. If Washington became a free city, they said, slaves would rush to it, or even be encouraged to start their own rebellions in nearby slave states. To prevent the petitions from being acted on, southerners persuaded Congress to pass resolutions known as "gag rules," which forbade the House from even accepting the petitions to stop slave trading. After nine years the gag rule was finally repealed, but southern states continued to suppress protests against slavery within their own lands.

Then came the war with Mexico and the debate over new territories. General Zachary Taylor, hailed as a war hero, was elected president in 1848. Nicknamed Old Rough and Ready, he was blunt in speech. Should slavery be allowed in the new territories? Taylor's rough-and-ready answer was to just skip the territory stage and bring in two very large states: New Mexico (which included most of present-day Arizona, Colorado, and Utah) and California. Californians clearly didn't want slavery. As for New Mexico, Taylor proposed outlawing it there as well. He thought the climate was too dry for slavery ever to flourish.

Southerners were astounded. Old Rough and Ready was from Louisiana and a slaveholder to boot! Instead of pairing off a slave state and a free state, he was proposing to give the North two free states and so upset the balance in the Senate—which stood at fifteen free and slave states each. The angriest southerners, nicknamed "fire-eaters," called a meeting in Nashville, Tennessee, to consider seceding from the Union.

Once again Congress drew new lines and compromised. California would come in free, but the remaining new lands would be made into two territories, New Mexico and Utah. And both would have the chance to vote slavery up or down. This solution was known as "popular sovereignty"—let the voters choose. It allowed at least the possibility that two more slave states might be created. Southern representatives were still unhappy about the thousands of slaves escaping to the North, so Congress passed a new and tougher Fugitive Slave Law that required northerners to assist southerners in capturing runaway slaves. Anyone who refused could be jailed or fined up to $1,000. Finally, to soothe northerners, the slave trade was outlawed within the District of Columbia. Slavery itself would remain legal, but there would be no more buying and selling humans on the auction block in the nation's capital.

Together, these measures were known as the Compromise of 1850. They probably would not have passed without the maneuvering of an energetic senator from Illinois, Stephen A. Douglas. But with Douglas's help, they squeaked through. It seemed as if the Union had been saved.

But the Compromise of 1850 proved to be one more bitter pill. True, many white northerners didn't strongly oppose slavery. African Americans living in the North knew all too well that public places such as theaters and stagecoaches were segregated—divided into areas for whites only and blacks only. Occasionally rioters hostile to African Americans had even attacked black communities in cities such as Boston, Pittsburgh, and New Haven. For all that, people in the North resented being forced to help federal officials capture runaway slaves. Harriet Beecher Stowe, a reformer, wrote a best-selling novel called *Uncle Tom's Cabin,* which was turned into a play with scenes of slave catchers and bloodhounds chasing an escaping mother and daughter across the icy Ohio River. "I never saw so many white pocket handkerchiefs in use," commented one theatergoer. "I was not the only one in that large audience to shed tears I assure you."

Meanwhile, a new fight over slavery broke out in the recently proposed territories of Kansas and Nebraska. For thirty-four years, the line drawn by the Missouri Compromise had decreed that these lands remain free. But California had already tipped the balance in the Senate toward free states—and here were two more free states in the making. Southern senators refused to admit them; and once again Stephen Douglas stepped in to patch up the quarrel. Douglas, who was short but spirited, had gained the nickname the Little Giant. In his Kansas-Nebraska Act, he proposed that residents of these territories be allowed to vote slavery up or down—again, the idea of "popular sovereignty." To make perfectly clear that slavery *could* be established, southern members of Congress insisted that the Kansas-Nebraska Act say flat out that the Missouri Compromise was repealed.

Immediately, settlers from both free and slave states rushed into Kansas Territory to support their cause. As the first elections were held, proslavery mobs from neighboring Missouri crossed the line into Kansas and voted, even though they didn't live there. "We will be compelled to shoot, burn and hang, but the thing will soon be over," boasted Senator David Rice Atchison of Missouri, who organized the mobs. "If we win, we carry slavery to the Pacific Ocean." Northerners fought back against "the slave power," as they called it, and a shooting war broke out. With cannons and banners proclaiming

"Southern Rights" and "Superiority of the White Race," a new Missouri posse attacked the free-state settlement of Lawrence, Kansas, in June 1856. A few days later a northern abolitionist named John Brown took revenge at nearby proslavery farms, brutally executing five men. None actually owned slaves or had even participated in the raid on Lawrence, but Brown didn't care. A devout but extreme man, he believed "God had raised him up on purpose to break the jaws of the wicked."

The dispute over slavery was tearing up the old system of political parties. Many northern Whigs and Democrats joined new organizations—and with proslavery violence in Kansas on the rise, northerners paid special attention to one new party, the Republicans. Strongly antislavery, the party didn't even bother to organize in the South. One member, Senator Charles Sumner of Massachusetts, gave a speech that condemned slavery in the harshest terms. Sumner particularly insulted Andrew Butler, an elderly senator from South Carolina, whom he accused of taking slavery as his "mistress." Several days later, Butler's nephew, Representative Preston Brooks, strode into the Senate to punish Sumner according to the southern code of honor. As the senator sat at his desk, Brooks began striking him with his cane, continuing so long and hard that the senator staggered as he stood up. Then, blinded by the blood streaming down his face, he collapsed unconscious on the floor. "Every lick went where I intended," Brooks told his brother. Sumner did not return to the Senate for four years.

News of the caning was like a shock of "electricity to 30 millions," one northerner commented. Violence in distant Kansas was one thing, "but to see a senator assaulted in the Senate Chamber no one can find any excuse for it," agreed a Detroit editor. In the South, on the other hand, Preston Brooks was sent souvenir canes and honored at dinners.

"Bleeding Kansas" and "Bleeding Sumner" aroused so many northerners that in 1856 the Republican candidate for president nearly won. And events continued to create Republican converts.

A Missouri slave named Dred Scott lived for several years with his master in free territory and afterward, back in the slave state of Missouri, he sued for his freedom. The Supreme Court rejected Scott's claim, ruling that African Americans "had no rights which the white man was bound to respect." More shocking to northerners, the court ruled that Congress had no right to outlaw slavery in *any* territory. Only a state could outlaw it. Two years later, in 1859, southerners were horrified when the abolitionist John Brown struck again. He and twenty-one followers seized a federal arms depot at Harpers Ferry, Virginia. Brown hoped to take the weapons stored there and roam the countryside encouraging slaves to revolt. The plan was harebrained, for few slaves lived anywhere near Harpers Ferry; and Brown was quickly caught, tried, and hanged. But he conducted himself with such dignity at his trial that many northerners agreed with Ralph Waldo Emerson that he was "a saint, whose martyrdom will make the gallows as glorious as the cross."

Compromising had failed. The lines drawn to contain slavery had been crossed again and again. In 1860 the Republicans nominated for president a man who saw the problem clearly. His name was Abraham Lincoln. Born in the slave state of Kentucky, raised in rough cabins in free Indiana and Illinois, the tall, gangly boy had received little formal schooling. But he had read much on his own. Even after he became a lawyer and politician, his speech never lost its Kentucky twang—he said *thar* for *there, heerd* for *heard, kin* for *can.* His high-pitched voice sometimes seemed awkward, but his humor charmed listeners. And his words had logic. Lincoln saw how difficult it was to keep slavery in its place, to wall it off, to agree to disagree. In a famous speech entitled "The House Divided," he picked a proverb from the Bible to make his case:

A house divided against itself cannot stand.

I believe this government cannot endure, permanently half *slave* and half *free.*

I do not expect the Union to be *dissolved*—I do not expect the house to *fall*—but I *do* expect it will cease to be divided.

It will become *all* one thing, or *all* the other.

Either the *opponents* of slavery, will arrest the further spread of it, and place it where the public mind shall rest in the belief that it is in course of ultimate extinction, or its *advocates* will push it forward, till it shall become alike lawful in all the States, old *as well as new—North* as well as *South.*

The election of 1860 showed how divided the nation had become. Four candidates ran, but neither Lincoln nor his closest rival, Democrat Stephen A. Douglas, had any real backing in the South. When the votes were counted, Lincoln was victorious. For the first time, a president had been elected with the support of the free states alone. For the first time, a candidate won who was committed to stopping slavery from expanding.

Led by South Carolina, the seven southernmost states seceded from the Union to form the Confederate States of America. They were the states where slavery was most deeply entrenched. The remaining eight slave states hesitated, hoping that some final compromise could be reached.

But none was. The Union whose motto had been *Out of many, one* now broke apart over the issue of who should be equal, who should be free. The final line had been crossed. And what was coming, no one could say.

22

What Was Coming

NO ONE COULD QUITE SEE what was coming. When Lincoln first heard that the Deep South had seceded, he thought it was a bluff—to push the North to make bigger compromises. Reaching out, he promised to enforce the Fugitive Slave Law and even back a proposed amendment to the Constitution guaranteeing that slavery would never be abolished in states where it existed. Lincoln believed that most southerners didn't want to leave the Union— and in truth, many didn't. The crisis was set in motion by "our Big Men," one Georgian grumbled. By that he meant wealthy slaveholders. When Lincoln took the oath of office in March 1861, the eight slave states of the Upper South still had not decided whether to secede.

But Lincoln would not—could not—bend too far. Republicans had won the election fair and square, he pointed out, on a pledge to keep slavery out of the territories. And, like Andrew Jackson, Lincoln believed that "no state can in any way lawfully get out of the Union without the consent of the others." Yet Confederates were already taking over federal forts; and in April their new president, Jefferson Davis, ordered that cannons bombard Fort Sumter in Charleston harbor. When Sumter surrendered, Lincoln declared that a rebellion was under way and called for seventy-five thousand troops to put it down. That pushed most white southerners into the arms of their Big Men. "Lincoln has made us a unit to resist," said a North Carolina man, "until we repel our invaders or die." North Carolina, Tennessee, Arkansas, and Virginia joined the Confederacy. The Civil War had begun.

Both sides rushed to recruit armies, and the first big battle came near a stream called Bull Run, twenty-five miles outside Washington. Some members of Congress rode out in carriages to picnic, watch the battle, and celebrate what they were sure would be a northern victory. At first, the sea of Union blue surged forward, but it was halted by Virginia grays who did not yield—troops led by a college professor, Thomas Jackson. "There is Jackson standing like a stone wall!" cried an officer nearby. "Stonewall" Jackson earned a nickname and went on to lead his brigade brilliantly. More Confederate units soon reached the battlefield, letting loose a full-throated wail that came to be called the rebel yell. "There is nothing like it this side of the infernal region," one Union soldier recalled. "The peculiar sensation that it sends down your backbone . . . can never be told." Union forces fled back to Washington—and so did the panicked picnickers.

Unlike George Washington, Lincoln had little military training. So he looked for a strong general with the ability and determination to lead. His first choice was Robert E. Lee, a gentlemanly officer from Virginia. Though Lee owned slaves himself, he had doubts about slavery and wasn't sure secession was legal. Still, he couldn't bring himself to take up arms against his home state, and so he joined the Confederates. Lincoln next turned to a thirty-four-year-old railroad executive named George McClellan. Handsome, though not especially tall, and sporting a broad mustache, Little Mac promised to "crush the rebels in one campaign." He planned to do so by fighting a strictly limited war. If southerners truly wanted to rejoin the Union, he reasoned, the army shouldn't plunder their farms to feed the troops. And certainly it should not free the slaves of southern planters. Lincoln agreed. Several slave states had not yet joined the Confederacy: Delaware, Maryland, Kentucky, and Missouri. Lincoln worried about these border states, especially Maryland. If it seceded, Washington would be surrounded by Confederate territory and cut off from the North. But by the beginning of the war's second year, the border states seemed in no danger of leaving the Union.

Unfortunately, neither did Little Mac and his army. Month after month he drilled and prepared the troops, but never made a move to attack. Lincoln became uneasy. "If General McClellan does not want to use the army," he said, "I would like to borrow it." McClellan, for his part, thought Lincoln was "nothing more than a well meaning baboon." The president suffered such insults patiently. "I will hold McClellan's horse," he promised, "if only he will bring us success." In the spring of 1862, the Union Army of the Potomac finally marched to within five miles of Richmond, capital of the Confederacy. Success seemed within reach. But then Robert E. Lee took command of the rebel armies in the east—and Lee was a man who "would take more chances, and take them quicker than any other general in the country," as one friend put it. Lee's smaller, more nimble forces stung Union troops from several sides. Little Mac retreated, hoodwinked into thinking that Lee's army was twice the size of his own.

McClellan's caution frustrated Lincoln, especially because the president was beginning to think that a limited war would never bring victory. Many Republicans were pushing to attack slavery head-on as a way to win the war. To free the slaves would be more than a moral act. It would steal valuable manpower from the rebels, since African Americans made up more than half of all southern workers. Lincoln, still worried about losing the border slave states to the Confederacy, twice tried to persuade their representatives to pass a law freeing their slaves gradually. Let it take effect over the next thirty years, he suggested. He even promised that Congress would pay planters for freeing their slaves. But the border states refused to act. The night of his final meeting with their representatives, Lincoln came away resolved to issue a proclamation. "We must free the slaves or be ourselves subdued."

It would be too simple, though, to say that Lincoln freed the slaves. His Emancipation Proclamation, which took effect January 1, 1863, freed only slaves living behind the lines in Confederate territory. That meant *no* slaves were freed, critics complained, except those the Union had no power to free. But news of Lincoln's act spread like wildfire. Thousands of slaves had freed themselves long before the proclamation was issued. In doing so, they were forcing Lincoln, the Union, and even white southerners to decide what to do about slavery.

At first many Confederates thought their slaves would prove to be a "tower of strength" in the fight. They were wrong. From the beginning, slaves worked to turn the war to their advantage. They overheard conversations at their masters' dinner tables, passed along news from friend to friend, and ran for freedom when they had the chance. Slaves guided Union troops along southern back roads, told them where Confederate troops were stationed, and forced Confederates to devote valuable soldiers to guarding slaves rather than fighting Yankees. By war's end, over 180,000 African Americans had joined the Union army and "fought as bravely as any troops," testified one Yankee officer.

The Union's fortunes began to turn by the third summer of the war—but not easily. Lincoln fired McClellan and tried a number of other generals, some just as cautious, others hard-charging but reckless. The president was "wrung by the bitterest anguish" over their defeats. But hope came from Union armies in the west, which fought their way through Tennessee to the Mississippi River. Meanwhile, Union warships captured New Orleans at the mouth of the Mississippi and worked their way north. If the North could control the entire river, it would cut rebel country in two.

The unlikely star among western generals was Ulysses S. Grant. Though Grant had graduated from West Point, he was working as a lowly store clerk in Illinois when the war broke out. A man of few words, shabby in dress, a cigar usually clenched between his teeth, he was determined and calm in battle. He memorized maps at a glance, then galloped down back roads and through fields to coordinate an attack. "The art of war is simple," he explained. "Find out where your enemy is, get at him as soon as you can and strike hard as you can and keep moving on." By the spring of 1863 the Union controlled most of the Mississippi—but not the key town of Vicksburg. In a daring move, Grant left behind his supply boats and marched inland, living off food from southern farms. He surrounded Vicksburg and starved it into surrender on July 4. "I can't spare this man," said Lincoln. "He fights."

A turning point in the East came during those same July days. Surprising everyone, Lee marched his army north into Pennsylvania —Union territory. He had become convinced that the South needed to take the offensive if it meant to win. In an intense battle near the village of Gettysburg, Pennsylvania, rebels assaulted Union lines hard for two days running. On the third, Lee ordered Major General George Pickett to attack the center of Union defenses, convinced that the exhausted Yankees would yield. They did not. Valiantly, Pickett's men charged uphill into a withering hail of bullets. Half of them died; the others were captured or forced back. Discouraged, Lee rode among the survivors, consoling them. "It's all my fault. . . . You must help me. . . . All good men must rally." Then he retreated south. There were no more rebel campaigns in Union territory.

Lincoln thought Grant's victory at Vicksburg was "one of the most brilliant in the world." As the fourth year of the war began, he put Grant in charge of all northern armies. Both men agreed

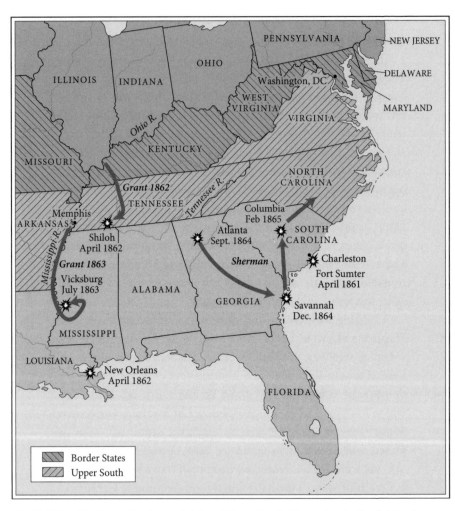

The Civil War. The Lower South seceded first, followed by the Upper South after fighting began at Fort Sumter. Lincoln managed to keep the border states in the Union as well as the western part of Virginia, which became the new state of West Virginia. Meanwhile, Union general Grant made progress in the western battles of the war during 1862 and 1863 (left map). After Lincoln put him

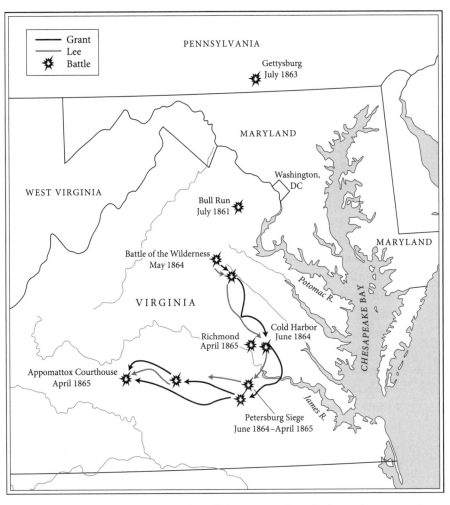

PENNSYLVANIA

Gettysburg
July 1863

MARYLAND

WEST VIRGINIA

Washington,
DC

MARYLAND

Bull Run
July 1861

Battle of the Wilderness
May 1864

VIRGINIA

Cold Harbor
June 1864

Potomac R.

CHESAPEAKE BAY

Richmond
April 1865

Appomattox Courthouse
April 1865

James R.

Petersburg Siege
June 1864–April 1865

in charge of all Union forces, he chased Confederate general Lee (right map) in 1864 and 1865
until Lee was cornered and surrendered at Appomattox Courthouse.

that to save the Union, they could no longer fight a limited war. To defeat the Confederate army, the food and supplies that kept it going would also have to be destroyed. While Grant hammered Lee month after month, General William Tecumseh Sherman advanced into Georgia, whose fertile farms had until then suffered little damage. Get into "the enemy's country as far as you can," Grant ordered, "inflicting all the damage you can against their war resources."

But even with the Confederacy on the defensive, the North nearly lost the war because of politics. Lincoln was up for reelection in 1864 and his Democratic opponent was George McClellan. McClellan wanted to negotiate peace and end the war quickly, even if it meant allowing slavery to survive. Lincoln refused to pay that price. More than 130,000 former slaves were already fighting for the North. Under such a peace, they would become slaves once again—and for making such a bargain, Lincoln said, "I should be damned, in time and in eternity." Yet if he didn't seek peace, his defeat in the election seemed certain. Four years of war had left the North heartsick over the deaths of thousands of sons. Grant was still locked in a grinding campaign against Lee, while in Georgia Sherman's army had stalled outside the well-fortified city of Atlanta. "Lincoln is deader than dead," gloated one Democratic newspaper.

Then in September the red-haired, grizzle-faced Sherman telegraphed news: "Atlanta is ours, and fairly won." With the soldiers in the field among his strongest supporters, Lincoln, the "well meaning baboon," handily beat his ex-general.

General Sherman set out on a campaign from Atlanta to the Atlantic Ocean designed to "make Georgia howl," as he put it. "We are not only fighting hostile armies, but a hostile people." The army cut a path of destruction fifty miles wide in this "March to the Sea," which deepened the Confederacy's severe sufferings. Already food had become so scarce that in several southern cities women rioted, demanding bread. To pay for the war, the Confederacy ended up simply printing money, which over time became nearly worthless. By 1865, a barrel of flour in Richmond cost $1,000 in Confederate currency. "We haven't got nothing in the house to eat but a little bit o meal," wrote one Alabama woman to her soldier husband. She and the family would lie "in the grave yard" if he didn't come home soon. Jefferson Davis was so desperate that he proposed drafting three hundred thousand slaves to fight for the Confederates. A "monstrous" idea, protested more than one southerner. "The South went to war to defeat the designs of abolitionists and behold! In the midst of war we turn abolitionist ourselves!"

Davis's proposal came too late to be put into effect. And by then, Lincoln had convinced Congress to pass the Thirteenth Amendment to the Constitution, abolishing slavery forever within the Union. Republicans cheered when the measure passed, as African Americans looked on from the galleries and wept for joy.

Lincoln was relieved at the news, but the war had taken a tremendous toll on him: the ceaseless letters to be read and answered, the officials who called all day, the telegraph office the president haunted at night for news of the day's battles. Men pestered him for jobs in the government, mothers who had lost several sons arrived in tears, begging that their remaining boy be spared from service. Lincoln's secretaries tried to hold back the flood but the president often ignored them, saying, "They don't want much and get but little, and I must see them." Toward the war's end some pointed out the "great black rings" of fatigue under his eyes; others noticed he would suddenly change the subject and launch into one of the innumerable funny stories he seemed to have at hand. When a friend protested such humor in the midst of dark times, Lincoln broke down, the tears seaming his cheeks. "I should die," he explained, without some relief "from the crushing burden I am constantly carrying."

Three-quarters of a million soldiers dead, a million and a half horses perished, $20 billion spent on the war. That sum was more than eleven times all the money paid out by the federal govern-

ment between 1789 and 1861. Who could have foreseen the cost or
guessed what was coming? That thought was on Lincoln's mind
when he spoke at his second inauguration in March 1865, perhaps
the most remarkable speech an American president has ever given.
The war was all but over, the North victorious. But the president
did not claim that justice was on his side nor that God had blessed
the victory. Slavery was at the center of the conflict, he said. Everyone knew that. But

> neither party expected for the war the magnitude or the du-
> ration which it has already attained. . . . Each looked for an
> easier triumph, and a result less fundamental and astound-
> ing. Both read the same Bible and pray to the same God, and
> each invokes His aid against the other. It may seem strange
> that any men should dare to ask a just God's assistance in
> wringing their bread from the sweat of other men's faces, but
> let us judge not, that we be not judged. The prayers of both
> could not be answered. That of neither has been answered
> fully. The Almighty has His own purposes.

What were they? Lincoln would not, could not say. But slavery was
an offense in God's sight, that much he believed. And if, in order
to remove it, God gave "to both North and South this terrible war,"
who could deny the justice? For centuries American slavery had
grown up side by side with American freedom. If God willed that

> this mighty scourge of war continue until all the wealth piled
> by the bondsman's two hundred and fifty years of unrequited
> toil shall be sunk, and until every drop of blood drawn with
> the lash shall be paid by another drawn with the sword, as
> was said three thousand years ago, so still it must be said "the
> judgments of the Lord are true and righteous altogether."
>   With malice toward none, with charity for all, with firm-
> ness in the right as God gives us to see the right, let us strive on

to finish the work we are in, to bind up the nation's wounds, to care for him who shall have borne the battle and for his widow and his orphan, to do all which may achieve and cherish a just and lasting peace among ourselves and with all nations.

Only a month passed from the time Lincoln spoke these words until Ulysses Grant cornered an exhausted Confederate army near the village of Appomattox Courthouse in Virginia. There Robert E. Lee surrendered, nearly four years to the day after the Civil War had begun.

Who could have foreseen the cost, or known that there was yet more to be paid? Lincoln could not, did not. But more than once he had glimpsed, as through a glass darkly, what final sacrifice might have to be made.

23

How Do You Reconstruct?

LINCOLN HAD BEEN WARNED OF one assassination attempt even before the war, when he was on his way to Washington as president-elect. The detective in charge of security, Allan Pinkerton, advised Lincoln to take a special midnight train through Baltimore, a city with many secessionists who despised this "Black Republican," as they called him. Though he doubted the report of a plot, Lincoln agreed to don an overcoat, soft hat, and a scarf that could hide his face. Later, the new president was mocked for creeping into Washington like "a thief in the night." From then on he resolved to go about business as usual, despite the threatening letters he received. One evening in 1864, as he rode alone on horseback, a shot rang out and his top hat spun away. Soldiers later recovered it with a bullet hole through the crown. "I know I am in danger," he told a newspaper editor, but added that in his opinion, no precautions would stop a determined assassin.

On April 14—Good Friday—Lincoln attended a play at Ford's Theatre. The audience cheered when he and his wife, Mary, appeared in their balcony box seats, for it was only five days after General Lee's surrender. In the middle of the performance a Confederate sympathizer and actor, John Wilkes Booth, snuck into the president's box and shot Lincoln in the back of the head with a derringer. Booth then jumped from the balcony onto the stage and escaped through a side door. He was eventually tracked to a Virginia tobacco barn, where he was shot and killed after refusing to surrender. From Ford's Theatre the president was rushed across the street to a private home, but the wound was fatal. He died at 7:22 the next morning.

Two years earlier, Lincoln had honored the men who fell on the battlefield at Gettysburg as citizens who gave to the nation "the last full measure of devotion." Now the president, too, had given it. Thousands of mourners paid their respects as his funeral train returned him to Illinois; many must have recalled his final words at Gettysburg, "that we here highly resolve that these dead shall not have died in vain—that this nation, under God, shall have a new birth of freedom—and that government of the people, by the people, for the people, shall not perish from the earth."

But how to achieve that new birth? How to knit together a nation so badly torn? Eleven states had seceded, and had spent a great deal of blood and treasure fighting the United States. What should be required of the rebel states before allowing them back into the Union? How should Confederate officials be treated? Which southerners would be able to vote in the new elections? How would life change for 4 million former slaves, who became known as freedpeople? (The original term was *freedmen,* but historians today use *freedpeople* to include women as well as men.)

The process of bringing the Union together again was called Reconstruction; and it was the hardest peacetime task the nation had faced. Days before Lincoln's death, a Union general had asked the president how the conquered South should be treated. "I'd let 'em up easy," he advised, "let 'em up easy." Lincoln had a way with people. He was willing to talk, ready to compromise on many issues, but clear about when to stay firm. Now he was gone; and the president who replaced him was a very different man indeed.

Before entering politics Andrew Johnson had been a modest tailor from Tennessee who could barely read. He had long resented the South's rich planters. "Some day I will show the stuck-up aristocrats who is running the country," he vowed. When Tennessee seceded, Johnson remained a strong Union man. He was even shot at as he fled the state. As president, his program for Reconstruction required southerners to swear loyalty to the United States if they wanted to vote. High Confederate officials and rich southerners would have to do more. They would have to ask for special pardons from the president.

By the time the war ended, some planters had come to see that slavery "was wrong, and that the Declaration of Independence meant more than they had ever been able to see before," as one Confederate cavalry captain put it. But the fierce war left much anger. A North Carolina innkeeper commented that Yankees had stolen his slaves, burned his house, killed his sons, and left him with only one privilege: "To hate 'em. I git up at half-past four in the morning, and I sit up till twelve at night, to hate 'em." Southerners recognized that slavery must end, but even so, their new state governments passed "black codes," laws restricting former slaves. While African Americans could now own property, be married legally, and sue in court, black codes forbade them from testifying against whites or serving on juries. The codes also allowed freedpeople to be arrested on vague charges, such as having no home or regular work. Once arrested, they could be hired out to planters and forced to work. To northerners, this seemed little more than slavery under a different name. Southern voters also elected high rebel officials to Congress, including the former Confederate vice president, Alexander Stephens.

President Johnson could have rejected the actions of the new southern governments. But since he had approved those governments to begin with, that would have meant admitting he had misjudged the situation, and Johnson was stubborn. He wanted Reconstruction over and done with. When former Confederates flocked to the White House, asking for special pardons, he changed his tune about "stuck-up aristocrats" and issued over thirteen thousand pardons in two years. Many northerners were shocked to hear that ten former Confederate generals had been elected to serve in Congress. Worse, when Republicans objected, Johnson began calling *them* traitors, for giving black citizens too many rights. Meanwhile, white mobs attacked African Americans in major southern cities, including Memphis and New Orleans.

Over Johnson's protests, Congress laid out a stricter approach to bringing the South back into the Union. It insisted on a Fourteenth Amendment to the Constitution guaranteeing that no citizen, including African Americans, could be deprived of "life, liberty, or property, without due process of law." Every citizen deserved "equal protection" under the law—which meant "black codes" or other laws aimed at only some citizens were unconstitutional. Second, Congress rejected the South's new state governments and divided the region into five military districts supervised by Union officers. In this new order, only white men who took a loyalty oath to the United States could vote and hold office. So could freedmen.

The political war that followed was fierce. President Johnson vetoed every Reconstruction bill Congress passed, but Republicans easily overrode his vetoes. He tried to fire his secretary of war, Edwin Stanton, who sided with Congress, but Stanton barricaded himself in his office day and night for two months to keep Johnson from locking him out. Congress supported Stanton. Finally, the House of Representatives voted to impeach the president—the process laid out in the Constitution for removing someone from office. At Johnson's trial before the Senate, enough senators agreed that he had not committed "high crimes" or broken the law, so he was allowed to serve out the remaining few months of his term.

When events turn out so badly, it is natural to wonder *what if?* What if Lincoln hadn't been shot? Would Reconstruction have gone more smoothly? What if white southerners had not passed black codes? What if northerners had not demanded so much change? But such questions glide over the real difficulties of Reconstruction, which involved more than just political fights in Washington. Reconstruction changed nearly everything and everyone in the South—not only personal lives, marriages, and families, but also work and play and even physical things such as houses, churches, and schools. Think about it. For over two hundred years, free people and slaves had lived side by side, as customs grew up over how each group treated the other. Reconstructing the Union meant putting together a world without slavery—a "new birth of freedom," as Lincoln put it, in large ways and small.

How do you reconstruct work? White planters faced huge changes in the way they managed their fields. They were used to telling slaves what to do—not bargaining over how much workers should be paid or when they got time off. Now, planters could no longer use the whip to keep field hands in line. Yet tobacco still needed to be planted and cotton harvested on time, and freedpeople could stay or go as they pleased. Thousands left their old homes, "*without notice, just when the notion takes them,*" complained one Alabama planter. How irresponsible! Or so it seemed to former masters, desperate because their crops were at risk of failing.

Now consider the freedpeople, reconstructing their own lives. Under slavery, millions of husbands had been sold away from their wives. Children had been torn from their parents. After the war, the roads were clogged with former slaves in search of loved ones. Was it irresponsible to leave a plantation to look for your long-lost daughter or husband? Surely freedom meant the right to leave a planter who treated you cruelly.

It may seem far-fetched to talk about reconstructing houses, churches, and schools, but not so. On most plantations, slave quarters had been built in a central location, where masters could keep an eye on slaves. Freedpeople wanted to spread out, to have their own cabins with a little privacy for their families. As for worship, for the first time freedpeople had the right to choose their own preacher and their own church. Beale Street Baptist Church in Memphis was at first just a "brush arbor"—a rough shelter at the corner of Beale Street and Lauderdale, made from branches and bushes. But the church grew quickly to over two thousand members, who worshiped in a massive stone church with twin towers. As for schools, before the war slaves could be whipped if they were even caught reading. During Reconstruction, northern teachers and missionaries came south to start schools and even colleges. Blacks were not merely "anxious to learn," a school official in Virginia reported, they were "crazy to learn." Many who did became teachers, too.

To speak of reconstructing sidewalks seems even more far-fetched, but the effects of Reconstruction changed the smallest things. Before the war, slaves had to get off a sidewalk quickly if a white person came along; they also had to bow and take off their hats. (Remember how colonial students had to doff their hats to superiors?) Reconstruction meant the right to walk on sidewalks, and many whites were angered when black soldiers who had fought for the Union refused to hop into the muddy street.

For a time Reconstruction was truly a revolution that turned the world upside down. In voting, freed African Americans joined with white Republicans to elect governments and to serve in them all across the South. Freedpeople held about 15 to 20 percent of state offices, and sent two senators and fifteen representatives to Congress. The new governments helped rebuild railroads destroyed during the war. They began the first statewide system of public schools in the South, and built new roads and bridges. Often, if not always, elections went forward peacefully, without "the least ill feeling between the blacks and the whites," as one white woman from Georgia commented.

Sadly, the revolution did not last. A civil war filled with death and destruction had left many Americans sick of reform and high ideals. Politicians across the nation found it all too easy to cut corners, to do favors for their friends, to steal from public funds. This behavior infected Reconstruction governments as well. "There is a *mint* of money in this, or I am a fool," commented one South Carolina Republican. Such corruption made Democrats determined to throw out Republican officials. Even more important, Reconstruction failed because it was hugely difficult to overcome two centuries of inequality. White southerners who refused to treat African Americans as equal began to push back. They launched a battle, you might say, over reconstructing the night.

Under slavery, masters had organized patrols to prevent slaves from sneaking out at night to hunt, visit family on nearby plantations, or run away. During Reconstruction freedpeople took back the night. In election campaigns they marched in torchlight political parades just as whites did. They went to meetings in the evening and visited friends as they pleased. But as early as 1866 some whites organized semi-military groups to put a stop to these freedoms. One group, the Ku Klux Klan, wore various disguises, such as white sheets and hoods that hid their faces. On nighttime rides, they took away the guns of black citizens, broke up Republican political meetings, and even murdered political leaders.

At first such attacks outraged northerners. In 1868 and again in 1872 General Ulysses Grant was elected president, and he directed federal troops to arrest Klan members and others who tried to put "white rule" into effect. But as time went on, northerners began to tire of Reconstruction—even strong abolitionists. "We have tried this long enough," complained one. "Now let the South alone." Southern Democrats became quite open about their plans to win power—through elections if they could, but by force if necessary. Riots and more terror kept perhaps a quarter of a million Republicans from voting in the election of 1876, in which Republican Rutherford B. Hayes of Ohio ran against Democrat Samuel Tilden of New York.

By then Democrats had come to power in all but three southern states. In those states—South Carolina, Louisiana, and Florida—both the Democrats and Republicans claimed victory. To sort out the dispute, Congress appointed a special commission, but the final agreement was hammered out in a private meeting at the Wormley Hotel in Washington. Democrats reluctantly agreed to let Hayes become president—so long as Reconstruction ended. And so it did in 1877. The nation reunited, but at the expense of the freedpeople's rights.

Civil war had torn the nation apart, Lincoln had warned, because 250 years of slavery could not easily be washed away. Reconstruction was a valiant effort to overturn those years of inequality. A century more would pass before the march toward equality surged again.

24

The Next Big Thing

ONE OF THE CONQUISTADORS WHO explored for treasure in Spanish America liked to display a motto below his portrait. It read, "By compasses and the sword: more and more and more and more." Sometimes it seems as if all American history has been a scramble for more and more, from one boom country to the next. The search for gold and silver. Sugar plantations in the Caribbean. Virginia tobacco, Carolina rice. Fur traders roaming the Rockies. Cotton kingdoms and textile mills. Each boom seemingly bigger than the last. How big was big? By 1860, a large southern plantation put over 250 slaves to work. In Maine, the Pepperell Cotton Mills hired about eight hundred people, from mill girls and Irish immigrants to the boys paid to spear the eels that clogged the mill's waterwheels. In 1860, eight hundred workers seemed a huge number for one company.

But only twenty-five years later, the Pennsylvania Railroad listed fifty thousand people on its payroll. Near Pittsburgh, not far from where George Washington tried to stop the French from building a tiny two-acre fort, the sixty-acre Homestead Steel Works belched smoke into the sky as its furnaces turned out two hundred tons of steel rails *every day*. The railroads gobbled them up as fast as they could get them. Steel transformed American cities, too. For centuries churches had been the tallest buildings, their steeples stretching toward heaven. Now, new steel girders made it possible for buildings to climb ten, twenty, even thirty stories high—"sky-scraping apartment houses," one newspaper called them.

But there was more to bigness than getting bigger. You couldn't just triple the size of a railroad and have done with it. To grow truly big, Americans had to create new *systems*. These systems were crucial for mastering the thousand and one details that went into becoming big.

Consider the difference between a steamboat and a locomotive. Someone who wanted to get into the steamboat business could pretty much just buy a boat and cast off downriver, stopping at one town or twenty-two. A railroad, on the other hand, needed not merely a locomotive and railcars; it had to buy the land its tracks would run on, clear a path through trees, fill in swamps, construct bridges over rivers, lay gravel and track, and build railroad stations. All that and more was necessary before the company could earn money carrying freight or passengers. In the 1850s many small rail-roads already crisscrossed the eastern United States, so companies like the New York Central Railroad began to buy them up to make "trunk lines" that ran smoothly between big cities like New York, Philadelphia, and Chicago. Still, no one had settled the question of how wide railroad tracks should be. Many companies laid rails four feet eight and a half inches apart. Others preferred a five- or six-foot width. At least half a dozen sizes were in use. In order for one railroad to send freight to many different destinations, miles of tracks had to be adjusted so that the systems worked together. One of the biggest changeovers came on Sunday, May 30, 1886, when thousands of workers in the South pulled up the rails of their five-foot tracks and nudged them three inches closer together.

With crews racing each other to get the most track adjusted, some thirteen thousand miles were narrowed in about thirty-six hours. From then on, southern trains could run on northern lines.

The biggest railroad dream was a route across the continent. No company was large enough to build such a transcontinental line, let alone pay for it. So the federal government stepped in. Congress gave the Union Pacific Railroad the right to head west across the Great Plains and allowed the Central Pacific Railroad to build east from California. To help pay for the job, the government also gave these corporations 45 million acres of federal land free, which the railroads sold to people who wanted to settle along the route. Looking for workers, the Union Pacific hired veterans from the Civil War along with Irish immigrants. Crews laid two miles of track a day across the hot, dry Plains. On the Pacific side, nine out of ten workers were Chinese, many newly arrived in the United States. They faced the grueling task of laying track over the Sierra Nevada Mountains, where in winter, snowdrifts piled as high as sixty feet. That stopped most work, but the dynamiting of tunnels through the mountains continued. Snow slides, falling boulders, and explosions killed more than a few laborers, and some bodies weren't found until the snow melted in spring. But in 1869 the tracks of the Central Pacific and Union Pacific railroads were at last joined at Promontory Point, Utah.

With trains running for hundreds, even thousands of miles, think about the difficulty of making schedules. To keep time, villages set their clocks to noon when the sun was highest in the sky. But "noon" varied from one town to the next. When the sun was highest in Chicago, it was only 11:50 in St. Louis, but already 12:31 in Pittsburgh. To a traveler on horseback, such differences hardly mattered. But for railroads stopping at dozens of towns in a single day, making timetables was a nightmare. Each line had to choose its own "standard" time, different from local times in villages. Some train stations placed several clocks on their walls to help passengers keep matters straight. (The main station in Pittsburgh displayed six.) Finally, in 1883, the railroads got together and created time zones, dividing the country into four sections, each with its own standard time. The new system helped railroads to become big.

In fact, railroads grew so much, they hired managers whose only job was to organize thousands of engineers, brakemen, locomotives, depots, repair shops, roundhouses, porters, conductors, and station agents. The managers developed charts in the shape of a large tree, with the president and officers of the railroad at the trunk and the different divisions and workers spreading like branches with a thousand leaves.

Inventions of every sort contributed to these new industrial systems. Americans patented more than half a million new designs and machines in the thirty years after the Civil War. The era's greatest inventor was a young telegraph operator, Thomas Alva Edison. Edison figured out how to send more than one message at a time over a telegraph wire, and made so much money from his idea that he was free to devote his life to thinking up new inventions— everything from a phonograph that would record and play back sound to the electric lightbulb, which turned night into day in cities across the country. About the same time, Alexander Graham Bell discovered how to send voices over wires. His system was much better than the dots and dashes of Morse code used by the telegraph. Edison's biggest idea was to create a *system* for inventing things, rather than just dreaming up ideas one by one. If you could have cotton and steel factories, why not start an invention factory? Edison bought electrical generators and chemical supplies and hired technicians and toolmakers to work in what became known as a "research laboratory." Its purpose was to put new knowledge to practical use. Big companies quickly copied the idea.

Inventions helped overcome technical problems, like how to carry electric current between neighborhoods or how to brake railroad cars smoothly. But there were more down-to-earth problems to solve. Many small companies competed against each other trying to get big; and that competition often got rough. Railroads raced to build more track in order to lure customers away from their rivals. They gave secret discounts called rebates to their best and biggest shippers, while charging small customers more. Other companies bribed members of state legislatures to pass laws favorable to them. People spoke of "railroad wars"—and in fact rival railroads sometimes hired armed guards and even street gangs to protect their interests. Cornelius Vanderbilt, who owned the New York Central Railroad, knew that his competitor Jay Gould at the Erie Railroad charged $125 to ship a railcar full of cattle from Buffalo to New York. So Vanderbilt dropped his price to $100. Gould struck back by charging $75. Vanderbilt went to $50, Gould to $25. Enraged, Vanderbilt finally set his price at $1 for an entire car full of cattle. He was losing a huge amount of money, but at least the Erie Railroad wouldn't get the business! His freight cars were filled. Gould was cleverer: he rushed off and bought every steer in Buffalo. When Vanderbilt learned "he was carrying the cattle of his enemies at great cost to himself and great profits" to them, he "very nearly lost his reason," recalled one friend. Such competition ruined many businesses.

Those who survived learned ways to eliminate the competition. John D. Rockefeller got into the new business of oil. People had begun to drill wells that gushed a thick, slippery liquid, known as petroleum, out of the ground. It could be refined into kerosene, which burned in lamps, or into oil, which helped machine engines run smoothly. Oil became even more valuable once engines themselves were designed to burn petroleum as fuel. Rockefeller saw a good thing and jumped in. His Presbyterian father had taught him to work hard and trust no one. "I cheat my boys every chance I get," the father boasted. "I want to make them sharp." Young Rockefeller was sharp and then some. He bankrupted rivals by slashing prices, started "shell" companies that looked like someone else owned them, or simply bribed competitors to sell out. He used any strategy to win. But his Standard Oil Company also produced high-quality oil because its owner watched over every detail of the business like a hawk. Rockefeller was the first to arrive at his offices in the morning and the last to leave at night. Even on the day of his wedding, he worked all morning. If he could save even a tenth of a penny on every gallon of petroleum, he would. That might not seem like much, but Standard Oil refined 700 million gallons of oil a year. Saving a tenth of a penny earned an extra $600,000 in profit.

By 1880 Rockefeller controlled 90 percent of all the oil refined in the United States. As the only big supplier left, he had a monopoly and could set his prices higher without worrying about losing business to a competitor who charged less. Pretty much everyone who wanted oil had to deal with him. And other big corporations followed his lead, trying to drive out their rivals and build monopolies.

Steel was another business that became big. It was led to new heights by a young Scottish American, Andrew Carnegie. For years railroads used iron rails for their tracks, but when iron was purified into steel, it became stronger and lasted longer. Carnegie's steel furnaces used the latest technology to turn iron into steel. Carnegie did not follow Rockefeller's strategy, buying up every big steel company (though he did buy many). Instead, he protected himself by purchasing the *other* businesses a steel company needed to survive: the iron mines supplying his furnaces with iron ore, the railroads that shipped it to him. Then nobody could interfere by cutting off his supplies or charging high prices for things he needed.

Big railroads, big oil, big steel. And last, but surely not least, big money. Huge corporations needed cash for their projects. So bankers created marketplaces where "capital"—the money used for investment—was bought and sold. Thousands of ordinary people could buy a piece of a large company by investing in shares of stock available at money markets like the New York Stock Exchange. The old Dutch lane called Wall Street became the nation's center for capital. And bankers at the center of this business were masters at buying and selling stock, putting together millions of dollars to buy corporations, and combining them into even more powerful businesses. The biggest banker of all was J. Pierpont Morgan, a bear of a man who almost always got his way. "Meeting his blazing dark eyes was like confronting the headlights of an express train bearing down on you," recalled a photographer who took Morgan's portrait. In 1901 the banker combined Carnegie's steel company with the eight next-biggest steel operations in the country to create the United States Steel Corporation, the nation's first billion-dollar company. In doing so, he had gobbled up two hundred companies, a thousand miles of railroad track, Minnesota's biggest iron ore range, and 170,000 workers. More and more and more and more. "I like a little competition," said Morgan, "but I like combination more."

Newspapers hailed people like Carnegie, Rockefeller, and Morgan as captains of industry. Hadn't they tied together the continent with rails? Forged steel to build bridges and towering skyscrapers? The nation was being reconstructed into a world that was grander than anything that existed before the Civil War. And yet . . .

Where were ordinary Americans in this story? We've talked about some of the giants of these years. What about the common folk—the thousands of workers who were only tiny leaves at the end of so many branches in those complicated business charts? They, too, had to adjust to the industrial world—sometimes it was a matter of life and death. Consider a rough-looking fellow, middle aged, who appears one day at the offices of the Pennsylvania Railroad asking for a job as a switchman. The manager looks him over and asks if he has any experience. Likely enough, the man can get the job simply by raising his hand.

The reason why is a story for the next chapter. And it shows, in the age of the Next Big Thing, why ordinary folk had to find a way to get big, too.

25

THE COLOR OF YOUR COLLAR

WHEN THE ROUGH-LOOKING fellow applied for a job as a rail-road switchman, the manager asked if he had any experience. The worker nodded and held up his hand. A couple of fingers were missing.

Missing fingers were one sign of experience on the railroads. The new world of industry was not only glittering and glamorous but also dangerous and deadly. For a railroad passenger in 1885, a journey cross-country was nothing like it had been on the primitive early railroads, where a ride meant "a great deal of jolting, a great deal of noise . . . not much window, a locomotive engine, a shriek, and a bell." Now, trains served meals in wood-paneled dining cars. Breakfast might include bacon, sausage, trout, oysters, fruits, hot breads, rolls, chocolate, and more—all for 75¢. More wonderful yet, George Pullman of Illinois had manufactured sleeping cars, in which beds swung down from the ceiling and were made up with fancy linens. Pullman porters—they were African American —stowed ladies' hats in boxes, shooed flies from the corridors, and propped spittoons by the bed for men who chewed tobacco. George Pullman called his creations "palace cars," and he intended his passengers to be treated like royalty.

Railroad workers, on the other hand, lived differently. Never mind rain, sleet, or freezing hands: the work had to be done. A switchman who let down his guard at the wrong moment could easily get a finger smashed or lopped off. Being a brakeman was even more dangerous. When a train approached the station, the engineer tooted the "down brakes" whistle, and the brakemen all clambered up ladders to the tops of their cars to turn the braking wheels. If a wheel was tightened too quickly, the train might jolt, throwing one of the brakemen to his death. A thousand brakemen a year died in accidents. And not just brakemen: engineers, boilermen, machinists, carpenters, car oilers, and flagmen all risked their lives. Here are a few of the 198 injuries reported in a single year by a single railroad, the Chicago, Burlington & Quincy: *instep broken, skull fractured, hand and thumb mashed, leg amputated, jaw broken, foot crushed, hand run over by cars, fingers cut off, leg and arm scalded, leg crushed.* At least these men survived. Another thirty died that same year: *struck by train, crushed between cars, fell from train, fell down stairs, fell off bridge, fell from smokestack, killed when engines derailed, crushed between car and platform, drowned.*

Danger was a part of the new world of work. Men walking into Andrew Carnegie's Homestead Steel Works faced a blast of fiery heat. The furnaces were "giant caldrons," as one man put it, "big enough for all the devils of hell to brew their broth in, full of something white and blinding, bubbling and splashing, roaring as if volcanoes were blowing through it." The workmen's sweaty bodies were quickly coated with dust and tiny grains of steel. Machine saws screeched so loudly, the noise deafened workers. To keep Homestead running twenty-four hours a day, two crews took turns on their shifts, working twelve hours a day one week, twelve hours a night the next. The furnaces stopped only on the Fourth of July and Christmas. On "swing shift," the exhausted Saturday night crew took Sunday off, while the next crew worked twenty-four hours straight. "Home is just the place where I eat and sleep," explained one worker. "I live in the mills."

Another odd thing happened as factories got bigger. The jobs themselves got smaller. In Thomas Jefferson's day, a shoemaker made a pair of shoes from start to finish, choosing the proper leather, cutting the shoe patterns, stitching and gluing the pieces together . . . about forty different steps. Factories got big by dividing a shoemaker's job into smaller tasks, each done by a different person, who could be taught the job with little training. Women and girls sewed the upper parts of the shoe, men and boys put on the bottoms, machines made the tasks simpler. In a lightbulb factory, some women inserted filaments into bulbs, one tiny wire after another: that was all they did all day. Others used a vacuum machine to suck out the air and seal each bulb.

An old-fashioned shoemaker took pride in his skills. But these jobs? Who could feel proud of doing the same small thing a thousand times? A shoemaker was paid out of the profits from selling his shoes. Factory workers were paid wages by the hour, a custom that became common only after the Civil War. Such workers were often treated badly by the foremen who watched over them. Women working in a glove factory or making shirtwaists knew that the factory doors were locked, so no one could sneak away. Workers had to ask permission even to use the bathroom.

Children as well as women worked: in textile factories where fibers clogged the air and damaged their lungs. Young children fixed broken textile looms because they were smaller and could crawl beneath the clattering machines. Boys went into the coal mines with their fathers and were glad to come back up with nothing worse than a blackened face: there were so many gas explosions, cave-ins, and sharp, heavy machines. In a cannery, eight-year-old Phoebe Thomas sliced her thumb badly while cutting off sardine heads with a butcher's knife. She was sent home alone screaming, her hand bloody, "her mother being busy" elsewhere. In steam laundries, harsh chemicals in the wash water left sores on workers' arms. Despite such risks, women's work paid only about half of men's wages for similar jobs. Husbands were expected to earn what the family needed; women only got "pocket money."

Not all factory jobs were as grueling. Cigar making could be dreary work, done in small dingy apartments where a father, mother, and their children slept by night and turned out three thousand cigars a week by day. But in bigger cigar factories, where many Puerto Ricans and Cubans worked, the men were allowed to hire a *lector,* or reader, who sat atop a table and read to the workers from newspapers or novels to help pass the time pleasantly. Women in the collar factories of Troy, New York, were permitted to sing songs.

There were so many collar factories in Troy that it became known as Collar City, which points to another change. More men and women were working in jobs that didn't require hard physical labor—a job that didn't "soil the clothes or the hands," as one woman explained. Women working as telephone operators or secretaries were required to wear a proper skirt and a "shirtwaist" (a blouse that looked more like a man's shirt) when they came to work. For men in the new office buildings, work attire meant a jacket, tie, and shirt with a clean white collar. The collar was separate so the shirt could be worn for several days: every morning you put on a new collar, stiff, white, and starched. For the first time people in such jobs were referred to as members of "the middle class" or "white-collar workers." That contrasted with the "blue-collar" jobs, in which the work required rougher clothing.

The new white-collar men began talking about having not just a job but a "career." In the old days, a young man who wanted to be a lawyer "read law" with an older lawyer who taught him the job. Now law schools sprang up at universities, and other schools were created to teach students the special knowledge needed for careers as doctors, dentists, engineers, and other professions. Women were not welcome in many of these jobs. But they worked as postmistresses, schoolteachers, and secretaries, despite warnings by some men that female brains might suffer nervous breakdowns from thinking too much! The reformer Elizabeth Cady Stanton had no use for such nonsense. "The talk of sheltering woman from the fierce storms of life is the sheerest mockery," she protested. Any woman should have the right to "use all her faculties for her own safety and happiness."

When times were good, people in this new world of work managed to survive or even prosper. But times were not always good. One time or another, almost every boom country goes bust. Colonial Virginians got rich growing tobacco . . . until they shipped so much that its price sank like a stone. Fur traders made fortunes . . . until the beaver were all gone. And when things turned from boom to bust so suddenly, merchants lost businesses, farmers lost lands, and ordinary folk lost jobs and even their homes. Small wonder people referred to these hard times as "panics"—the Panic of 1819, the Panic of 1837, the Panic of 1857. Such ups and downs had always been around. But in the era of the Next Big Thing, as the booms got bigger and the rich became richer, the bad times got even worse and the poor even poorer. Three major panics, or depressions, hit America during these years: from 1873 to 1879, from 1882 to 1885, and from 1893 to 1897.

If you were a John D. Rockefeller with an empire of oil or a Jay Gould with several railroads to your name, you cut expenses and kept on going. But the way for businesses to cut back was to pay their workers less. Or make them speed up in order to get more work for less money. A brakeman was responsible for stopping two cars? Make him tend three or four. Can't he scramble across the tops of the cars a little faster? If business was really bad, the owners simply laid off workers—thousands, if need be. During the Panic of 1873, Andrew Carnegie commented that there were so many out-of-work people sleeping on the streets of New York, he had to step over them to get to his office.

In such a world, what could ordinary workers do? What power

did a buttonholer in a collar factory have, when she could be replaced so easily? If the brakemen were told they were going to be
paid less, how could they convince the president of a company that
they would starve on such wages?

Sometimes the anger boiled over. In 1877, twelve hundred brakemen and firemen took over a railroad depot at Martinsburg, West
Virginia. Officials sent the state militia in to run the railroad, but
the militia joined the protesters. In Pittsburgh twenty out-of-work
trainmen were shot and killed when a mob marched on the Pennsylvania Railroad to protest starvation wages. ("Give them a rifle
diet and see how they like that kind of bread," suggested Thomas
Scott, the president of the railroad.) Angry workers struck back,
destroying over a hundred locomotives and two thousand railroad
cars. Finally, President Rutherford B. Hayes sent federal troops to
put down the protests. The workers gained little and lost much.

If getting big was a key to succeeding, how did ordinary folk
become big? Just as big businesses needed systems to become big,
so did workers. Even before the Civil War, some had joined together in labor unions—organizations that workers formed to protect themselves and improve their lives. Early unions most often
united skilled workers such as carpenters, tailors, or printers. They
campaigned for public education and an end to twelve-hour work-
days and debtors' prisons. But each time that boom was followed
by bust, the unions did badly. Hard times made it harder to stand
up to bosses, who could hire other folk just as desperate for a job.

Some unions tried to grow bigger by getting different kinds
of workers into a single organization—carpenters, cigar makers,
trainmen, steelworkers—skilled or unskilled, blue collar or white,
all speaking with one voice. "Eight hours for work; eight hours for
rest; eight hours for what we will!" demanded the National Labor
Union. The Knights of Labor tried the same approach to gather up
the "toiling millions." Why not allow workers to own factories, railroads, and mines so they could share in the profits in good times
and help each other in the bad? Why not band together to elect

officials who would protect workers? Make it illegal to put children to work. But this was easier said than done because all workers did not have the same interests. One group would go out on strike—keep the factory from running in order to win their demands. But other workers would not agree, and the public would condemn the union if the strike turned violent. The Knights won some victories. But there were too many different sorts of workers with too many different interests for them to unite and become big in a lasting way.

Samuel Gompers, the son of a Jewish cigar maker, tried a different tactic. He didn't have any grand plans for reforming society, like the Knights of Labor. Unions should stick to simple demands, he believed, and get big by pulling together only skilled workers, like the cigar makers he knew. These craft workers joined together as the American Federation of Labor (AFL) and had simple goals: more pay, fewer working hours, safer jobs. By 1900—the beginning of the twentieth century—the AFL had a million members. But progress came slowly. And Gompers didn't want to try to organize unskilled laborers, like the steelworkers.

Labor unions were one way for workers to get big. And there was no turning back. The nation had become bigger, for better and for worse. You could see the changes not just in the size of factories and railroads but also in what was perhaps the greatest marvel of all, the new American city.

26

A Tale of Two Cities

GETTING BIG, WE'VE SEEN, meant more than just growing larger. It meant creating new systems to speed trains across time zones and keep steel mills white-hot twenty-four hours a day. Systems to let money flow into stock markets and out. Labor unions to fight for workers' rights. Which is why we need now to look at the way cities were growing up—because cities were where so many systems met. In fact, we can think of cities themselves as giant systems—living and breathing, groaning and straining—as they brought together people and markets and industries.

The cities of the 1880s were quite different from those of a hundred years earlier. In 1789, when George Washington took the oath of office in New York City, only 33,000 people lived there and you could walk from one end to the other in an hour. (Compare that with the Aztec capital of Tenochtitlán, where over 150,000 people once lived.) But American cities were growing. By 1840 so many people had crowded into New York it was more than double the size of old Tenochtitlán. And the strain had begun to show—which was clear enough to one particular newspaper reporter who liked to wander around town: a jaunty, footloose fellow by the name of Walt Whitman.

As young Whitman sauntered down New York's noisy avenues, his eyes took in carts, coaches, and walkers, all jostling for space. Here, an auctioneer clambered onto a table to sell a pile of chairs and beds to a gathering crowd. There, butcher boys with a bit of spare time threw off their blood-spattered "killing clothes" to dance a jig. Whitman's ears were open, too, to catch "the blab of the pave[ment]" as people chatted, or to hear the clanking "tires of carts and sluff of bootsoles." Boots in these streets had to step carefully because manure was everywhere, left by the horses that pulled carts, by stray dogs, and even by herds of pigs roaming the avenues. The pigs at least did some good because they ate garbage that people threw out their windows.

And people as well as animals were disorderly. Whitman visited crime scenes for his newspaper: "the sudden oath, the blows . . . the policeman with his star" making an arrest. Street gangs such as the Bowery Boys were common. These "b'hoys" (so they called themselves) sported greased sideburns, red shirts, stovepipe hats, and high-heeled leather boots. They strolled arm in arm with their "g'hals" and battled bitterly with rival gangs, including the Shirt Tails, the Roach Guards, and the Dead Rabbits. Fires were always a danger. Volunteer firefighters would rush to a blaze, but rival companies often fought with each other instead of pumping water—and might even let a building burn down if they didn't like the owner.

Making matters more difficult, in the 1840s and 1850s a wave of immigrants flooded the cities. Germans were among them, but the greatest number came from Ireland, where a blight had infected potatoes, causing "the Great Hunger." Potatoes were a huge part of the Irish diet—sometimes the only food poor folk could afford. As the crop rotted in the fields, a million people died from starvation. Another million and a half fled the country. "They are all gone—

clean gone," wrote one Irish priest. By 1855 one out of every four New Yorkers was Irish. The hubbub, the dangers, and the over-crowding in cities worried Americans. Many also feared the Irish, who were not only poor but also Catholic, a religion distrusted by Protestants.

Walt Whitman sometimes complained about the city's "Irish rabble." But his years on the streets and his sunny approach to life helped him see that the rough jumble of cities was actually an important part of what it meant to be American. At some point he began to think less about his reporting and more about larger dreams. Walking here and there, he had been "absorbing a million people, for fifteen years." And so he poured out his memories and feelings in the most remarkable book of poetry an American has yet written. Titled *Leaves of Grass,* it was a kind of song of America, celebrating its people, moods, and colors:

> I am of old and young, of the foolish as much as the wise. . . .
> Of every hue and trade and rank, of every caste and religion,
> Not merely of the New World but of Africa Europe or Asia . . .
>   a wandering savage,
> A farmer, mechanic, or artist . . . a gentleman, sailor, lover or
>   quaker,
> A prisoner, fancy-man, rowdy, lawyer, physician or priest.

The poem's frank scenes shocked some readers. "Whitman is a rowdy, a New York tough, a loafer, a frequenter of low places, a friend of cab drivers!" sniffed the proper Boston poet James Russell Lowell. But Whitman realized that when it came to cities—and even to America itself—he could not separate "the white from the black, or the native from the immigrant just landed at the wharf." That mixture was what made the United States what it was: "not merely a nation, but a teeming nation of nations." Thomas Jefferson had always distrusted "the mobs of great cities" and compared them to "sores" on the human body. Not Whitman. He put cities at the center of the American spirit.

And in the course of his seventy-two-year life, cities truly became that vital center. When *Leaves of Grass* was published in 1855, only one in six Americans lived in cities. Within fifty years, nearly half of all Americans did. This movement of millions—out of farms and villages into cities—happened not only in the United States but all over the world. Oceangoing ships powered by steam made it easier and cheaper to start new lives all across the globe.

For a time, one unlikely spot in America became the fastest-growing city on the planet. Unlikely because only two people lived there when George Washington took office: a black French fur trader named Jean-Baptiste-Point du Sable and his Potawatomi Indian wife, Kitihawa. Their five-room cabin stood where the Chicago River flowed into Lake Michigan. Americans from the East moved to the settlement in large numbers only after Andrew Jackson's policy of Indian removal pushed the Potawatomis beyond the Mississippi River. The city's growth was halted in 1871 by fire, as a sharp wind blew flames and sparks from one rooftop to the next. A hundred thousand people were left homeless, but Chicago roared back and rebuilt. By 1890 more than a million people lived there. It was a perfect example of the new city that was remaking America.

How new? In a city expanding so quickly, the answer can be found by considering a series of directions: *up and down; in and out; high, middle, and low.*

Up and down. First, Chicago expanded not just outward but also up, for it led the way in building the new skyscrapers. And if you want to transport people high enough to scrape skies, you require a smarter solution than stairs. When Potter Palmer of Chicago advertised his luxurious new hotel, he wasn't quite sure what to call the new system of transport. It was a kind of "perpendicular railroad connection, floor with floor, rendering passage by the stairs unnecessary." In other words, an elevator! And as skyscrapers pushed Chicago upward, city officials dug down as well. Chicago was first to build a citywide sewer system belowground to carry away the waste created by hundreds of thousands of residents. Other pipes brought drinking water from Lake Michigan. The new system meant less sickness from the sort of unhealthy wells used in older cities. By building down, the new city became healthier and safer.

In and out. As cities grew, residents could no longer walk easily from one end of town to the other. To move people more quickly, horses at first pulled streetcars along iron rails. But in a city Chicago's size, that required over six thousand animals that needed to be fed and cared for. (Sadly, the great fire of 1871 killed many of them.) Small steam locomotives called "dummies" were tried as a substitute, but they spewed smoke and sparks. Eventually electric trolleys saved the day, for their engines didn't smoke. And like New York and other big cities, Chicago began building elevated railways above the streets to get people in and out of town. The "el" reduced the crowds on busy avenues. Then subways were dug, since clean electric engines didn't foul the underground tunnels.

Railroads transported more than people in and out of the new cities. In the simplest terms, cities grow by acting as go-betweens. Go find some raw material—trees, for example. Or wheat or cows. Bring them into the city and turn them into something more valuable: flour or lumber, for example. Then ship the products out to people who need them. In and out. Chicago's location made it an ideal go-between. It stood on the edge of the Great Lakes, where ships could depart Chicago's ports for the bustling East. Rail lines spread like spokes on a wheel, linking the two halves of the nation. Their cars brought cattle by the millions; these were killed, cut up, and the meat shipped east, thanks to refrigerated railroad cars invented by Gustavus Swift. Wheat, oats, and barley flowed into Chicago and were sorted into different types and qualities using grain elevators. (For indeed, the city needed elevators to move grain as well as people.) North of Chicago, in Michigan and Wisconsin, majestic white pines were chopped down and then "skidded" on sleds along icy paths through the forest and floated down streams into Lake Michigan; mills then sawed the logs and shipped them to Chicago. Chicago hummed, day and night.

As always, people powered the systems. In the 1880s a new wave of immigrants came to America. Most ended up in cities. The earlier Irish and Germans were joined by newcomers from southern and eastern Europe. Jews persecuted in Russia and Poland fled their villages. Hard times drove many Chinese across the Pacific; they landed at Angel Island outside San Francisco. That city soon had its own "Chinatown," with "groceries and vegetables overflowing on the sidewalks," one Chinese newcomer reported. There, Americans marveled at the men's long pigtails and their "loose pajamalike pants and coats." Too often, surprise turned to suspicion and discrimination, as Chinese immigrants found themselves barred from more desirable jobs. On the East Coast, European immigrants funneled through Castle Garden in New York and then nearby Ellis Island, beginning in 1892. For many of these newcomers, the only jobs available were rough manual labor, building skyscrapers, bridges, and streets. "In Italy, they told me the streets were paved with gold," one immigrant recalled. "When I got here, I found the streets were not paved with gold, they were not paved at all, and they expected me to pave them." At "Packingtown" in Chicago, where butchers slaughtered cows and packed meat into tins, the men's faces and clothes became so clotted with blood and grease that the meat cutters seemed to "have neither the body nor the face of humans," said one Italian visitor. By 1890 three out of four Chicago residents were either immigrants or the children of immigrants.

Finally—*high, middle, and low.* Just as the distance between one end of a city and the other continued to grow, so did the distance between the highest and lowest classes of people living there. The richest Americans had become so wealthy and the poorest workers were paid so little that rich and poor hardly seemed to live in the same universe. Chicago's workers crowded into dingy shacks near the steel mills and slaughterhouses in a neighborhood known as Back of the Yards. In New York, six- or seven-story apartment buildings packed a dozen people into a single room at night—no elevators here. These "tenements," as they were called, were dank and filthy. On one occasion, a fire broke out among some papers and rags hanging on an apartment wall and a frightened visitor ran to a policeman for help. The officer only laughed. "Why, don't you know that's the Dirty Spoon? It caught fire six times last winter, but it wouldn't burn. The dirt was so thick on the walls it smothered the fire."

How different the houses of the rich! Where once Jean-Baptiste-Point du Sable's cabin stood, mansions reared up along Lakeshore Drive, built in the style of Italian palaces or made to look like castles out of the Middle Ages. Perhaps a room was decorated to resemble a hideaway in Turkey or a Chinese parlor. "Everything riots riotously," complained one visitor; "dragons writhe, bronze figures flourish swords, and painted dancing girls wave tambourines. . . . The more money to the square inch, the better." Potter Palmer, who built the hotel with elevators, had his own mansion, stuffed with servants and topped off by turrets. In colonial days, when someone knocked at your door, the custom was to call, "Walk in." Potter Palmer ordered that none of the doors on his mansion should have outside doorknobs. The doors could be opened only from within. To see Mr. Palmer, you presented the lowly doorkeeper a calling card with your name engraved on it. He passed it to another servant, who passed it to another—your card might go through the hands of well over twenty servants before a decision was made on whether to admit you.

Between the high and low of the rich and the poor stood that growing "middle class"—of managers and secretaries, doctors and engineers, schoolteachers and salesclerks. They could afford no mansions, but they did adopt some customs of the rich, such as calling cards. Middle-class dining rooms were not littered with statues, but meals might include unusual new foods, such as bananas imported from Central America and whisked to cities by rail. A businessman might show off his purchase of one of Edison's splendid new gramophones, playing recordings of opera solos or popular ballads. The woman of the house might be lucky enough to have a refrigerator, though it still depended on the local iceman to deliver blocks of ice to keep the food cold.

As these new cities were being pushed up and down, in and out, high, middle, and low, Walt Whitman watched. He marveled at "steam-power, the great Express lines, gas, petroleum. . . . This world all spann'd with iron rails." As a young reporter, he had sometimes worried about the growing distance between rich and poor. Did he still? If so, he left the problem for a new generation to solve. In March 1892 the champion of rowdy cities and the singer of America drew his last breath. Four thousand ordinary folk flocked to see his coffin taken to its final rest—even homeless children, attracted by the bands playing and the street vendors selling fruits and treats. Whitman would have loved it—the blab of the pave, the sluff of bootsoles, the never-ending hubbub of a city full of life, even in the midst of death.

27

THE NEW WEST

IN CHAPTER 5, I SPOKE of the blank space in history books between the time Hernando de Soto explored America around 1542
and the voyage of the French explorer La Salle down the Mississippi River in 1682. During those missing 140 years, North America
seemed to have been made over. Where de Soto saw many Indian
kingdoms crowding the Mississippi, La Salle saw only a village here
and there. Where de Soto had sighted not a single bison roaming
the land, La Salle reported hundreds. European diseases seem to
have created a new world out of the old. Historians and archaeologists are only beginning to guess how those changes occurred.

On the other hand, we have a very good idea of what happened
to the great West during the 1800s. In the lands beyond the Mississippi River, another new world came into being. And this time it
took only half a century to create, from about 1840 to 1890.

Consider these lands about the time Walt Whitman came to
New York City. Covered wagons had begun to cross the Plains,
heading for Oregon and California. President Polk's war with

Mexico redrew the map of the United States. The changes told a simple story: the nation now stretched from sea to shining sea. Or so it seemed. But in truth, Indian nations still controlled much of this territory. The Comanche were the most powerful people on the southern Great Plains, while farther north, the Cheyenne and Sioux hunted buffalo on vast grasslands. Perhaps 30 million of the shaggy beasts lived there, and in late summer the separate herds gathered together "into such masses in some places," one visitor reported, "as literally to blacken the prairies for miles together," the animals "bellowing . . . in deep and hollow sounds."

Then the world began to change. The first sign was not the coming of white settlers but of their horses. We've already seen how Indians valued horses from Europe, because riding bareback enabled hunters to kill many more bison than stalking them on foot. Even the poorest Comanche family owned a half dozen or more horses. These animals threatened buffalo, too: they competed for the grasses that both buffalo and horses ate. That problem became worse in the 1850s, when a long spell of dry weather began on the Great Plains. And just at that time pioneers began to swarm into the land, their horses, cattle, and sheep eating more grass, especially in the river valleys, where Indians sheltered in winter from the harsh blizzards. By 1857, the country along the Platte River had become a "lifeless, treeless, grassless desert" littered with "hundreds of dead and frozen animals," an American soldier reported.

Then railroads began pushing west. And the buffalo, already hunted by thousands of Indians, were also shot at by white men looking for adventure and fun. As a train passed a herd, "sports" would throw open a window and fire without even getting out. Worse, in 1870 eastern merchants discovered a way to treat buffalo hides to make them soft and attractive to city dwellers. With money to be made, professional hunters rushed out to shoot as many animals as possible. Four million died within a few years, leaving "myriads of carcasses. . . . The air was foul with sickening stench." By the 1880s, a population of 30 million bison had dwindled down to only about five thousand.

On top of these changes, some of the most isolated spots in the West were turned into yet another boom country. In 1848, flecks of gold were discovered at a sawmill along the American River in California. At Sutter's Fort, the nearest settlement, Captain John Sutter was not sure what to do with the news. He had long been in debt and the discovery of gold could mean great wealth. But it could also mean hordes of newcomers and chaos. The Coloma Indians who lived on these lands told Sutter of a legend that "gold was bad medicine because it belonged to a jealous demon in a mountain lake of gold-lined shores." For the Indians, gold proved bad medicine indeed. For the white man, it made too many act like demons. In the sleepy town of San Francisco, a merchant ran down the street waving a glass bottle full of bright flecks and yelling, "Gold! Gold! Gold from the American River!" Within days, most men cleared out of town for Sutter's Mill. When the news reached the East, thousands of gold seekers set out for California in 1849.

And these "Forty-Niners" were only the beginning. A decade later, not only gold but also silver was found. Twenty thousand miners flooded into Idaho, another twenty thousand into Montana, and as many as one hundred thousand to the diggings in Colorado. The greatest riches came from Davidson Mountain in Nevada, where the tents, mud-and-stone huts, and shacks of Virginia City sprang up beside the new silver mine known as Comstock Lode.

In all these spots only a few prospectors got rich. Most had the same bad luck as a greenhorn from the East named Sam Clemens, who bought a flannel shirt and big slouch hat, grew whiskers and a moustache, and started digging. The country, he joked, was "fabulously rich in gold, silver, copper, lead, coal, iron, quicksilver, marble, granite, chalk, plaster of Paris (gypsum), thieves, murderers, desperadoes, ladies, children, lawyers, Christians, Indians, Chinamen, Spaniards, gamblers, sharpers, cuyotès (pronounced ki-yo-ties,) poets, preachers, and jackass rabbits." For five months

Sam hopped around as madly as a jackass rabbit. He lived in a leaky cabin, enduring cold nights, bad food, and worse luck. "Send me $50 or $100, all you can spare," he wrote his brother. "I mean to make or break here . . . my back is sore and my hands blistered." He broke, and ended up taking an exhausting job in a mill that crushed minerals from the mines. It paid a measly $10 a week. After receiving his first paycheck, Sam told his boss he wanted a raise: $400,000 a month. He was fired on the spot.

Miners had learned that the only way to make a lasting profit was to become bigger. Success came to the businesses that could afford stamping machines to crush silver or huge high-powered hoses whose water jets blasted apart whole mountainsides to loosen the ore. As for Sam Clemens, he finally struck it rich—but only by changing jobs. The failed prospector began writing about his adventures using the pen name of Mark Twain. Eventually he went back east and created the most celebrated book in American literature, *The Adventures of Huckleberry Finn.*

As the world of the West was turned upside down by horses, settlers, miners, and disease, Indians were the hardest hit. The bison were disappearing. The sheltered river valleys had been picked clean. Whites settled on Indian lands, usually without permission. The state of California passed a decent-sounding law, the Act for the Government and Protection of Indians. But the law "protected" Indians by selling them to the highest bidder and putting them to work. Kidnapping Indian children "has become quite a common practice," reported one California newspaper. "Nearly all of the children belonging to some of the Indian tribes in the northern part of the state have been stolen" to be sold in the southern part of the state. The government even paid a group called the Eel River Rangers to capture or kill Indians straying from their new reservations. "However cruel it may be," their leader insisted, "nothing short of extermination will suffice to rid the Country of them." In twenty years, California's Indian population dropped from around 150,000 to 30,000.

Across the West Indians fought back, often in small bands that attacked a farmer's cabin or a miner's camp. But by the 1860s and 1870s, whole Indian nations were going to war with whites. Rumors of new goldfields in the Black Hills of South Dakota sent prospectors onto land that a U.S. treaty had reserved for the Sioux nation. Here animals were abundant and lodge poles could be cut from trees, which were so scarce on the Plains. The Black Hills were sacred to the Sioux. A vain, publicity hungry army general led an expedition onto the land that only fanned the rumors of gold. Whites knew him as General George Armstrong Custer. The Sioux called him Long Hair because of his blond, shoulder-length locks; they also called him Chief of All the Thieves. The federal government tried to buy the land by treaty; when the Sioux refused, the United States ordered them off the reservation. Custer rode out with his cavalry to round up the Indians, boasting that he could conquer the entire Sioux nation with only six hundred soldiers. He underestimated the seven thousand Sioux and their chief, Sitting Bull. Custer charged into battle along the Little Bighorn River. He and all his men were lost. "Those men who came with 'Long Hair' were as good men as ever fought," admitted Sitting Bull later. But Custer's pride cost them their lives—and his.

Sitting Bull's victory was a high-water mark for the Indians. They couldn't turn back the forces changing their land. Neither could the army control the eager prospectors and settlers, though some wanted to. General George Crook, one of the smartest and toughest Indian fighters, was one. "The trouble with the army," said Crook, "was that the Indians would confide in us as friends, and we had to witness this unjust treatment of them without the power to help them. Then when they were pushed beyond endurance and would go on the war path we had to fight when our sympathies were with the Indians." The U.S. Army chased the Sioux until, exhausted and starving, most surrendered. Similar stories were told across the West: in the forests of Minnesota and Washington and in Arizona Territory, where Apaches under their leader,

Geronimo, held out until 1886. Even the Nez Perce of Idaho, who had not taken up arms, were chased off their lands on a thousand-mile retreat across Oregon, Idaho, Wyoming, and Montana before finally surrendering. "Hear me, my chiefs," said their leader, Chief Joseph. "I am tired; my heart is sick and sad. From where the sun now stands I will fight no more forever." His people were carted off in unheated railroad cars to a bleak spot in Indian Territory (present-day Oklahoma), far from home.

As badly treated as they were, Indians were not "exterminated," as the Eel River Rangers wished. They endured harsh conditions for years on reservations or were taken to missions where their long hair was cut and they were encouraged to learn white customs. Gradually their numbers began to increase.

Meanwhile, the West was being filled by new families and new animals. For years, easterners had referred to the Great Plains as the Great American Desert. Who could make a living on such dry land? But as the buffalo were hunted away, the cattle of white settlers took their place. Columbus had brought the first cows to the Caribbean in 1493, and over the centuries they had spread across Mexico and north into Texas. These cattle survived on little water and defended themselves with horns that spread eight or even nine feet from tip to tip. Mexican *vaqueros,* or cowboys, developed the equipment needed to herd the beasts, such as branding irons to mark a cow with the owner's symbol, lariats to lasso steers, wide-brimmed hats—sombreros—for shade from the scorching sun, and leather boots with high heels, spurs, and pointed toes to fit snugly in the saddle's stirrups. The Americans from the East—*gringos,* the Mexicans called them—adopted these techniques, and many Mexicans continued to ride herd as well. Jesús Lavarro was one. Born in Mexico, Jesús moved with his family to Idaho as a boy and grew up spending most of his time on horseback. He "had few equals," said one cowboy who knew him, and one year he was hired to guide a herd of three thousand cattle home. The gringos "did not appreciate working under a Mexican," especially when Lavarro brought along his Indian wife, named Almost an Owl Woman, and his nine-year-old son, Joe. But he got the cattle safely home and taught the cowboys new skills in the process.

Cattle would never make ranchers rich unless they found a way to sell them. Only when the railroads reached far enough west did ranchers begin rounding up their herds for the "Long Drive," herding them more than a hundred miles to cow towns like Abilene, Dodge City, and Kansas City. There, railroad cars rushed them to Chicago, where they were butchered in Packingtown.

Farmers also swarmed onto the Plains to raise new varieties of wheat and corn. Almost immediately trouble erupted. Ranchers were used to letting their cattle roam free before the annual roundup. Farmers fenced in their land. With few trees for building wooden fences on the Plains, settlers depended on a new invention, barbed wire, to protect their crops. As more farmers fenced in land, "range wars" broke out, with cowboys cutting fences in the middle of the night. And neither farmers nor ranchers liked another Mexican import: sheep. These beasts nibbled the grasses so close to the ground that cattle and horses couldn't eat it.

The West of 1890 was a new world indeed. Where the tall-grass prairie once stretched for miles in Illinois and Indiana, corn and wheat now grew on large fenced-in farms. Where thousands of Indians had chased 30 million bison across the short-grass Plains, cattle and wheat farms were spreading, and the remaining Indians had been driven onto reservations.

At first glance it may seem as if this world of wide-open spaces had nothing to do with the crowded cities and the smokestacks of Homestead Steel. But in fact both lands were part of the vast system making over America. "Without farmers there could not be cities," admitted one Chicago resident. Nor could Packingtown's slaughterhouses survive without the cattle shipped to them. City and country depended on each other, in good times and bad.

28

Luck or Pluck?

IT'S NOT TOO MUCH TO say that in the last four chapters, we've seen the United States being made over from top to bottom. Even if the process took a few decades rather than a few years, it would be hardly an exaggeration to call it a revolution.

Gazing at this hubbub of expanding cities, fiery blast furnaces, and sprawling cattle herds, have you noticed what's missing? We've said almost nothing about government, elections, and political campaigns. It's not that those activities stopped. But none of the presidents or Congresses that the voters elected contributed much to these changes. President Rutherford Hayes left office in 1881 after only one term, relieved to be "out of a scrape." James Garfield was shot and killed after only a hundred days in office, by a man angry that the president wouldn't give him a government job. Of those who followed—Chester Arthur, Grover Cleveland, Benjamin Harrison—none seemed nearly big enough to fill the boots of Washington, Jefferson, Jackson, or Lincoln.

But there was another reason the federal government played a fairly small part in transforming the land. Most Americans didn't think it *should* get involved in such matters. To be sure, Alexander Hamilton and the Federalists had wanted government to encourage manufacturing in a land where few factories existed. And the Whigs who opposed Andrew Jackson believed that government should actively support the building of roads, canals, and railroads. (The transcontinental railroad, after all, couldn't have been built without government aid.) But early on, Jefferson set a different tone. Citizens should be left alone, he argued, "free to regulate their own pursuits of industry and improvement." The idea of keeping government out of economic affairs had a French name: *laissez-faire.* That was because a famous French minister of finance once asked some businessmen what the government could do to help them. "Leave us alone!" they replied. "Laissez-nous faire."

Then, too, the followers of Andrew Jackson insisted that when the Declaration of Independence said that *all men are created equal,* it meant everyone should be given an equal opportunity, not that the government should step in to help make them equal. As long as everyone began the race of life at the same starting line, individuals should be free to run the race on their own. *Strive and Succeed,* you might say. At least, that was the title of a popular children's book that made the point. It was published in 1872 and written by a former teacher and minister, Horatio Alger.

Alger beat the drum loudly for striving and succeeding. He wrote dozens of children's books, all recommending the same lessons of success. Alger's heroes were mainly homeless boys "adrift in the streets," with nicknames like Ragged Dick and Tattered Tom. Fourteen-year-old Dick slept in a box half full of straw, dressed in baggy, torn pants, a shirt "which looked as if it had been worn a month," and a scruffy vest with only two buttons. Dick was a bootblack; he shined shoes and was thrilled if even 50¢ ended up in his pocket. "I guess I'll go to Barnum's [Show] to-night," he said when he did well, "and see the bearded lady, the eight-foot giant, the two-foot dwarf, and the other curiosities, too numerous to mention."

This was Dick's idea of a good night out. But Alger's heroes meant to get ahead, through *Luck and Pluck,* to use the title of another story. "I mean to turn over a new leaf, and try to grow up 'spectable," Ragged Dick vowed. As he rode a ferryboat to Brooklyn one day—so Alger imagined—he saw a six-year-old boy wander too close to the edge of the deck and fall into the river. "My child!" exclaimed the horror-struck father. "Who shall save my child?" Dick plunged in, of course, without even thinking; and though he might have drowned, he reached Little Johnny, keeping him afloat until the two were hauled out of the water by people in a nearby rowboat. "You're a plucky boy," said one of the oarsmen, in case readers hadn't noticed. Even better, Little Johnny's father was a merchant who gave Dick a new suit of clothes and a job as a clerk. "My lucky stars are shinin' pretty bright now," exclaimed Dick. "Jumpin' into the water pays better than shinin' boots." Who needed the government when you were lucky as well as plucky?

Other Americans turned to science to explain why government should let things alone. In 1859 the British naturalist Charles Darwin proposed a new scientific theory: evolution. Darwin overturned the long-accepted idea that animal species never changed—that giraffes and woodpeckers and speckled trout had always been the way they were, from the beginning of creation. Darwin showed that species changed, evolving over thousands and even millions of years. If a certain kind of finch was born with an unusually long beak, which by chance helped it to dig up more grubs, then over time long-beaked finches, because they were more successful, would replace short-beaked finches. Competition in nature selected the fittest and allowed them to survive.

Now, in truth, Darwin never associated "the survival of the fittest" with *human* societies. But other thinkers applied ideas about evolution to politics and government. They argued that day in and day out, individuals competed for wealth and success, just as finches competed for grubs. "The growth of a large business is merely a survival of the fittest," said John D. Rockefeller, the wealthy oilman. "This is not an evil tendency of business. It is merely the working out of a law of nature and a law of God." For some people, known as social Darwinists, the theory of evolution suggested that government shouldn't interfere with business. Let the fittest survive and society would only get better.

The most famous Englishman who wrote about evolution and politics was a rather strange man named Herbert Spencer. Spencer was bald on top but had bushy muttonchop sideburns that stopped just above his chin. He seemed not at all like one of nature's fittest. He suffered nervous breakdowns, had trouble sleeping, and was driven to distraction by noise in public places. Sometimes he even brought his own hammock on train trips, which two servants set up, so he could lie down as he traveled, as if in his very own private Pullman palace car. Spencer's books on evolution became popular in America, and he had no bigger fan than that captain of the steel industry, Andrew Carnegie.

Andrew's father had been a poor weaver in a Scottish village, but the son was full of enthusiasm, even as a baby. Little Andrew shoveled down his oatmeal porridge breakfast with two spoons, one in each hand, and then cried in his Scottish accent for "Mair! Mair!" As an older boy, he fetched water from the village well, which sometimes meant waiting in line for an hour. Andrew thought it unfair that some of the women lined up their pails the night before, reserving a place so they could cut to the front of the line. Fed up, he boldly kicked the pails over and went to the head of the line. The women called him Daft Andrew—meaning foolish and crazy. But like Ragged Dick, Daft Andrew meant to become "'spectable" when he and his family moved to America. Though he first worked as a lowly laborer in a Pittsburgh textile mill, he soon got a job as a telegraph messenger. From there, he rose to sending telegrams over the wires and later was hired by a high official of the Pennsylvania Railroad. Finally his hard work and long hours led him to the steel business. To Carnegie, Herbert Spencer's books explained how nations improved through competition and struggle, just as boys like him had competed to be the best. "*All is well, since all grows better* became my motto," Carnegie said. "Before Spencer, all for me had been darkness."

After he grew rich and famous, Carnegie determined to meet the great philosopher. That was no easy task, for Herbert Spencer hated travel. But finally he announced a trip to America to promote his books. Carnegie immediately arranged to be on the ocean liner that brought him over. Then he persuaded the dining steward to assign him a place at Spencer's dinner table so they could talk. Come to Pittsburgh, Carnegie begged. See the world's most advanced steel mills! What better demonstration of how the United States had evolved? Reluctantly, Spencer agreed. Alas, the banging, screeching, and clanging in the factories left the nervous thinker in a state of near collapse. Worse, he was staggered by the "repulsiveness of Pittsburgh." The poor were jammed into grime-covered shacks. The Ohio River was fouled with pollution. No green and pleasant public parks could be seen anywhere. Pittsburgh the height of evolution? "Six months' residence here would justify suicide," Spencer announced.

Carnegie got over these criticisms from his hero; but they were one sign that *strive and succeed* could not solve all the world's problems. What about the thousands of workers who strived and barely survived? Brakemen showed plenty of pluck as they scrambled across the tops of railcars. But if luck ran out and a man plunged to his death, would it help his children if his wife read them another tale by Horatio Alger? When a laundress became so tired that she let down her guard for just a few seconds and washing-machine rollers pulled her hand in and crushed it, the motto *All is well, since all grows better* seemed small comfort.

In any case, captains of industry like Carnegie didn't like it when labor unions tried to help ordinary folk compete with million-dollar corporations. At Carnegie's Homestead Steel plant, the union refused to accept a new contract that reduced workers' wages. The employees went on strike in the summer of 1892. The union knew that Carnegie's manager, Henry Frick, would try to reopen Homestead by bringing in several hundred armed "Pinkertons"—private detectives—to fight the strikers. (The detectives got their name because their company had been founded by the same Allan Pinkerton who years earlier had guarded President-elect Lincoln on his trip to Washington.)

Day and night, union sentries waited for Frick to make his move. Finally two barges were spotted sneaking up the Monongahela River late one steamy July night. Union men sounded the alarm with factory whistles and sirens—and instantly the entire town of Homestead swarmed out to do battle. For twelve hours they fought the "Pinks," taking potshots with rifles, firing a cannon, and throwing sticks of dynamite. Workers' wives were even more desperate. They filled stockings with scrap iron and beat the Pinks as they retreated. Sadly, the detectives were mostly poor workers, too, out of a job and desperate enough to accept $1 a day to fight for Henry Frick. Frick would have agreed with a remark made by railroad boss Jay Gould during another strike. "I can hire one-half of the working class to kill the other half," he said.

Where was the government? It stayed away until fighting broke out. Then Pennsylvania's governor called in the militia on the side of the business owners. The troops took control of Homestead, let Frick back in, and the strike was put down. That same July in Coeur d'Alene, Idaho, federal troops crushed a protest by miners after their pay was cut at the same time that they were made to work ten hours a day instead of nine. In disputes between workers and business, the government usually ignored workers' problems until strikes and protests broke out. Then it left behind "laissez-faire" and stepped in to help business.

Worse was to come. When a large railroad went bankrupt six months later, a financial panic broke out. Five hundred banks failed; fifteen thousand businesses went bust. In cities across the country desperate people wandered homeless, out of jobs, out of money, out of luck. It was one thing to sleep in the street when the weather was warm, as Ragged Dick had. But now newspapers reported people freezing to death in winter and starving to death in summer. Times were just as hard out in the country. "The suffering is terrible," a Nebraska banker reported. "Scores of women and children have to stay in their sod shanties bare-footed for the want of something to cover their feet. All this was brought on these people through no fault of theirs." Where was the government? Governor John Altgeld of Illinois warned workers of "a long dark day ahead of you. It will be a day of suffering and distress, and I must say to you there seems to be no way of escaping it, and I therefore counsel you to face it squarely." The government could do nothing. *Laissez-faire*—leave it alone.

Jacob Coxey, a businessman from Ohio, believed that the government could and should do something. Determined that things must change, he organized the first protest march on Washington, with the goal of proposing that the government hire the unemployed to improve the nation's roads. About one hundred supporters began their journey on a chilly Easter morning, a black man leading the way with an American flag. They called themselves the Commonweal of Christ, but newspapers nicknamed them Coxey's Army. They passed through Homestead, where a brass band and hundreds of supporters greeted them. Elsewhere friendly citizens gave them food and a place to sleep. Across the country other "armies" formed and began to march. Arriving in Washington, five hundred of Coxey's Army marched to the steps of the Capitol, as fifteen thousand spectators looked on. Coxey led the march, accompanied by his wife and baby boy—named Legal Tender, of all things. But the moment Coxey doffed his hat to speak to the crowd, two policemen tackled him and other officers began clubbing the marchers. Instead of receiving a serious hearing from the leaders of government, Coxey was arrested for walking on the grass, the only law the police could come up with as an excuse to jail him. Relieve

unemployment? Nonsense, exclaimed a congressman from Massachusetts. That would be "immoral, for unemployment was an act
of God."

Four hundred years after Columbus landed in America, the
United States had become a colossus, a land made over. But this
powerful nation faced a depression more serious than any before
in the nation's history. The systems of industry were not strong
enough to weather hard times. The nation needed more than luck
and pluck, more than the survival of the fittest, if it was to become
truly great.

29

The Progressives

COXEY'S ARMY CALLED itself the Commonweal of Christ. And the word *commonweal* takes us back to the idea of a holy commonwealth held by John Winthrop and the Puritans. Their thoughts about government were rather different from the calls of the new industrial world to strive and succeed and let the fittest survive.

Winthrop wanted his "city on a hill" to be more than just individuals going their own way. In a commonwealth, people were "knit together in this work as one man. We must delight in each other," he insisted; "make others' conditions our own; rejoice together, mourn together, labor and suffer together." Like Winthrop, Jacob Coxey wanted a government that acted for the common good, "to aid the people in their day of distress. We are here to tell our representatives . . . that the struggle for existence has become far too fierce and relentless. We come and throw up our defenseless hands and say: 'Help, or we and our loved ones must perish.'"

Coxey was jailed for proclaiming such a strange idea. President Grover Cleveland made matters clear: "While the people should patriotically and cheerfully support their Government, its functions do not include the support of the people." But as the depression spread desperation and ruin, reformers pushed the government to take action.

Farmers in the South and West led the way. For decades they had suffered from the coming of the Next Big Thing. They had borrowed money from big banks to buy their farms. They had delivered their crops on big railroads, which charged small farmers more than big corporations paid. And when a dry summer ruined their harvests or the price of wheat fell, many didn't have enough money to pay off their loans. So they borrowed more—they had to, just to buy seed for the next year's crops. When they finally dug themselves so deep into debt that they could borrow no more, the banks took over their farms and threw them off their land.

At first farmers banded together in local groups known as granges. There, farm folk met at community suppers, fairs, and lectures to talk over their problems. The granges also helped them pool their money to buy supplies and store their crops more cheaply. When the depression struck in 1892, southern and western farmers formed a "People's Party." The Populists, as they were called, campaigned to break up big banks and have the government take over the railroads. By the election of 1896 the Populists had done so well that the Democrats decided they had better abandon Grover Cleveland's idea that government could do little. Instead, they nominated the energetic William Jennings Bryan, a candidate the Populists supported, too. Bryan set crowds afire, speaking as often as twenty times a day in favor of a government that took action. Republican William McKinley, on the other hand, had no talent for speechifying. So he spoke only to small groups from his front porch in Canton, Ohio, promising prosperity and "a full dinner pail" for workers if he were elected. McKinley may have been dull, but many middle-class Americans worried about fiery Populists and angry, out-of-work Democrats. The poor wanted mostly "the

chance to get something for nothing," Republicans warned. Mc-
Kinley won the election and the Populist Party faded.

Strikes and riots, homeless people wandering the streets, cities swarming with strange immigrants . . . such scenes frightened
many Americans. America should be *American,* they protested.
It should be more pure—which was another way of saying more
like themselves. The nation would become one rather than many
by setting apart people who looked different, thought differently,
or acted differently. During the 1890s, groups of Americans who
seemed foreign began to be looked down upon and kept apart—
segregated. Colleges, social clubs, and resorts decided not to admit
Jews, even if they had before. Groups like the American Protective
Organization worked to pass laws keeping out immigrants. (The
pope, they falsely claimed, was encouraging Catholic immigrants to
murder Americans.) In dozens of ways, life in the United States became segregated in hopes of making it more "pure." Baseball's major
and minor leagues shut out black players after 1898, leaving them
to form their own "Negro leagues." Schools were segregated, separating not only blacks but also Mexican Americans from whites.
In the South, state legislatures passed laws to complete the process
of segregation, right down to separate water fountains for "whites"
and "colored." Worse, the new laws made it all but impossible for
southern African Americans to vote. When blacks challenged the
whole idea of segregation, the Supreme Court ruled, in the case of
Plessy v. Ferguson, that so long as states treated each group equally,
segregation was legal. The policy was called "separate but equal."

In truth, *separate but equal* was never equal. Railroad cars for
African Americans were not as comfortable, black schools received
far less money for education, and black citizens were kept out of the
best restaurants and hotels. By walling off so-called inferior people,
segregation encouraged more scorn, hatred, and violence toward
them. In the West, Chinese immigrants were beaten and driven
from farm work. In the East, unarmed Polish miners were shot by

police when tensions over strikes ran high. Jewish merchants in the South had their shops destroyed by nighttime raiders. By far, the violence hit African Americans hardest. Some three thousand were lynched in the years to come—hanged, tortured, and burned alive by white mobs, mostly in the South, but in other states as well. The mobs often made no secret of their plans, and large crowds gathered to watch, including mothers and even children let out of school, as if on holiday. In the rush to keep America "American," too many Americans forgot their nation's ideals: that all were created equal and that "we must be knit together in this work."

The growing middle class was as guilty of discrimination as the contented rich or the angry poor. Yet, strangely, that same middle class inspired a new reform movement that energized government and set it to work for better purposes. Whereas the Populists had largely failed in their efforts to stir up change, the Progressive movement succeeded.

Who were the Progressives? They didn't speak with a single voice or come from a single party. But they all agreed that government should do more for the common good. They questioned the idea that, in the real world, each individual really had an equal opportunity in life. Did the son of wealthy parents truly begin at the same starting line as the daughter of someone who lived in a dirty tenement and worked long hours? It was common then to blame the poor for being poor. "No man in this land suffers from poverty, unless it be more than his fault," insisted one minister, "—unless it be his sin." Progressives disagreed. People were shaped by the conditions they lived in. If you changed those conditions, you gave people a chance to do better. Progressives firmly believed that poverty was not a sin but a problem with the way society worked. To help, society had to be changed.

Reformers started locally. Jane Addams bought a rundown building in Chicago, named it Hull House, and opened its doors to neighbors in need. As Hull House grew, it provided a kindergarten for young children, a coffeehouse for adults, a library, a gym, and apartments. All sorts of people came. A fifteen-year-old girl, just married, looked for shelter. Her husband had beaten her every night for a week because she'd lost her wedding ring at work. A ninety-year-old woman, losing her memory, had been thrown out of several apartments because she would aimlessly pick plaster off the wall all day. Her adult daughter couldn't watch over her because she had to work. Hull House staff taught the mother how to make paper chains, decorating the walls instead of ruining them. A poor neighbor died; Hull House helped prepare the body for burial. Garbage piled up on the streets; Jane Addams became a city garbage inspector to push the city to do its job. Hull House performed many tasks, many missions; the list of what was needed was seemingly endless. But now a rundown neighborhood had a community center that gave it hope. Hull House was the first "settlement house" in the United States. By 1910 Progressives had founded over four hundred throughout the country.

Addams was only one of many women reformers. Perhaps their most determined campaign was to gain suffrage—the right to vote. Women had been pushing for this since the Women's Rights Convention at Seneca Falls in 1848. A few western states allowed women to vote by the 1890s. Where life was more informal, women were treated more equally. But men in the East and South resisted. A new generation of younger women protested day after day in front of the White House, standing as "Silent Sentinels." Quaker Alice Paul and her followers gained sympathy after Washington police arrested them, pulled off their clothes, and threw them naked into jail. Gradually, the tide of public opinion turned, until finally in 1920 the Nineteenth Amendment to the Constitution gave women the right to vote in all elections. Only one woman was still living who had attended that convention in Seneca Falls seventy-two years earlier: Charlotte Woodward Pierce.

Meanwhile, Progressive men and women alike were reforming city government. They were fed up with dirty streets, streetcars that charged too much, high gas, electric, and water bills. Cities usually gave only one business the right to run such utilities because it made no sense to have three water companies each digging their own water pipes or several electric companies stringing competing wires. But that meant that if you wanted water or electricity, you had only one choice and had to pay whatever the utility company charged. Progressive mayors got their cities to take over the utility companies and charge fair prices. They also relied on experts to run city services rather than the friends of old-style political bosses who got jobs because they knew someone or were owed a favor.

If cities could be reformed, why not whole states? Progressives ran for the legislature and for governor, winning most often in the Midwest. Governor Robert La Follette of Wisconsin, known as "Fighting Bob," pushed through reforms that were widely copied. States began to regulate unfair railroad rates. They formed commissions to hold hearings about bank fraud or accidents in the workplace. The commissions then used the information to create laws regulating banks, railroads, and other corporations.

In 1898 a brash forty-year-old Republican named Theodore Roosevelt became governor of New York. As a boy, Teddy had been sickly, with weak eyes, skinny legs, and asthma that made it hard to breathe. But with luck (he came from a wealthy family) and a lot of pluck, Roosevelt built up his strength. For a time he lived in the Dakotas, hunting, riding, and tending cattle. He climbed the snow-capped Matterhorn Mountain in Europe and boxed or wrestled with anybody who was willing. Raising a family in the governor's mansion, he played "bear with the children almost every night" and even lowered them by rope out a second-floor window. Thomas Platt, the Republican party boss who ran affairs in New York, was suspicious of this new governor—a reformer who might play bear with *him!* Over Platt's objections, Teddy pushed through a law making streetcar and telephone companies pay taxes. Such companies, after all, had received a monopoly from the state government—the right to provide services to the public without any competition from rivals. Once that reform was passed, Roosevelt got rid of the state insurance commissioner, a man handpicked by Platt. That official had received $400,000 from one of the very companies he was supposed to watch over. Boss Platt raged: Teddy was beginning to act like a Populist! Worse, people had already begun to talk about reelecting him to a second term.

Platt, wanting to prevent that, hit on a brilliant plan. President McKinley was running for reelection in 1900. Why not nominate Roosevelt as McKinley's vice president? Vice presidents had almost no power, either to do good or to make mischief. Other Republican bosses liked the idea, but not Mark Hanna. "Don't you realize that there's only one life between this madman and the White House?" he asked. Nobody listened. McKinley was reelected and Teddy became vice president. Then, in 1901, a desperate worker shot the president at the Pan-American Exposition in Buffalo, New York. McKinley held on to life but soon took a turn for the worse. When the news reached Roosevelt, he was deep in the woods climbing Mount Marcy, the tallest peak in New York State. He rushed down muddy, rain-swept roads in a midnight ride, finally reaching the tiny train station in North Creek. A telegram was waiting for him: "THE PRESIDENT DIED AT TWO-FIFTEEN THIS MORNING." The "madman" was now master of the White House.

Of course, Roosevelt was hardly mad, and he was not even a Populist. He simply supported Progressive reforms and promised a "square deal" for every individual. As president, he worried when the powerful banker J. P. Morgan formed a vast new corporation named Northern Securities. Morgan, as we've already seen, had created the nation's biggest company, U.S. Steel. Both it and Northern Securities were known as trusts: a kind of supercorporation that brought many smaller companies under one big umbrella. The Northern Securities trust was going to control the Northern Pacific Railway, the Great Northern Railway, and just about every major rail and shipping line in the West—plus quite a few beyond. As one reporter put it, a person could travel "from England to China on regular lines of steamships and railroads without once passing from the protecting hollow of Mr. Morgan's hand." Roosevelt feared so much power in the hands of the richest men in America. He took Northern Securities to court to break it apart.

Morgan was shocked and rushed to the White House. "If we have done anything wrong," he told Roosevelt, "send your man to my man and they can fix it up." Teddy's "man," the attorney general of the United States, jumped in. "We don't want to fix it up, we want to stop it," he said. And they did. The Northern Securities trust was broken up and Teddy got a reputation for being a "trust buster."

In truth, Roosevelt thought that some trusts were fine, so long as they didn't use their size and power against the public good. But bad trusts needed to be stopped, he said. Should the government just ignore corporations that sold "patent medicines" to cure everything from baldness to backaches? Especially when science proved that their remedies were worthless, or even contained harmful ingredients such as acid or axle grease? What about conditions in the meatpacking industry, where millions of cattle were slaughtered in Packingtown for canned beef? The writer Upton Sinclair shocked the public with his novel *The Jungle,* which revealed that rats were allowed to fall into the cooking vats. "These rats were nuisances," wrote Sinclair, "and the packers would put out poisoned bread for them, they would die; and then rats, bread and meats would go in the hoppers together." At Roosevelt's urging, Congress passed the Pure Food and Drug Act to deal with such abuses.

Should the government just stand by as huge corporations cut down mile after mile of majestic pines for lumber? In a single year, a quarter of a million trees were shipped to Chicago alone. Should mining companies be free to rip open the sides of mountains and leave behind polluted streams and wastelands of gravel? Roosevelt insisted that the federal government should preserve some of these priceless lands for future generations. It needed to manage the nation's natural resources. The president added some 200 million acres of land to forest reserves and carved out more national parks.

Two more Progressive presidents followed Roosevelt, as the next chapter will show. But Teddy pointed the way. Like John Winthrop, he wanted a commonwealth that would "get from every citizen the highest service of which he is capable." Ordinary citizens could and should use political power to work for the common good. "Property shall be the servant and not the master of the commonwealth," Roosevelt insisted. "The citizens of the United States must effectively control the mighty commercial forces which they have called into being." Laissez-faire—simply "letting alone"—was not enough.

30

Smashup

THEODORE ROOSEVELT became president at the dawn of the twentieth century and was elected to another term in 1904. Four years later, William Howard Taft, the man Roosevelt favored, followed him. Taft was a quiet fellow with a big heart and a bigger body (he dieted constantly to keep his weight under three hundred pounds). As president, he busted more trusts than Roosevelt and protected more federal lands. But he didn't do as well in the rough-and-tumble of politics. The Republican bosses thought he was *too* progressive; and Progressives thought him not progressive enough. "He's all right, but he's weak," Teddy told a reporter. "They'll get around him. They'll *lean* against him." And here he gave the reporter a big nudge to illustrate his point.

Teddy went off on a grand safari to Africa, but when he returned a year and a half later, he, too, began leaning on Taft. Disappointed in his old friend's caution, Roosevelt ran again for president in 1912. The bosses backed Taft rather than face another four years of the Madman, so Teddy formed a Progressive Party of his own. "I'm feeling like a Bull Moose!" he bellowed, and Bull Moose became the party's nickname. Meanwhile, the Democrats nominated a reform governor from New Jersey, Woodrow Wilson, who held progressive views too; and labor leader Eugene Debs ran as a Socialist, most progressive of all. With the Republicans divided, Wilson won the election. But far more people voted for Progressives than ever before. It was their high-water mark.

Thomas Woodrow Wilson was a man with high ideals, a strong Presbyterian faith, and no love of political bosses—even those who helped him win. "I owe you nothing," Wilson told one party leader. "Whether you did little or much, remember that God ordained that I should be the next President of the United States." Unlike Roosevelt, Wilson didn't believe that some trusts were good and others bad. *Any* business that became big would be tempted to use its power unfairly, he argued. So he strengthened the laws against trusts. In addition, Wilson sponsored a new income tax. Until then, the national government had raised most of its money by selling off federal lands, taxing liquor, or imposing tariffs on imported goods. An income tax provided a different way to pay for the active government favored by Progressives. Furthermore, the tax was graduated: that is, people who had bigger incomes paid at a higher rate. Progressives believed that wealthier citizens, who benefited more from their country, owed their country more as well.

Wilson helped pass many progressive laws, including an eighthour workday and limits on children working in factories. But despite these victories and others, the Progressive movement was turned back by something unexpected: a war so vast that it engulfed the entire world. Sadly, this "Great War" turned out to be the Next Big Thing. And the same Industrial Revolution that had helped corporations become large now helped nations expand and make war more fearful and deadly than ever before.

To see how war and nations became big, we must back up a decade or two. In a way, we've already seen the process. When Andrew Carnegie wanted to protect his steel mills from competitors, he purchased entire mines so he would always have a supply of iron ore. Nations—especially European nations—also reached out to control lands on other continents that were rich in raw materials. For centuries, of course, kings and queens had built empires by conquering lands. But the new inventions of industry greatly helped Europeans expand. Steamships, railroads, and the telegraph made it easier to send traders and armies abroad. As for weapons, newly invented machine guns spit death at the rate of eleven bullets a second. People with only spears or even a few rifles stood no chance of stopping such armies.

Europeans called this drive for empires *imperialism*. And they told themselves they were doing a world of good. Cecil Rhodes, a British businessman who made his fortune from African diamond mines, put it plainly. "We are the finest race in the world, and the more of the world we inhabit, the better it is for the human race." Whether it was diamond or copper mines in Africa, rubber plantations in Brazil, tea plantations in India, or tin deposits in the East Indies, European nations took control. The people living where European empires spread were not as happy about imperialism. Slavery or near slavery continued in many colonies. Revolts broke out, but they were put down.

Americans were often pleased to think *they* were not imperialists. They had no colonies overseas! But the United States had already scooped up a huge amount of territory, stretching across North America. While Europeans scrambled for gold and silver abroad, Americans rushed after precious metals in their own West. While Europeans put down revolts in India and China, Americans drove the Indians from their lands and herded them onto reservations. The United States didn't need to establish far-flung colonies for raw materials. It took control of a continent of riches at home.

As a new century neared, some U.S. leaders looked more favorably on imperialism. American businesses were already trading throughout the world. The Tropical Fruit Company imported bananas by the ton from Central America. Sixty thousand agents sold Singer sewing machines everywhere from Africa to China. American plantation owners grew sugarcane and pineapples in the Hawaiian Islands, midway across the Pacific. In 1893 some of those planters overthrew the island's ruler, Queen Liliuokalani, and asked the United States to annex Hawaii. President Grover Cleveland refused. He was against "stealing territory," he said. Five years passed before a different president and a different island drew the United States into the race for empire.

That president was William McKinley and the island was Cuba, only ninety miles from Florida. In 1898 it was still a colony of Spain, but Cubans were in revolt. Should the United States recognize Cuba's independence? McKinley didn't want a war with Spain. But he did send the battleship USS *Maine* to Cuba to protect American businesses there. On a peaceful February morning, the *Maine* exploded while anchored in Havana harbor. A fire in the ship's coal supplies may have been the cause, but U.S. newspapers immediately blamed Spanish secret agents for planting explosives. "Remember the *Maine* and to hell with Spain!" proclaimed the *New York World*. Little more than two months later the Spanish-American War began.

It was a summer war, over in nearly the blink of an eye. The American navy had recently replaced its old wooden vessels with new ships of steel. They trounced Spain's forces. On land, Lieutenant Colonel Theodore Roosevelt won a well-publicized battle against the Spanish with a volunteer troop of cowboys, ranchers, hunters, and college athletes. Known as the Rough Riders, they followed Teddy's victorious charge up Kettle Hill, although his voice was so high and scratchy he had to yell twice before his men heard his order. Within six months, Roosevelt was governor of New York; within three years, president of the United States.

When Congress declared war, it promised that the United States would not take over Cuba. It didn't want to be accused of gobbling up colonies. But wars are always unpredictable. In Asia, Admiral

George Dewey sailed U.S. ships to the Philippine Islands and drove Spain out of its colony there. Most Americans could hardly locate the Philippines on a map, but imperialists argued that those lands certainly shouldn't be left for some European nation to exploit. And if the United States occupied the Philippines, then Hawaii would become a key port where American ships could stop on the way to Asia. McKinley convinced Congress to annex Hawaii that same summer. As a territory, it would have the chance one day to become a state and its residents to become American citizens.

On the other hand, Congress had no intention of doing the same for the Philippines. Or for Cuba's neighbor Puerto Rico, which Spain had also given up at war's end. American imperialists wanted to control these lands as "protectorates," not territories. Sounding like Cecil Rhodes, Senator Albert Beveridge of Indiana suggested that God had been preparing America and Britain to become "the master organizers of the world . . . that we may administer government among savage and senile peoples." That was not how Filipinos viewed the situation. They began a war for independence against their new American rulers—and the brutal battle was no summer war. It cost the lives of five thousand Americans, twenty-five thousand Filipino soldiers, and some two hundred thousand Filipino civilians. Both sides burned villages, destroyed homes, and tortured each other savagely. Perhaps the saddest moment came when a U.S. commander ordered his men to seize all copies of a dangerous document that Filipinos were spreading. It was a Spanish translation of the Declaration of Independence. The Philippines remained an American protectorate until 1946.

It almost seemed as if the United States had stumbled into the quest for colonies. But in truth, imperialism was the all-too-easy next step in the race to become big. After the Spanish-American War, the United States began to interfere regularly in the affairs of its southern neighbors. It *leaned* on them, as Roosevelt might have said: and the biggest leaner was Teddy himself, as he built a U.S.-controlled canal across the isthmus of Panama. When the nation of Colombia refused to deal with him, he encouraged some of its people to break away and form their own nation of Panama. Then Teddy signed a treaty with them to build the canal. He also warned Europeans not to found any new colonies in the American half of the world. Each "big power" would police its own area of influence.

The problem was, big powers enjoyed being big. They could never quite agree where *their* areas of influence started or ended. Each nation wanted the largest navy, the most modern army, the biggest guns. Ordinary folk supported their leaders in this race for power, marching by the thousands in parades through streets where flags two stories tall waved in the breeze. In a way, the flags were a symbol of the changes we've seen in the past seven chapters, which have been a parade of Next Big Things. Big industries, big banks, bigger cities, larger empires, deadlier ships and guns. And biggest of all in the summer of 1914—the Great War.

It began in central Europe, where the archduke of Austria-Hungary was shot and killed by a man who wanted independence for Serbia, which Austria-Hungary controlled. This tragic event by itself affected few nations. Still, the big powers had created a series of alliances with partner nations in order to increase their powers. *If one of us is attacked,* they pledged, *we both go to war.* So when Austria-Hungary attacked Serbia in retaliation for the archduke's death, Serbia's ally Russia jumped in to help the Serbs. Germany, the ally of Austria-Hungary, then went to war against Serbia and Russia; and France, Russia's ally, was drawn in, too. Like dominoes toppling one after another, Europe fell into chaos. Twenty-eight nations banded together as the Allies and fought against the Central Powers: Germany, Austria-Hungary, Bulgaria, and the Ottoman empire. Before the war was over, 8 million soldiers had died and the fighting spread over the lands and oceans of the world.

This was a war like none before. Old-fashioned cannons were replaced by artillery guns the size of railroad cars. Machine guns mowed down anyone who charged an enemy's line. Both sides dug trenches to hide from the bullets and bombs—twenty-five thousand miles of trenches. Chemists who had once used science to improve health or fertilize crops now created poison gases that rolled in deadly fogs across battlefields, killing anyone who didn't pull on a gas mask. Sixteen years earlier, Teddy Roosevelt had charged up Kettle Hill with cavalry troops. Now he wanted to organize a division of "horse riflemen." But what use were horses in trenches or amid swirling poison gas? Roosevelt never got his division. The nature of war had changed so much he was hopelessly out of date.

When the war began, President Wilson announced that the United States would remain neutral. If imperialists wanted to fight over land and colonies, America would stay out of it. But war is never predictable. Germany set up a blockade around Great Britain and France using a potent new weapon, the submarine. Hidden underwater, it fired torpedoes that sank ships bringing food or weapons to the Allies. Being neutral, Americans wanted the freedom to trade with Britain and France, or even to travel on Allied ships. In 1915, a German submarine sank the British ocean liner *Lusitania* in waters off Ireland. Some twelve hundred passengers died, including Americans. And the situation only worsened in the next two years, as Germany became more desperate. Finally, its submarines began attacking American ships as well as British. When Woodrow Wilson was reelected in 1916, his supporters cheered, "He kept us out of war." But in the end, he didn't. The United States entered on the side of the Allies in 1917. "The world must be made safe for democracy," Wilson proclaimed.

Two million American soldiers sailed to France and helped turn back the German army, which had advanced to within fifty miles of Paris. Exhausted by four years of cruel war, the Central Powers agreed to stop fighting on November 11, 1918—a day still remembered by Americans as Veterans' Day.

The war exhausted Wilson, but his ideals remained high. He announced a peace plan, known as the Fourteen Points, designed to end not just this war but all wars. The peace treaty should not punish the losers, he said, but instead be a "peace among equals." The big powers should destroy their heavy weapons and stop dividing up the world through backroom deals. Crowds showered Wilson with flowers when he arrived in Europe to help work out a treaty. The leaders of the big powers were less thrilled. "God gave us the Ten Commandments, and we broke them," joked the prime minister of France. "Wilson gives us the Fourteen Points. We shall see." He and other Allied leaders insisted on making the losers pay heavily for the war. But Wilson did win some points. The treaty agreed to at Versailles created a dozen new nations in Europe, all established on democratic principles. And most important to Wilson, the League of Nations was founded, a world organization for settling future disputes.

Most Americans favored the new League. But Wilson was a Democrat, and the Senate, controlled by Republicans, had to approve the peace plan, known as the Treaty of Versailles. Some were flat out opposed to it, but others were willing to compromise, if changes in the treaty were made. Stubborn in his ideals, Wilson refused to budge. "Anyone who opposes me in that, I'll crush!" he said angrily. The president took his case to the people, touring the nation at a grueling pace. After giving one of the finest speeches of his life, he collapsed in Pueblo, Colorado. Four days later he suffered a stroke that left him paralyzed on one side. Though his wife and advisers hid the worst of his illness from the public, Wilson was spent, physically and politically. The Senate voted against the treaty and the United States refused to join the League of Nations, instead signing a separate peace.

The Great War would not end all wars. In fact, in only twenty years, the coming of an even greater conflict would cause the Great War to be renamed World War I. But for a time, peace returned to a world weary of fighting.

31

THE MASSES

THE NEW PRESIDENT IN 1921 was a Republican from Ohio named Warren Gamaliel Harding, and he looked and spoke like a president, even if he liked to drop rather large words into the middle of speeches, just as his parents had dropped his big middle name between two more ordinary ones. Harding reassured people that despite the worst war in human history, fought with machine guns and poison gas and cannons the size of railcars, there wasn't "anything the matter with world civilization, except that humanity is viewing it through a vision impaired in a cataclysmal war. Poise has been disturbed, and nerves have been racked . . . and men have wandered far from safe paths." But never mind the wandering, elephantine words. In 1920 it was Harding, not Woodrow Wilson, who knew what people wanted. "America's present need is not heroics, but healing," said Harding, "not nostrums, but normalcy." People were tired of progressive campaigns for new laws and weary of war. Americans wanted to return to the old ways: to normalcy.

But could they return? Were the old ways even normal any more?

The Nineteenth Amendment had just given women the vote, a right they had pursued for decades, and they were not going back. In fact, women's lives had been changing so much that people were talking about a "New Woman" of these modern times, more independent and freethinking. This woman wanted a simpler style of dress, to begin with. She discarded her bulky petticoats and heavy woolen skirts that dropped to the ankle in favor of sleeker garments made from silk or a new artificial fiber, rayon. Sometimes her skirts barely covered her knees. She "bobbed" her hair, cutting it short, and she shocked many by wearing makeup, tight felt hats, and galoshes that flapped when left fashionably unbuckled. A "flapper girl," the newspapers called her. Rather than stay at home, the New Woman was more likely to take a job as a secretary, teacher, nurse, or beautician. In Texas and Wyoming women even ran for governor—and won.

Of course, the women who could afford to dress and behave so independently were largely from the middle class. The plain truth was, most women who took jobs outside the home were blue-collar folk. They worked not as secretaries or teachers but as poorly paid servants or as factory workers, perhaps standing all day preparing tobacco or working as "kidney pullers" in meatpacking plants. Despite such hardships, what was important was the idea that women could do more than tend the home. "We cannot believe it is fixed in the nature of things that a woman must choose between a home and her work, when a man may have both," said one student at Smith, a college for women.

And the lives of women were hardly the only things that were changing. Steam engines had been the marvel of the nineteenth century, powering everything from cotton looms to locomotives. As electric service spread, factories replaced their old steam engines with electric "dynamos." The research labs of large corporations turned out hundreds of new products, and Americans marveled. Imagine—a watch small enough to wear on your wrist! New chemical products were developed, like rayon and cellophane, a transparent wrap for packages. There were electric sewing machines that didn't need to be pumped by foot and electric refrigerators that kept food cold without the need for the iceman to deliver a block of ice every day. Jazz, a new style of music pioneered by black musicians, spread its catchy melodies across the nation and sparked a dance craze, the Charleston. "Some dance, some prance, I'll say, there's nothing finer / Than the Charleston, Charleston. Lord, how you can shuffle!" Older Americans frowned upon such sinful "wriggling" and so did younger folk used to traditional ways. One Mexican ballad complained about wives who wore "a bob-tailed dress of silk" and kids who "speak perfect English / And have no use for our Spanish / They call me 'fader' and don't work / And are crazy about the Charleston." But like it or not, normal or not, Americans in all walks of life were living differently. Small wonder the 1920s came to be called the New Era.

What set apart this era was not simply the new. It was the way new products were used and new experiences shared by millions of people—masses of people. Imagine the biggest crowd you've been in. At a football game, perhaps, where thousands flock to a stadium, or a presidential inauguration. But you've almost certainly joined a much larger crowd without leaving your living room— if you've watched the Super Bowl, the Oscars, or a hit television show. The idea of millions upon millions of people watching a single event is so common today it seems odd to speak of this sort of "mass culture" as new. The 1920s were when people began sharing such experiences.

Two key inventions led the way toward mass culture: motion picture films and the radio. The first machines for projecting "moving pictures" spread in the 1890s, in cities where working-class folk eagerly lined up to see shows. (The theaters were called nickelodeons because tickets cost a nickel.) Films projected sights never seen before indoors: crashing ocean waves, the Grand Canyon, lions and tigers. Then filmmakers had the idea of telling simple stories. *The Great Train Robbery,* a ten-minute extravaganza, played all across the country. But movies really came into their own in the 1920s when huge theaters were built in big cities, boasting grand names like the Roxy (in Manhattan) or Grauman's Chinese Theatre (in Hollywood, which became the movie capital of the world). These theaters seated thousands and their spaces felt like cathedrals. Doormen wearing white gloves greeted customers, even offering the shelter of an umbrella on rainy days. Ushers escorted patrons to their seats. The films had no sound, but a live pipe organ provided music to go with them. And unlike live theaters, Americans all around the country could see the very same show, swoon over the same movie actors or actresses—see them in close-ups, their faces filling the screen. By 1926, twenty thousand movie theaters had been built across the nation.

At about the same time, inventors found a way to broadcast radio waves through the air; these could be picked up by anyone who owned one of the new radios being sold. In November 1920, the first real broadcast went out from a shack on the top of a Westinghouse Electric Company building in East Pittsburgh. Station KDKA announced the election returns giving Warren Harding his victory. Americans loved this new way of bringing news and entertainment directly into their homes. Within a few years 3 million residences had radios; and the president broadcast a speech from St. Louis during a cross-country tour. (Being Harding, he did not just call it a tour to meet Americans; it was his "Voyage of Understanding.") Midway through the journey he had a heart attack, fell dead on his bed, and understood no more. The new president, Calvin Coolidge, spoke to a much wider radio audience a few months later. It was a marvel: not just to read a president's words but to actually hear his *voice,* coming from thousands of miles away.

The new masses were traveling differently, too. Inventors had long dreamed of making a carriage that moved on its own power. A "steam wagon" appeared in France as early as 1771. But more than a century passed before practical motorcars were made, using engines that ran on gasoline. The contraptions frightened horses and were widely distrusted. Vermont passed a law requiring drivers to send someone with a red flag to walk ahead of the vehicle to warn other travelers. Tennessee drivers had to take out newspaper ads a week in advance announcing their travels. By the beginning of World War I, more than a million autos were on the road, but they were so expensive that they remained the toys of the rich. That changed after a racecar buff named Henry Ford got into the car business. "Everybody wants to be somewhere he ain't," Ford commented. In his Michigan factory he created an "assembly line": instead of mechanics putting together cars one at a time, a chain pulled each auto along a line at the rate of about a foot a minute from one worker to the next, and each did a separate job. Ford's black Model T cars cost $845 apiece—much cheaper than others—and the price dropped to only $290 by 1925.

It was a car for the masses—and built by them. Ford paid his thousands of workers $5 a day, twice as much as most wages in the auto business. But the work was mind-numbing. You stood all day doing your single task over and over, relieved only by one fifteen-minute lunch-and-bathroom break. And Ford demanded that there be no whistling, laughing, or talking on the assembly line. Workers learned to speak without moving their lips. This was too much for the wife of one worker, and she wrote the boss: "The chain system you have is a slave driver! My God! Mr. Ford. My husband has come home and thrown himself down and won't eat his supper—so done out! Can't it be remedied? . . . That $5 a day is a blessing—a bigger one than you know but oh they earn it."

The sale of so many autos helped the economy to boom. With the taxes collected from the sale of gasoline, states and the federal government began a highway system that turned dirt roads into gravel, and gravel roads into concrete or asphalt, a gooey tar left over from refining gasoline. With millions of people making cars, building roads, and constructing skyscrapers, Americans experienced a higher standard of living than ever before. They had usually been cautious about buying what they couldn't afford, but companies were offering "installment plans" so that people could purchase cars, pianos, washing machines, or vacuum cleaners even if they didn't have the money to pay the full price right away. In short, they bought on credit. Why not? Prosperity had come to stay.

President Coolidge applauded the good times. As a Republican he championed the businesses that led the boom, large and small. "The man who builds a factory builds a temple," he said. "The man who works there, worships there." Coolidge rejected the Progressives' worry that too many workers were "living in industrial slavery." Businesses should be free to do as they wished, the president said, boasting that he governed best by "minding my own business." In other words, laissez-faire—let business alone. Though voters elected him to a term of his own in 1924, Coolidge chose not to seek reelection four years later. His secretary of commerce, Herbert Hoover, easily followed him into the White House in 1928, boasting that "the poorhouse is vanishing from among us."

Millions of Americans shared his confidence. They had begun to pay attention to the New York Stock Exchange on Wall Street— the place where investors bought shares of exciting new businesses like RCA, Radio Corporation of America. In the spring of 1928 RCA was selling for $94 a share. If you bought a hundred shares, the cost was $9,400. Even better, you could buy stocks on credit. Pay only $5,000 and get your broker to loan you the rest on "margin." RCA jumped from $94 to $108 in a week, then to $120 the next day. Another week and it roared along to $138—and so many new investors wanted it, the price then zoomed to $168. If you had paid $5,000 for a hundred shares, you could sell now for $16,800. "Everybody Ought to be Rich," proclaimed a popular ladies' magazine. The excitement of making a fortune in the stock market spread everywhere—to "the elevator man, the barber, the bootblack, the engineers, the porters, the newsstand man," remarked one businessman. Stockbrokers had offices with a stock ticker machine, a contraption that clattered as it spit out the latest prices on a long slim paper ribbon.

And then the great "bull market" crashed. Panic set in on October 24, 1929, as investors worried that stocks were headed for a fall. Millions of orders came in to brokers' offices: sell, sell! Almost nobody wanted to buy, so stock prices plummeted. Investors who bought on margin suddenly found their brokers demanding that their loans be paid back immediately, just as their profits were disappearing in smoke. Anxious crowds gathered on Wall Street while traders bellowed on the floor of the stock exchange. "The whole place is falling apart!" reported one clerk.

Prosperity had seemed as if it would go on forever. The American people had created a mass society in which millions gazed at movie stars, bought automobiles and radios, went to work on assembly lines, bought stocks—and now sold them, or what was left of them. The New Era was over and done in a whirlwind of weeks.

In the midst of the turmoil, a man staying in a New York hotel tried to make a phone call. He couldn't get a line. He went downstairs and finally located the hotel telephone operator. She was modern and up-to-date. Perhaps she even thought of herself as one of the New Women. Now, as she got off the phone, she was in tears. "That was my broker," she said. "I'm ruined. All I have left in the world is my sealskin coat."

32

A New Deal

THE TWO MOST FRIGHTENING days of the Great Crash, October 24 and 29, 1929, became known as Black Thursday and Black Tuesday. But the stock market plunge lasted months, not days. This is important, because it wasn't just money that people lost, it was confidence. Now and then stocks rose slightly, and hopes would flutter. But the plunge resumed, deeper and deeper; and hope began to fade.

If the "roaring" economy had been strong, Americans might have ridden out the crash, simply enduring a year or two of hard times. But the economy's weakness was much more serious. True, factories had been turning out cars and appliances by the millions. But the same workers who made those products—the new masses—were also the customers buying these items. And workers weren't being paid high enough wages to be able to afford all the goods being produced. Many had bought items on the installment plan, with money they hoped to earn in the future. Now, who wanted to buy more? If times were tight, the idea was to cut back. It was only common sense.

But as people cut back, so did businesses. With so few people buying, factories let go workers they no longer needed. It was only common sense. And now *these* workers weren't buying either. About one hundred thousand Americans were losing their jobs every single week. By the end of 1932, 13 million were out of work.

At least people had their savings. Or did they? During the Roaring Twenties, banks took savers' deposits and invested them in stocks to make money. But a lot of that money went into "surefire" stocks like Radio Corporation of America. And way too many banks were giving their officers huge bonuses or even cheating customers. So banks lost a lot of ordinary people's money—even that of Americans who never went near the stock market. And once rumors of trouble spread, people flocked to the banks to withdraw their hard-earned savings. Big banks closed, like the National Bank of Kentucky, but also small ones, formed to serve workers or farmers. Which bank would be next? In Nebraska John Farr, an African American rancher, heard talk and "moseyed" into town. "Sure enough. There was a big sign. . . . Closed. And people were lined up outside screaming and crying." The Jewish Noel State Bank of Chicago—failed. Smulski's Bank for Polish immigrants—gone. Over five thousand banks went out of business between 1930 and 1932.

Then there were the farmers. Most hadn't prospered even during the 1920s, and the 1930s brought a new calamity. Hundreds of windstorms swept up millions of tons of soil from farm fields on the Great Plains and just blew it away. These "black blizzards" darkened skies, blasted crops, and carried so much dirt east that a single storm in 1934 "rained" 12 million pounds of dust on Chicago alone. That winter red snow, filled with dust from the Great Plains, fell on New England. A change in climate was partly to blame for turning the Plains into a dust bowl, but humans were at fault, too. Farmers were growing crops on land whose soil had been anchored for thousands of years by the deep roots of prairie grass. Once those roots had been plowed up to make way for corn and wheat, the soil had little to anchor it and was more easily swept loose. Some 3 million people packed up and began a long trek to California in hopes of a better life—Okies, they were called, because so many were from overwhelmed Oklahoma.

Herbert Hoover had been president only six months when the Great Crash struck. A decade earlier, he had won fame directing aid that saved millions from starvation in war-torn Europe. Grateful cities named streets after him, including at least three Hooverstrasses (Germany and Switzerland), two Avenue Hoovers (France), and a Hooverplein in Belgium. As the economy worsened in 1930, the president resisted advice to do nothing. "Let nature take its course," recommended the head of the New York Stock Exchange. Instead, Hoover pushed through a tax cut so people would have more money to buy necessities. He got pledges from businesses not to lower their wages or cut jobs. And he convinced Congress to spend over $1 billion to hire workers for projects like the construction of Boulder Dam along the Colorado River. (The dam was later named after Hoover.)

All this was not enough. In the end businesses had no choice but to lay off workers. Meanwhile, Hoover began following the same commonsense advice as everybody else: if the government was taking in less money, it ought to cut back and spend less. To balance the budget, Hoover gave up his tax cut and raised taxes instead. Further, he didn't want to give money to the unemployed for fear that people would become lazy and not work. What was left to do? The president fell back on *encouraging* people. Instead of referring to the bad times as a "panic," the usual term, he talked about a "depression," as if that were a milder condition that would soon go away. "We have passed the worst," he announced in 1930.

But by the end of 1931 desperate people out in the countryside were eating weeds to survive. In the cities, men pawed through garbage for scraps to eat. Schoolteachers who had gone unpaid for months fainted from hunger in their classrooms. People who had lost their homes began to gather in shantytowns, living in canvas tents and cardboard shelters. There were no more Avenue Hoovers bringing honor—instead, the shantytowns were scornfully nicknamed Hoovervilles. The president meant well. He worked tirelessly, rose early, went to bed late. His eyes became bloodshot from lack of sleep. "What this country needs is a good big laugh," he said hopefully. "If someone could get off a good joke every ten days, I think our troubles would be over." Unfortunately, the jokes were at Hoover's expense. (*Hoover:* Can I borrow a nickel to call one of my friends? *Adviser:* Sure, here's a dime. Call both.) The so-called mild depression turned into the worst hard times in American history. In the election of 1932 the president was roundly voted out of office.

The man who replaced him was a very different person. While Hoover was a master of facts and figures, a brainy engineer, he had never been elected to any public office before becoming president. Franklin Delano Roosevelt, on the other hand, was a politician to his bones, ready to talk, bargain, and hobnob. While Hoover looked glum and hoped someone would make jokes, Roosevelt beamed with a cheerful, sunny energy. In a way, this optimism was surprising. Young Franklin had started out along the same track as his distant cousin Teddy Roosevelt—though as a Democrat rather than a Republican. Like Teddy, he went to Harvard, became assistant secretary of the navy and a candidate for vice president (though Franklin Roosevelt's ticket lost). But suddenly, at the age of thirty-nine, he contracted polio. The disease left him paralyzed from the waist down, a misfortune serious enough to discourage anyone. Not Roosevelt. He had himself fitted with steel leg braces and then worked tirelessly to walk even a few steps. His arm muscles, he boasted, had become bigger than those of the famous boxer Jack Dempsey. Encouraged by his wife, Eleanor, Franklin plunged back into politics and was elected governor of New York—again like his cousin Teddy. As president, Teddy had promised each American a "square deal." Franklin promised "a new deal for the American people."

What would that deal be? Roosevelt had no straightforward plan. Like the Progressives, he believed that in hard times, the government must act: "not as a matter of charity, but as a matter of social duty." His approach was experimental. "Take a method and try it: If it fails, admit it frankly and try another. But above all, try something." When he was sworn in on March 4, 1933, Roosevelt assured his fellow citizens that he would try, and that he would succeed. "The only thing we have to fear," he said, "is fear itself."

In fact, there was a great deal to fear. In the weeks before the inauguration, the banking system collapsed almost entirely, setting off new panic. The stock market shut down. To calm the situation, Roosevelt proclaimed a "bank holiday," ordering that every bank in the country be closed for four days. Holiday! It sounded almost jaunty. Then he rushed a law through Congress that reopened all the banks that were in good health, aided the ones that were a little shaky, and closed those that were badly failing. His decisive action relieved Americans and restored some confidence. When the banks reopened, more people put money into them than took it out.

The first hundred days of the New Deal were a whirlwind. The president gathered a band of professors and other experts to advise him. (The newspapers called them his "brain trust.") They were determined to experiment, to be bold and to change the very way the government worked. Roosevelt created dozens of new agencies to carry out his New Deal, although the program could be boiled down to three avenues of attack: relief for the needy, recovery of the economy, and reform of the system that had produced the Great Depression.

Of these three Rs, relief for Americans in need was the most pressing. Roosevelt created the Federal Emergency Relief Administration and put Harry Hopkins in charge—a pale, wisecracking, chain-smoking social worker from Iowa. Within three hours of getting his marching orders, Hopkins had set up a desk in a hallway and spent $5 million. The money went to state and local agencies to help those with no homes, no work, no food; and over the following months, another half a billion dollars followed. Meanwhile, the new Civil Works Administration hired 4 million unemployed to work directly for the federal government. A third agency, the Civilian Conservation Corps, sent over 2 million young men into the outdoors to do needed work. Altogether, laborers in these three programs built forty thousand schools, one thousand airports, and improved half a million miles of road. They planted trees, constructed athletic fields, restored Revolutionary and Civil War battlefields, built fire towers, and stocked waterways with over a billion fish.

Critics complained that the government was going into debt instead of balancing its budget and raising much-needed taxes. But some economists were beginning to realize that what was common sense for individuals wasn't always good advice for the entire economy. If everyone cut back, including the government, business would grind to a halt. The government *needed* to go into debt in the short run so that people who got government aid and government jobs could now go out and buy groceries, clothes, and supplies. That meant grocers and other store owners could afford to spend more, too.

Roosevelt wanted his relief programs to be temporary. But he believed that government could make a more permanent contribution toward the second R—recovery. For example, one of the country's poorest regions lay along the valley of the Tennessee River. There, flooding regularly ruined farm fields and communities, timber cutting had left hillsides barren, and malaria, spread by mosquitoes, sickened nearly one out of every three residents. Roosevelt created the Tennessee Valley Authority (TVA), a government organization that revived the region by building dams to prevent flooding, reforesting bare hillsides, and teaching farmers better ways to raise crops. The dams also produced inexpensive electricity, bringing power to houses that before had used oil lamps for light. People living in the valley saw their incomes and health improve sharply. Other New Deal agencies worked with corporations to build transportation facilities: a port in Brownsville, Texas, and the Lincoln Tunnel into Manhattan.

Finally, the New Deal set in place reforms—the third R—to help prevent any future Great Depressions. One was an insurance program to protect the bank deposits of ordinary folk so that they would never again lose their savings. Other agencies set rules preventing banks and the stock market from making risky investments or misleading their customers. New laws guaranteed workers the right to bargain for better wages by joining a union. Perhaps most remarkable, Roosevelt's New Deal put in place a support system for workers who were old, disabled, or out of a job. The president put his secretary of labor in charge of the problem, an energetic woman named Frances Perkins. The first woman to serve in a president's cabinet, Perkins had worked at Jane Addams's Hull House and for other progressive causes when she was younger. The system of "Social Security" she helped create did more than just provide a safety net for individuals. It and other New Deal reforms made the economy more stable so that future downturns wouldn't be so severe.

Roosevelt's Republican opponents complained bitterly about the dozens of New Deal agencies, each with its abbreviation to shorten a long-winded name. (For example, CCC for Civilian Conservation Corps and FDIC for Federal Deposit Insurance Corporation.) Roosevelt himself was nicknamed FDR. It was true that the new agencies often wasted money and made their fair share of mistakes. (TVA dams, for example, forced thousands of residents out of their homes, despite their many benefits.) Then, too, Roosevelt's method of trying one thing and then another led some advisers nearly to tear out their hair trying to get him to choose the plan *they* favored.

But for all its faults, the New Deal revived a nation that had been badly shaken, even broken down. And Franklin Roosevelt and his wife, Eleanor, were the faces of this new hope. Eleanor crisscrossed the country constantly, viewing hundreds of New Deal projects and talking with ordinary folk—whether a worker in a Seattle diner, Chinese Americans at a San Francisco nursery, or a West Virginia coal miner's wife in her rough shack. FDR reached out through his radio "fireside chats," listened to by millions in their homes. It felt as if the president was almost actually sitting by the fire. "Every house I visited . . . had a picture of the president," reported one New Deal official. "These ranged from newspaper clippings (in destitute homes) to large colored prints, framed in gilt cardboard. . . . And the feeling of these people for the president is one of the most remarkable phenomena I have ever met. He is at once God and their intimate friend; he knows them all by name, knows their little town and mill, their little lives and problems. And though everything else fails, he is there, and will not let them down." Roosevelt was reelected in 1936 with more electoral votes than any president has ever received: 523 out of 531. And unlike any other president, he was reelected to a third and then a fourth term.

In the end, what mattered most was not the votes he received or the confidence he showered. It was the way he changed people's ideas about government. The nation had always valued its political rights, Roosevelt explained, "among them the right of free speech, free press, free worship, trial by jury. . . . As our Nation has grown in size and stature, however—as our industrial economy expanded—these political rights proved inadequate to assure us equality in the pursuit of happiness. We have come to a clear realization . . . that true individual freedom cannot exist without economic security and independence." Government had a responsibility to *act,* to provide economic security in hard times. In that sense, the New Deal was a big deal indeed.

33

GLOBAL WAR

THE DAY AFTER FRANKLIN Roosevelt was sworn in as president
—March 5, 1933—Germany voted to choose its own legislature,
the Reichstag. Elections had been called by the new chancel-
lor, Adolf Hitler. An intense man, Hitler had a pale face framed
by brown hair, a toothbrush moustache, and piercing eyes that
too often burned with resentment. Several times he had tried to
sweep his National Socialist (or Nazi) Party into power and fallen
short. This election was different. In a brutal campaign, the party's
military-style gangs—"brownshirts"—attacked the rallies of opponents and beat up their leaders. Hitler's right-hand man, Hermann
Göring, warned business leaders that they had better open their
purses for the party. "The elections will certainly be the last for
the next ten years," he predicted, "probably even for the next hundred years." The Nazis won control of the Reichstag, which then
passed an act giving Hitler the power to make any law he pleased.
As Roosevelt worked with Congress on the New Deal, Adolf Hitler
became a dictator who spoke of purifying Germany and strength-

ening it. His people needed land—*lebensraum,* he called it, room to live.

Caught in the midst of their own Great Depression, few Americans paid heed. Yet within seven years Hitler brought Europe and the world to a new war; one so immense that the "Great" War of 1914–18 seemed moderate by comparison. Sixteen million people died in the first war; the new one killed 60 million. In the long parade of Next Big Things, World War II was, quite simply, the biggest event in human history. Humans had never before set in motion anything so deadly.

The forces that made such a war possible had been building for more than a century. As industry and science helped nations grow bigger and more powerful, the so-called big powers raced to control more colonies, more riches, and more weapons. World War I was the first smashup. At its finish, Woodrow Wilson dreamed of a peace to end all wars, with the League of Nations to resolve future disputes. But the Treaty of Versailles, signed to end the war, satisfied no one. Defeated Germany was angry at being forced to pay billions of dollars to the victors to help rebuild Europe. Italy and Japan, whose soldiers fought on the winning side, complained that they had not received their fair share of rewards. Japan wanted to expand its island nation to include some of China's territory on the mainland, while Italy's new dictator, Benito Mussolini, dreamed of standing at the head of a new Roman empire. Great Britain and France, on the other hand, had lost hundreds of thousands of young men in battle. The last thing the leaders of these democracies wanted was to be dragged into another war over some quarrel like the shooting of an archduke.

The United States was just as determined to avoid war. Both George Washington and Thomas Jefferson had warned against making "entangling alliances" with the nations of Europe. Jefferson's words echoed through the years, so that when Warren Harding steered the country toward normalcy, he assured Americans that "we do not mean to be entangled" in "the destinies of the Old

World." Better to remain safely isolated across the wide Atlantic. "Let us turn our eyes inward," suggested one political leader. "If the world is to become a wilderness of waste, hatred and bitterness, let us all the more earnestly protect and preserve our own oasis of liberty." Those who agreed became known as isolationists; and in truth, most Americans shared this view.

But it became harder to turn inward as the world slid toward war. When Japan invaded China's province of Manchuria and the League of Nations objected, the members of Japan's delegation simply walked out. "We are not coming back," they announced. Germany withdrew, too, demonstrating that the League's fine words had no force. Soon Italy invaded Ethiopia in North Africa and Japan unleashed an attack to gain more of China. Hitler marched newly organized armies right up to the borders of France and sent other troops east to occupy Austria. The European democracies might have blocked him if they had stepped in early. "We would have had to withdraw with our tails between our legs," Hitler admitted privately. But memories of the Great War remained too strong in Britain and France. At a summit meeting in Munich, Hitler promised he would not grab any more land if only he were allowed to occupy a part of Czechoslovakia where many German-speaking people lived. Britain and France agreed that they would "appease" Hitler one more time, and Prime Minister Neville Chamberlain returned to London announcing that he had achieved "peace in our time." It took only six months before Hitler broke his promise and took the rest of Czechoslovakia. Another six months and he invaded Poland. This time, France, Britain, and Poland declared war, leading the Allied forces (which would eventually grow to over twenty nations) against the Axis powers—primarily Germany, Italy, and Japan.

The United States did not join the fight. Although Franklin Roosevelt had come to believe that there could be "no escape" from war "through mere isolation or neutrality," Congress didn't agree, even as German armies knifed through Europe and forced France to surrender. Britain's turn was next, as wave after wave of German planes bombarded London and other English cities. The new prime minister, Winston Churchill, begged for American ammunition, planes, and "the loan of forty or fifty of your older destroyers." But Roosevelt's generals worried that if Germany invaded and conquered Britain, American warships and other goods would fall into Nazi hands. Better to fortify America and leave Britain to fight alone! Roosevelt disagreed, and the ships went over, helping the English in some small way to win their dogged Battle of Britain. Hitler gave up his plans for an invasion.

In the end, the stroke that brought the United States into the war came from an entirely different direction. Japan had long watched with envy as the British, French, Dutch, and even the Americans acquired colonies in Asia. Why shouldn't Japan do the same? Southeast Asia was much more its home territory than it was Europe's or America's. As Germany and Italy won victories in Europe, Japan secretly launched a fleet eastward across the Pacific. It was commanded by Admiral Isoroku Yamamoto and its mission was to attack the key U.S. naval base at Pearl Harbor in Hawaii. Years earlier, Yamamoto had lived for a time in Washington as a naval diplomat, where he had gained a reputation for being a sharp poker player. In truth, the raid on Pearl Harbor was much like high-stakes poker. If successful, the gamble would pay off immensely. But there was a risk. "If I am told to fight regardless of the consequences," Yamamoto told his chiefs, "I shall run wild for the first six months or a year." But if that big push didn't bring victory, "I have utterly no confidence for the second or third year." The admiral well understood that the United States was such a large nation, with so much industrial might, that it could build up its armies and navies and fight back to the bitter end.

On December 7, 1941, Pearl Harbor was caught unawares. Japanese bombers sank eight battleships, killed twenty-four hundred men, and damaged three hundred aircraft. Roosevelt proclaimed the day "a date which will live in infamy," and four days later, Hitler and Mussolini declared war on the United States. Americans would now fight the global war they had hoped to avoid.

Fortunately, the raid on Pearl Harbor didn't destroy the supplies of fuel that were vital to America's navy and air force. And no American aircraft carriers had been in port during the attack—a great stroke of luck, for out in the vast Pacific, these newer ships were able to launch air attacks in mid-ocean. Still, Japan's fleet was more modern—and its commanders planned a new strike against the U.S. base at Midway Island. This time the Americans knew the enemy was coming, thanks to code breakers who had been working day and night to decipher Japanese radio communications. At the end of an exhausting day of battle, the Japanese had lost four of their prized carriers as well as many skilled pilots trained in the difficult art of taking off and landing from heaving aircraft decks. Yamamoto's "wild ride" had not paid off, and the United States was on its way to victory in the Pacific. It would take three more years, however, as Americans slogged from island to island, working their way toward Japan.

Hitler took even greater gambles. German troops swept across North Africa in a successful offense, while in Europe an entirely unexpected attack thrust eastward, against the Soviet Union (formerly the Russian empire). Hitler boasted that he was putting into place a new Reich, or German state, that would last a thousand years. He began a ruthless campaign to rid Europe of those he considered disloyal or not racially "pure." These included Gypsies, artists, and thinkers who criticized the Nazis and, above all, Jews. Some 6 million Jews were deliberately starved, shot, worked to death, or killed in more than forty thousand slave labor camps, concentration camps, and six extermination centers, where Hitler's security forces built gas chambers. Hitler considered these victims "rubbish"—inferior beings who were members of "subhuman races." Later his campaign of mass murder became known as the Holocaust.

But in trying to fulfill his twisted dreams, Hitler spread his forces too thin. In eastern Europe the Soviets were led by an equally ruth-less dictator, Joseph Stalin. At the battle of Stalingrad his troops doggedly outlasted the Axis forces, as armies of more than a million on both sides fought hand to hand through the worst winter in decades. In Africa, British and American troops finally turned back the Germans and then began planning an invasion of Europe from Britain. That immense undertaking was coordinated by Dwight David Eisenhower, a determined, detail-oriented American general. Hitler knew the attack was coming, but not when or where. The day of decision (D-Day) came on June 6, 1944, as nearly 3 million soldiers, eleven thousand aircraft, and two thousand vessels set forth. On the French beaches of Normandy the Allies gained a foothold and began a slow push toward Germany. At the same time Soviet troops advanced from the east, while British and American forces invaded Italy from the south. By the spring of 1945 the exhausted German army had to accept old men and young boys as soldiers. But the Germans had lost. Hitler, holed up in an underground bunker, shot himself. Japan fought on.

That, in outline, is the way the war played out. But to squeeze six years into a few pages barely hints at the sorrow and terror the conflict spread. World War II was like a swirling firestorm that swept up everyone, touching people in large ways and small.

For David Crook, an English pilot in the Battle of Britain, tragedy hit home with the sight of a single towel. Crook returned from a mission after his fellow pilot was shot down—and there was his friend's towel, still hanging from the bunkroom window. He couldn't blot out "the thought of Peter, with whom we had been talking and laughing that day. Now he was lying in the cockpit of his wrecked Spitfire at the bottom of the English Channel."

Or there was "Sledgehammer," an American Marine fighting in the Pacific. His real name was Eugene Sledge and more than anything he feared the sound of a screaming artillery shell: "You're absolutely helpless. The damn thing comes in like a freight train and there's a terrific crash." One shell passed "no more than a foot over my head. Two foxholes down, a guy was sitting on his helmet drinking C-ration hot chocolate." He went "straight up in the air. The other two kids fell over backwards. Dead, of course."

Nadia Popova was one of many Soviet women who flew bombing missions in old crop dusters made of plywood and canvas. No guns, no radios, no parachutes. She and her comrades took to the air at night when the Germans could hear only a whoosh as the planes passed over. The Nazis called the pilots Night Witches. If a stray tracer bullet hit their aircraft, it was all over: the planes burned like paper.

Hans Michaelis, a German Jew, spoke with his niece Maria after hearing he was to be sent to a concentration camp. He knew what was coming. "What should I do? What is easiest, what's the most dignified? To live or to die? To suffer a terrible fate or to end one's own life?" Maria talked with him as time ran out. "I have 50 hours left here, at most!" he said. "Thank God that my Gertrud died a normal death, before Hitler. What would I give for that!" As the two parted, Maria said, "Uncle Hans, you will know the right thing to do. Farewell." He ended his life with poison.

On the American home front, Peggy Terry assembled artillery shells in Viola, Kentucky. One ingredient, tetryl, turned the workers orange. "Our hair was streaked orange. Our hands, our face, our neck just turned orange, even our eyeballs. . . . None of us ever asked, What is this? Is this harmful?" Children helped tend "Victory Gardens"—food grown at home—or collected scrap metal to be melted down for use in the war effort.

Nieces, nephews, sons, and daughters—no one escaped. As I mentioned in the introduction to this book, my wife's father was caught up in the Bataan Death March in the Philippines. His wife's first child died from a tetanus infection because the doctors all had fled when the Japanese arrived. My own mother, recently out of college, sailed to Britain with the Red Cross. And my father, a chemist at the Eastman Kodak Company, was one day visited by a mysterious government agent who asked if he wanted to help his country. He could tell no one where he was going, the agent warned, and then gave him a railroad ticket to Chicago. There he received another ticket, which took him south to a strange factory-city, Oak Ridge, being built from scratch in the Tennessee countryside. At Oak Ridge, the ingredients for a new bomb were being prepared with the utmost secrecy.

The bomb's nickname was "the gadget." It was an atomic bomb, a weapon the world had never seen. The power of its blast came from splitting atoms, which released immense amounts of energy. Scientists fleeing Germany had warned Roosevelt that Hitler was trying to build such a weapon, and that the United States should not be caught unprepared. Germany never succeeded in its quest, but meanwhile, over 120,000 people worked on the American project at secret locations in Tennessee, Washington State, New York, and even in an old squash court built under a football field at the University of Chicago. The most important research was done in the New Mexico desert at Los Alamos, where physicist Robert Oppenheimer led a team whose first bomb was ready to test in July 1945. The scientists were anxious. One calculated that the atom blast might be so fierce it would set the earth's atmosphere on fire. The possibility was not outlandish. Allied planes were already carrying out massive firebomb attacks against Dresden, Germany; Tokyo, Japan; and other cities. Over a million people died in these assaults, as the firestorms boiled water in canals and consumed the oxygen in the air. Victims who were not boiled or burned alive suffocated.

At Los Alamos, the test explosion was so sharp that Georgia Green, a nearly blind college student traveling a desert road fifty miles away, saw and felt the flash. Word of its success was relayed immediately to the president—though by July 1945 he was no longer Franklin Roosevelt. FDR had begun his fourth term six months earlier, looking gaunt and exhausted. In April he died of a stroke. The new leader, Harry S. Truman, ordered a nuclear attack on Japan. On August 6, residents in the city of Hiroshima

were astonished to see a great *pika don*—"flash-boom" in the sky—
followed by a boiling black mushroom cloud. In a single stroke,
one bomb killed forty thousand people and left a hundred thousand
more dying from burns and radiation. A second bomb exploded
three days later on the city of Nagasaki. Within a week Japan surrendered. The war was over.

The United States, although determined not to go to war, had
once again found itself fighting. "We must live as men and not
as ostriches," Roosevelt reminded in his final inaugural address.
There could be no more sticking of heads in the sand—not with
airplanes that could span oceans and bomb cities into ash. Isolation was no longer an option.

34

SUPERPOWER

OUT OF THE FLAMES OF war an ashen world appeared, one hugely different from the prewar world of 1939. To begin with, there were the ruins. City buildings caved in, rubble, broken glass, streets black at night because electric plants had been bombed. Twelve million prisoners of war to be seen to. Food and money so scarce, people often traded goods: a bracelet for some bacon or an old coat for a chicken. Strange sights and sounds—sad, horrifying, or just plain odd. Young girls hitching a ride in a Russian tank. An old German gentleman in a business suit clubbing a duck to death with his cane. The eerie quiet outside a concentration camp. "The first thing you get is the stench. That's human stench," said one American soldier. "You begin to realize something terrible had happened."

That was the human tragedy and the physical wreckage. But the world of politics and nations was wrecked, too. The big powers that had once competed for empires now faced broken economies and uncertain futures. The defeated lost their colonies, of course. But so did victorious Allied nations, for after the war many peoples in Asia and Africa threw off their European masters. India won its independence from Britain, Indonesia from the Dutch, and Indochina launched a rebellion against the French.

What of the United States? The war had killed some four hundred thousand Americans, but that number looked small when set next to the 60 million deaths worldwide. Also, the United States had no ruined cities or bombed-out factories to rebuild. The country had been in the midst of a depression when the war began; by its end the economy was booming. The American navy was the world's biggest, the air force the largest, the army the best equipped. Winston Churchill put the matter simply: the United States now stood "at the summit of the world." It had become not just a big power but a superpower. No other nation could challenge it. Except perhaps one.

That was the Soviet Union, known formally as the Union of Soviet Socialist Republics. Two centuries earlier, it had been called the Russian empire, which had expanded east across Asia during the same years that the United States was pushing west across North America. Americans built a nineteen-hundred-mile transcontinental railroad to the Pacific; Russia's Trans-Siberian Railway snaked over fifty-seven hundred miles and also ended along Pacific waters. The United States spanned four time zones; Russian possessions stretched over twelve. Long ruled by powerful tsars, the empire had been overturned in 1917 by the Russian Revolution, whose leader Vladimir Lenin pushed the idea of equality in a radical new direction. Aristocrats would no longer have power; nor would the "capitalists" who built factories and ran banks or businesses. Instead, workers and peasants would set the government's course by meeting in revolutionary councils known as Soviets. Lenin rejected the equality of opportunity that Andrew Jackson proclaimed, whereby citizens could succeed—become *more* equal—through hard work or ingenuity. Instead, Lenin's Communist Party declared an end to private property. No one would be rich. Everyone would work to the best of his or her ability and receive only what each needed to live decently.

That was the ideal, at least, but in carrying out their revolution, the Communist rulers quickly made themselves as powerful as the old tsars. Lenin launched a campaign of terror to eliminate his opponents. His successor, Joseph Stalin, was even more brutal. During the 1920s and 1930s millions died from badly thought-out reforms; millions more were sent to labor camps or executed.

Most Americans condemned Stalin's acts. But when Hitler launched his surprise invasion of Russia, the Soviet Union immediately became an ally of Britain and the United States. Indeed, the Soviets were essential to victory, and their country paid dearly with blood and treasure. In their fight with Germany over 20 million citizens were killed, seventy thousand villages destroyed, and 25 million people left homeless. Yet the Soviet Union remained the only other nation strong enough to become a superpower. In the eastern European countries where it had driven Germany out, Stalin took power, doing away with free elections and setting up governments friendly to the Soviets. "An iron curtain has descended across the continent," Churchill warned, which served to wall off Communist nations. "A fairy tale," replied Stalin blandly. But it was not. And so a new conflict began: not a hot war in which the vast armies of two superpowers battled, but a Cold War that simmered for nearly fifty years, sparking constant crises and sometimes open fighting.

You can see the flashpoints by viewing the globe from above. To the east, the Soviet Union was joined by China, which fell to Communists in 1949 at the end of a twenty-two-year civil war led by Mao Zedong. To the west stood the United States and Canada along with their allies in western Europe. Around the edges of these rival territories hot spots flared. The most serious among many were Germany, Korea, Vietnam, and Cuba.

The American president who faced this changed world was Harry Truman, a former senator from Missouri who was little known be-

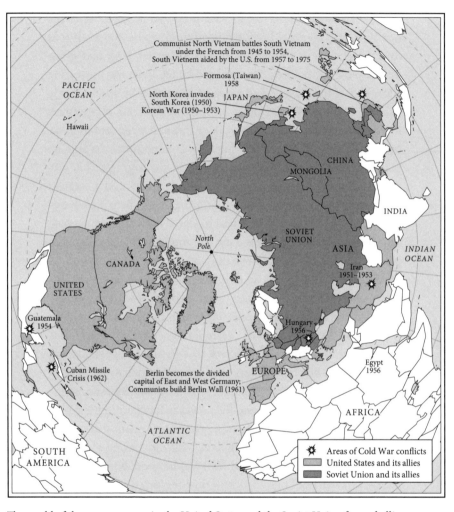

The world of the superpowers. As the United States and the Soviet Union formed alliances, conflicts flared. The most serious involved nations divided after World War II: East and West Germany, North and South Korea, and North and South Vietnam. But many other hot spots erupted in violence. The most serious, as we will see in chapter 35, involved Cuba.

fore FDR picked him to run for vice president in 1944. "Who the hell is Harry Truman?" asked one admiral when Roosevelt told him his choice. A scrappy, plainspoken farmer who had given up the plow for politics, Truman said he felt "like the moon, the stars, and all the planets" had fallen on him when he was suddenly ushered into the White House. But he was determined—perhaps too determined—not to seem weak or inexperienced and to make the hard decisions. "The buck stops here," announced the sign he placed on his desk in the Oval Office. At the urging of his secretary of state, George Marshall, Truman convinced Congress to create a billion-dollar foreign aid program to help Europeans build new factories, railroads, and bridges. With so many people starving and restless, it seemed the Communists might sweep into power much as Hitler had done during Germany's depression.

The Marshall Plan was an immense success in helping put Europe squarely back on its feet—and perhaps Truman's greatest achievement, along with the GI Bill, which helped over 2 million veterans go to college. ("GI," short for "government issue," was a nickname for American soldiers that became popular during World War II.) But Truman also used military and diplomatic pressure to deal with the Soviet Union, in a strategy known as "containment." If Stalin tried to expand his power in any part of the globe, Truman was ready to apply a counterforce to contain that expansion. Even the president's mother in Missouri passed along her own warning about Stalin. "Tell Harry to be good, be honest, and behave himself, but I think it is now time for him to get tough with someone."

At first, that seemed easy. After all, the United States possessed the most powerful weapon in the world—a weapon no one else had. Truman had been meeting with Stalin and Churchill during the war when he received the secret news of the atom bomb's successful test. Churchill noticed that the president suddenly seemed "a changed man. He told the Russians just where they got on and got off and generally bossed the whole meeting." Having a weapon like that gave great confidence. Indeed, many Americans rejoiced that the war had been ended by this mysterious but seemingly marvelous new technology. A bar in Washington began offering "atomic cocktails." A store on fashionable Fifth Avenue in New York advertised "atomic jewelry" offered in "a fury of dazzling colors." Kids could even order an atomic bomb ring from Kix breakfast cereal for 15¢ plus a box top. "Slide the Tail-Fin off—" read the instructions, "look in Observation Lens—and you'll see frenzied flashes of light—caused by released energy of atoms splitting like crazy." Amazingly, the rings actually contained tiny amounts of polonium-210, whose stream of slightly radioactive particles caused the view screen to light up.

At the same time, the fearsome dangers of atomic weapons began to sink in. American medics and reporters in occupied Japan saw what the bomb's radiation did to survivors, their skin covered by red blotches and their hair falling out. Magazines warned what could happen if other nations developed atomic bombs and put them on guided missiles. "Every city will be wiped out in thirty minutes," predicted one article. "New York will be a slag heap." And as radioactive energy from the bomb spread for hundreds of miles through the air as fallout, it would "leave the land uninhabitable" for decades or even hundreds of years. An atomic war, predicted a Chicago newspaper, could turn the globe into "a barren waste, in which the survivors of the [human] race will hide in caves or live among ruins." Truman began to realize that using atomic weapons was no routine matter. When a crisis in Berlin broke out after Stalin closed the roads into the American section of the German capital, the president organized a massive airlift to keep food coming. But he refused to give American officers control of atomic bombs. He didn't want to have "some dashing lieutenant colonel decide when would be the proper time to drop one." In the end, Stalin backed down, and Berlin became the divided capital of both West Germany and Communist East Germany.

Then in 1949 American scientists reported sobering news. Radioactive rain falling in the Pacific provided evidence that the Soviet Union had secretly tested its own atomic weapon. The United States was no longer the only nuclear nation. And the following year Communist North Korea invaded South Korea, an American ally. Truman sent troops immediately, though he stopped short of declaring war. The operation would be a "police action" on behalf of the United Nations, the new organization designed to replace the League of Nations. As Americans pushed North Korean forces back toward China's border with North Korea, hundreds of thousands of Chinese crossed into Korea, pushing the Americans back. On the defensive, Truman told reporters he would "take whatever steps are necessary to meet the military situation." Including using the atomic bomb? asked one reporter. "There has always been active consideration of its use," the president replied. This bit of news alarmed his European allies so badly that the British prime minister took the first plane to Washington to protest. Atomic war was not something to threaten so easily, he insisted. The war dragged on for two more years until a new president took office: Republican Dwight Eisenhower, the war hero from D-Day. Ike, as he was nicknamed, brought the Korean conflict to an end, though not before fifty-four thousand Americans had died.

With international tensions high, politics at home also heated up. Americans learned that a few scientists had passed atomic secrets to the Russians, helping them build their own bombs more quickly. A State Department official who had worked for Franklin Roosevelt was also accused of spying. Were there other Communists hiding in the government? Republicans accused Truman—a Democrat—of not doing enough to root out officials who were "soft" on Communism, and Truman—again on the defensive—set up a loyalty program requiring government supervisors to fire anyone who seemed suspect. In Congress, the House Un-American Activities Committee called a parade of movie stars to testify, hoping to expose Hollywood directors and actors who portrayed Communists too favorably. The accused were "blacklisted," often with little or no proof of any crime, which prevented them from working. In the Senate, Joseph McCarthy, a Republican from Wisconsin, made headlines when he announced that he had a list of 205 Communists working in the State Department. Or perhaps it was 57 or 81; at any rate, it was "a lot of" Communists. No one, including McCarthy, could ever be sure of the number he first used. These wild charges, which became more exaggerated every month, ruined the careers of many decent Americans until finally the public tired of the senator's grandstanding. President Eisenhower, who considered himself a "modern" Republican, refused to "get in the gutter with that guy." In 1954 the Senate formally condemned McCarthy's reckless behavior. By then Stalin had died of a stroke. The fear of Communist secret agents slowly faded.

But the Cold War continued, as both the Soviets and the Americans raced to build atomic missiles. People were learning to live with the threat of nuclear war. First graders were taught to cover their heads and duck under their desks if they should see the atomic flash. Some families built fallout shelters in their basements and filled them with canned goods and bottled water in case they needed to wait out a radioactive blast. Truman's secretary of defense encouraged one of his associates to write a question-and-answer book, *How to Survive an Atomic Bomb*.

> *All right. Let's say I've taken all the safety steps. I've gone down on my face with my head in my arms. The bomb has gone off. I've waited for the all-clear. . . . What do I do then?*
> The first thing is—get set for a shock. . . .
> *Why should I get set for a shock?*
> Because things are going to look different. . . . If the bomb hit within a mile and a half of the place where you are, things are going to look very different. Understand that beforehand. Then you won't get such a jolt when you come out later and see a lot of places that you knew very well—and find them damaged or destroyed.

Did people pay attention to such advice? Yes and no. Growing up during those years, my friends and I talked about fallout shelters and what we might do if the air-raid siren sounded. But we also played baseball in the backyard, watched westerns on the nifty new television sets our families had bought, and in summer splashed in our inflatable pools. Life went on.

All that changed suddenly in the autumn of 1962.

35

The End of the World

THE FIRST ATOMIC BOMB dropped on Japan had the power of fifteen kilotons of TNT. That is, you would need fifteen thousand tons of an "ordinary" explosive like TNT to get the same bang as the new five-ton atomic bomb. Lining up 150 railroad cars of TNT would about do it. But by 1962 the United States was testing *megaton* bombs, each megaton as powerful as a million tons of TNT. *One* fifty-megaton bomb had more power than a string of railcars stretching TNT from the Atlantic to the Pacific Ocean and halfway back. If a new world war broke out, American plans called for 3,423 nuclear weapons to be launched—weapons that would also spread poisonous radiation through the air. Even to consider such an event was horrifying. When the new president, John F. Kennedy, was briefed about the plan, he shook his head. "And we call ourselves the human race." Military planners hoped that such a catastrophe would never come. Surely neither side would start an atomic war if it knew the other had enough bombs to blast its own country into ruins. This idea was known as the theory of Mutual Assured Destruction—MAD for short. No one would be mad enough to risk ending life on earth as humans knew it.

Would they?

The planners crossed their fingers as the Cold War simmered through the 1950s. In Asia, the French were driven out of their colonies by Ho Chi Minh, a Communist revolutionary who afterward led the new nation of Vietnam. Russian troops put down a revolt in Hungary, while the United States used paid mercenaries to overthrow unfriendly governments in Guatemala and Iran. More than once during these skirmishes, President Eisenhower considered using atomic weapons, even though he knew it might take the world toward the brink of atomic war. "If you are scared to go to the brink, you are lost," warned Ike's secretary of state. Eisenhower edged toward that brink, but in the end held back.

Even so, the new Soviet premier, Nikita Khrushchev, kept Americans off balance. Bald, short, and stocky, Khrushchev had grown up on a farm in the Ukraine. Like another farm boy, Harry Truman, he was plainspoken and blunt. Khrushchev had "enough emotion for ten people—at least," commented one Russian who knew him. During a visit to the U.N. General Assembly, the Soviet leader pulled off one of his shoes and began pounding it on his desk. In the spring of 1962 he was particularly upset by the way the United States had hemmed in the Soviet Union. His vacation home was in Sochi, a resort town on the Black Sea only two hundred miles across the water from Turkey, a U.S. ally. The Soviet leader would hand guests a pair of binoculars and ask what they saw, looking out to sea. Water, they replied, baffled. "I see U.S. missiles," he shot back. For indeed, the United States had recently set up atomic missiles in Turkey that were able to reach Soviet territory in five minutes. Khrushchev wanted to turn the tables on his rivals. One afternoon in Sochi, he smiled and put a mysterious question to his defense minister: "What if we were to throw a hedgehog down the pants of Uncle Sam?"

Americans knew nothing of this conversation, of course. Only a few months earlier they had cheered John Glenn as the nation's first astronaut to orbit the earth. Glenn was playing catch-up because the year before a Soviet rocket had lifted a Russian astronaut into space. Still, Americans had much to celebrate, for they were living through the longest stretch of prosperity in the nation's history. The Great Depression and World War II had forced many couples to put off starting a family, but after 1945, so many children were born that the newspapers spoke of a baby boom. Many of these growing families spilled into new neighborhoods called suburbs, located around the edges of American cities. The owners of new suburban homes eagerly installed washing machines, dryers, and refrigerators, and proudly showed off a new invention in their living rooms, the television. Living in suburbs, they also needed automobiles to get around. No more boxy Model T's: the new cars sported tail fins that imitated the swept-back wings of a jet, each model year boasting fancier fins than the last. President Eisenhower helped the boom in new cars when he launched the biggest public works project in American history, a system of interstate highways crisscrossing the nation.

Khrushchev's surprise for the United States involved Cuba, his new ally in North America. Ever since Teddy Roosevelt had charged up Kettle Hill and helped kick Spain out of its colony, Cuba had been heavily influenced by U.S. business. By the 1950s, Americans owned half of Cuba's public railways, close to half of its sugar facilities, and 90 percent of its telephone and electric services. That changed after an uprising brought Fidel Castro to power in 1959. A fiery, full-bearded revolutionary who wore green military fatigues and smoked cigars (Cuban, naturally), Castro wanted to end what he considered America's unhealthy influence on his nation. When his government began taking over U.S. businesses, the United States cut off trade and Castro turned to the Soviet Union for help. Suddenly a Communist nation stood only ninety miles away from American shores.

When John F. Kennedy became president in 1961—at forty-three years old, the youngest in American history—he discovered that the U.S. government under Eisenhower had been secretly training fourteen hundred Cubans who had fled to the United States. The plan was to land these exiles in Cuba along the Bay of Pigs, where they could gather other Cubans to overthrow Fidel Castro. Kennedy approved the invasion, although he had his doubts. And rightly so, for the invaders were easily rounded up soon after they splashed ashore, leaving the president and the United States embarrassed. In the months that followed, Castro was convinced— also rightly—that the United States continued to look for ways to overthrow him. The Central Intelligence Agency (CIA) developed several rather wild assassination plots, including poisoning Fidel's favorite cigars and blowing up a big underwater seashell (Castro liked to scuba dive).

It was about then that Khrushchev began secretly shipping atomic weapons to Cuba to teach Americans "just what it feels like to have enemy missiles pointing at you." For several months the operation remained hidden; but on October 16, 1962, President Kennedy learned that a high-flying spy plane, the U-2, had photographed the missiles. Kennedy was furious. He had publicly warned that "the gravest issues would arise" if the Soviets put offensive missiles in Cuba; and the Soviets had pledged not to. Kennedy set up a secret executive committee, the ExComm, to discuss how to respond. Were the missiles ready to fire? Not yet, advisers said; but they might be soon. The joint chiefs of the army, navy, air force, and Marines recommended that the missile sites be bombed. "We're certainly . . . going to take out these missiles," Kennedy agreed. But Cuba is a large island. Flying from one end to the other is like flying from New York City to Chicago. Had the U-2 spy planes located *every* missile site? "It'll never be 100 percent, Mr. President," admitted one general. Clouds often covered parts of the island. In truth, the Soviets had already smuggled in more missiles than the Americans realized, along with forty thousand Russian troops. (They wore checked shirts rather than uniforms, which helped them go undetected.)

Then, too, if the United States launched an attack on Cuba without warning, it would look uncomfortably like Japan's surprise attack on Pearl Harbor. Kennedy decided instead to lay out the facts for the public. "Capital Crisis Air Hints at Developments on Cuba," read the *New York Times* headline. On October 22, the president revealed the missiles to a stunned nation. The U.S. navy quickly put in place a "a strict quarantine." Any ship bound for Cuba would be turned back if it contained offensive weapons. For a day and a half, the world waited anxiously as several Soviet ships approached. But they turned back short of the quarantine line. Secretary of State Dean Rusk was overjoyed: "We're eyeball to eyeball and the other fellow just blinked!" Still, the crisis was hardly over. The missiles already in Cuba looked as if they would be ready to fire in only three days and could then reach Washington, DC, or perhaps even New York City within ten minutes. How many deaths? asked Kennedy. As many as six hundred thousand for every missile. "That's the total number of casualties in the Civil War!" the president exclaimed. He thought it "insane that two men, sitting on opposite sides of the world, should be able to decide to bring an end to civilization."

Khrushchev, too, was having second thoughts. In a message to the president, he admitted that "if war should indeed break out, then it would not be in our power to stop it, for such is the logic of war. I have participated in two wars and know that war ends when it has rolled through cities and villages, everywhere sowing death and destruction." Two days later he sent a second message, insisting he would not remove his missiles unless Kennedy also removed the American ones in Turkey. The crisis, Khrushchev suggested, was like a rope with a knot, two enemies pulling from either end. "A moment may come when that knot will be tied so tight that even he who tied it will not have the strength to untie it. Then it will be necessary to cut that knot, and what that would mean is not for me to explain to you, because you yourself understand perfectly the terrible forces that our countries possess." The president decided to accept Khrushchev's offer of a trade, but only secretly. The U.S. missiles in Turkey would stay for another four or five months, then be quietly removed. Kennedy was also willing to promise not to invade Cuba.

But before the deal could be sealed, nuclear war seemed ready to break out anyway, on what came to be known as Black Saturday, October 27. Castro was convinced that the Americans were about to invade his homeland. The Soviet commander in Cuba, General Issa Pliyev, reported, "In the opinion of our Cuban comrades, we must expect a U.S. air strike" by dawn. "I have taken measures to disperse *tekhniki* within the operating zone." *Tekhniki* was the Russian code name for atomic missiles. If the Americans attacked, Pliyev said, "I have decided to use all air defense means available to me." On Saturday morning, Soviet radar picked up an American U-2 spy plane over Cuba. Was this the start of the invasion? Russian officers looked for General Pliyev for instructions, but he was nowhere to be found. They hesitated—then went ahead and fired. The U-2 plummeted out of the sky, killing its pilot. In Washington, the members of ExComm were shocked. "They've fired the first shot," said one. The Joint Chiefs of Staff unanimously recommended a large air strike within three days to take out the missile bases. Kennedy would not do it. A large air strike would kill who knew how many Russians? And then how would the Soviets respond? *Then it will be necessary to cut that knot, and what that would mean is not for me to explain to you.*

On Saturday evening, Kennedy sent his offer for a deal to Khrushchev. And waited. Robert McNamara, the secretary of defense, watched the sun go down on a beautiful autumn day. He worried he might "never live to see another Saturday night."

Khrushchev met with his advisers Sunday morning. To avoid "the danger of war and nuclear catastrophe, with the possibility of destroying the human race," he said, he had made his decision. "To save the world, we must retreat." The missiles would be removed. "I feel like a new man," Kennedy commented when the news came through. Half a year later, the American missiles in Turkey were taken down.

The Cuban missile crisis had come and gone in thirteen days. In the large scale of history, it was hardly a blip on the radar screen. Yet the world as we know it nearly ended. "The other fellow blinked," Dean Rusk had boasted. But both sides had blinked: Kennedy as well as Khrushchev. It was not an easy decision for either man. Castro was furious with the Soviet leader for not launching atomic missiles at America first. Kennedy showed no little courage in rejecting the advice of his military advisers. ("These brass hats have one great advantage in their favor," complained the president, speaking of the generals. "If we listen to them and do what they want us to do, none of us will be alive later to tell them that they were wrong.") Standing at the nuclear brink, Khrushchev had seen "death and destruction"; Kennedy a globe ruined by "fire, poison, chaos, and catastrophe." Both men stepped back.

And the people of the world took a deep breath and went about their business.

36

You or You or You

SOMETIMES, IT SEEMS AS if history revolves mostly around people in high places. "Two men, sitting on opposite sides of the world," as President Kennedy noted—deciding whether to "bring an end to civilization." But history bubbles up from below, too, moved by people no one has heard of, doing things that the powerful would never dare. Kennedy witnessed this the year after the Cuban missile crisis, when a quarter of a million Americans came to Washington to take up the unfinished business of slavery and freedom.

We've seen the uneasy link between equality and inequality that has long run through American history. Ideas of equality began to spread in the colonial era at the very time that slavery was increasing its hold. Later, abolitionists crusaded against "the peculiar institution" just as the cotton boom and the factory system were making it harder to root out. It took a civil war to end slavery—one so fierce that more Americans died in that war than in the Revolution, the War of 1812, the U.S.-Mexican War, the Spanish-American War, the Korean War, and World Wars I and II combined.

But even after emancipation had been won, American society became more divided through the policy of segregation. Laws in the old slave states were passed to ensure that there would be separate schools for each race, separate hotels, separate hospitals, separate drinking fountains. Alabama forbade whites from playing checkers with blacks. Oklahoma put up separate telephone booths for whites and blacks. The line between slave and free was replaced by a new color line between black and white, enforced more than ever by brutal lynchings.

African Americans didn't remain silent. In 1883 a young schoolteacher in Memphis, Tennessee, Ida Wells, sued the C & O Railroad after she was thrown out of a first-class "ladies car" because she was black. Wells became a journalist and eventually campaigned against lynching so loudly that she had to flee for her life from Memphis. But better to speak out and "die fighting against injustice," she said, "than to die like a dog or a rat in a trap." Wells was only one of many voices. Black and white Americans founded the National Association for the Advancement of Colored People in 1910. The NAACP campaigned for "equality before the law," and in the 1930s and 1940s, one of its brightest lawyers, Thurgood Marshall, traveled the South in his "little old beat-up '29 Ford," taking the cases of African Americans seeking justice. The Supreme Court had ruled in 1896 that segregation was legal so long as the separate facilities were equal. In court, Marshall showed that they virtually never were. A black state law school, for example, was hardly equal if it had five professors while the law school for whites had nineteen. But the NAACP became dissatisfied with this approach. The whole *idea* of "separate but equal" was wrong, they argued.

And at last, in 1954, the Supreme Court agreed. Oliver Brown, an African American in Topeka, Kansas, sued the school board because his eight-year-old daughter Linda was forced to walk along a dangerous rail yard every morning to get to her segregated school when a white school was only a few blocks away. In *Brown v. Board of Education,* all nine justices agreed that segregation was unconstitutional. Separate facilities were *always* unequal because they created "a feeling of inferiority" that affected students' "hearts and minds in a way unlikely ever to be undone."

The habits of a century were not overturned easily. Over one hundred southern members of Congress signed an open letter encouraging their states to defy the court. Segregation by law continued in most areas of the South. Then, on a city bus in Montgomery, Alabama, a seamstress named Rosa Parks refused to give up her seat to a white man who had boarded. She was arrested and taken to jail. Parks had not looked for trouble, but neither was she willing to be pushed around. When the NAACP asked if it could use her case to challenge segregation in court, she hesitated. "The white folks will kill you, Rosa," her husband warned—and he meant literally. But Parks agreed. That same night a group of black women met secretly and printed a leaflet calling for even bolder action. "Another Negro woman has been arrested and thrown into jail because she refused to get up out of her seat," they wrote. "Until we do something to stop these arrests, they will continue. The next time it may be you, or you or you. This woman's case will come up Monday. We are, therefore, asking every Negro to stay off the buses on Monday in protest of the arrest and trial." A new minister in town, Martin Luther King, Jr., was chosen to lead the boycott. As he and a friend drove to the Monday night meeting, a traffic jam forced them to park their car and walk the rest of the way. Over five thousand people had turned out, clogging the streets.

King addressed the crowd in church, with loudspeakers set up for the huge overflow outside. He began calmly but then, with increasing force, put into words why so many had come: "There comes a time when people get tired," he said. Slavery had ended nearly a century ago, only to be replaced by segregation. *Brown v. Board of Education* had struck segregation down—yet black Americans were still being "kicked about" and treated like second-class citizens. What else could they do but protest? The crowd erupted with cheers and *amens*. But King had more than a message of protest. He had a method—to use love and nonviolence to achieve his goals. He had read Henry David Thoreau on the moral duty to refuse to obey unjust laws. In divinity school he had studied how Mahatma Gandhi led India to independence from Great Britain using nonviolent tactics. Faced by violence and threats, he told his listeners to stand firm but not to strike back. There would be no midnight lynchings of whites by blacks wearing hoods. There would be no cross burnings or mobs roaming the roads at night. If his listeners followed these principles, King promised, history would remember them as a "great people—a black people . . . who had the moral courage to stand up for their rights."

The black community of Montgomery was roused and the buses stayed empty—costing the bus company over thirty thousand fares every day. To keep the boycott going week after week, and then month after month required nearly superhuman effort. Hundreds of drivers volunteered their cars and taxicabs to help residents who needed to get to work. Over the next year King's house was bombed, and he and others were arrested and jailed or harassed with trumped-up traffic tickets and menacing police cars. In the end the Supreme Court sided with Rosa Parks. The black citizens of Montgomery had won.

And they set a pattern in the fight for civil rights. Organizations were important in coordinating actions. The NAACP continued its work. King and other ministers formed the Southern Christian Leadership Conference (SCLC). And there was CORE, the Congress of Racial Equality, as well as the Student Nonviolent Coordinating Committee—SNCC (pronounced "Snick"). But these groups all depended on ordinary folk, who often took the first fateful steps on their own. Rosa Parks did. So did the women who printed leaflets in the dead of night. So also did Joseph McNeil, a college student who in January 1960 tried to get a meal one evening and was told, "We don't serve Negroes here." He and his roommates decided that, next day, they would "sit in" at a segregated lunch counter in Greensboro, North Carolina, until they *were* served. The astonished manager closed the counter, but the following day twenty-seven students joined the sit-in. The day after there were sixty-three. At the end of the week, sixteen hundred turned out— and the shop owners gave in. Such lunch-counter sit-ins spread from one city to another, opening up a once "whites-only" world to blacks.

Witnessing such deeds, people in power were often puzzled, astonished, or frightened. Neither President Eisenhower nor President Kennedy was a segregationist. But both tried to avoid being dragged into the crusade to integrate schools, buses, and restaurants. "Feelings are deep on this," said Ike. "And the fellow who tries to tell me that you can do these things by force is just plain nuts." In the end, Eisenhower decided he had no choice but to send federal troops to Little Rock, Arkansas, after a mob stopped nine black students from integrating Central High School. President Kennedy watched an even deadlier scene unfold when black volunteers rode Greyhound and Trailways buses through the South with the goal of integrating waiting rooms. These "Freedom Riders," both black and white, faced mobs several thousand strong who punched, kicked, and bloodied faces; beat their victims with lead pipes; knocked out teeth; and on one occasion even ambushed a bus and tried to burn the Freedom Riders alive inside. Kennedy had been elected in 1960 with the support of white southern voters. He knew quite well that they wanted federal troops to stay out of the South. But the violence became so serious, the president reluctantly sent federal marshals to protect the buses.

Partly in order to end the disturbing headlines about injured protesters, Attorney General Robert Kennedy (the president's brother) encouraged black leaders to focus less on integrating schools, buses, and waiting rooms. Why not concentrate instead on registering African Americans to vote? Ever since the late 1800s, only a tiny percentage of southern blacks had been given that opportunity. Unfair regulations made it easy for election officials to reject voters as they pleased. Kennedy was convinced there would be less white opposition to registering voters. After all, voting booths were different from schools, he said, where people could complain, "We don't want our little blond daughter going to school with a Negro." How wrong he proved to be!

The students of SNCC led the way, spreading out across the Deep South, encouraging black farmers who had never before dared do so to vote. But the violence only increased, with segregationists carrying out firebombings, beatings, and even cold-blooded murders. Living in such a hostile environment was exhausting. "You would be taking someone down to register, and you would simply be trailed by two cars of whites," recalled one volunteer. "Maybe they would do nothing, but you would never know. Maybe they would get out and whip you." Ten years after *Brown v. Board of Education,* over two thousand southern school districts remained segregated. Federal officials didn't want to get involved; northern whites paid little attention. "We've got to have a crisis to bargain with," suggested one of King's assistants. "To take a moderate approach hoping to get white help, doesn't help." King and the SCLC planned a nonviolent protest that would gain national attention by targeting the most segregated city in the country, Birmingham, Alabama. Among civil rights workers, Birmingham was known as Bombingham because some fifty terrorist explosions had been set there since the end of World War II. The city's police chief, "Bull" Connor, swore to stop any protest in its tracks.

Against Connor's strong forces—against the helmets, nightsticks, and guns—King sent forth the weak and powerless. In a desperate move, he gathered a thousand children—some teenagers, a few as young as six—and marched them out the doors of the Sixteenth Street Baptist Church singing protest songs, dancing, and clapping. Bull Connor's astonished troops swept them up and hauled them off to jail. "D Day," the protesters called it, and they promised there would be another thousand children next time, on Double-D Day. Connor was infuriated. He ordered his men to charge, beating protesters and onlookers alike. He let dogs loose to attack the protestors. He used electric cattle prods. He opened up fire hoses whose high-pressure jets were strong enough to rip the bark off trees. News photographs of the events went out across the nation and the world. Northerners who before had paid little attention were horrified. The pictures made President Kennedy "sick," he admitted. Birmingham's business leaders told Connor the protests had to end. They agreed to a timetable that would integrate lunch counters and other facilities. And for the first time, the president sent a strong civil rights bill to Congress. It allowed the federal government to take action in desegregating schools and guaranteeing the right to vote. "This nation," Kennedy declared, "will not be fully free until all its citizens are free."

Three months later, in August 1963, a quarter of a million Americans gathered in the March on Washington to champion the civil rights bill. Even then, Kennedy was wary. "We want success in Congress," he argued, "not just a big show at the Capitol." But the people came and the nation heard King remind Americans that a hundred years earlier, Lincoln had issued the Emancipation Proclamation. "I have a dream," he told them:

that one day on the red hills of Georgia, the sons of former slaves and the sons of former slave-owners will be able to sit down together at the table of brotherhood. . . .

So let freedom ring! . . . Let freedom ring from Stone Mountain of Georgia. Let freedom ring from Lookout Mountain of Tennessee. Let freedom ring from every hill and molehill of Mississippi, from every mountainside let freedom ring. And when this happens—when we allow freedom to ring from every village and every hamlet, from every state and every city, we will be able to speed up that day when all God's children, black men and white men, Jews and Gentiles, Protestants and Catholics, will be able to join hands and sing in the words of the old Negro spiritual, "Free at last! Free at least! Thank God almighty, we are free at last!"

The speech was a high-water mark for the civil rights movement, but hardly an ending to it. In the three months after Birmingham, almost eight hundred new protests erupted across the South. More than fifteen thousand protesters were arrested. A bomb exploded at the Sixteenth Street Baptist Church, killing four black girls. Strange, the way inequality and equality once again walked hand in hand— for King's Birmingham struggle would never have succeeded without the fierce attacks of Bull Connor. Astonishing that so many young people stepped forward, when warned that the next at risk might be *you or you or you.*

What would we have done? It's easy, now, to say we would have marched. But make no mistake: the decision was immensely difficult. During the Montgomery bus boycott, the phone in King's kitchen rang and a voice on the other end of the line warned him to get out of town or they would shoot him and blow his house up. "I couldn't take it any longer," King recalled. He agonized, trying "to think of a way to move out of the picture without appearing a coward." Praying out loud, he heard an inner voice saying, "Martin Luther, stand up for righteousness, stand up for justice, stand up for truth. And lo I will be with you, even until the end of the world."

He needed every ounce of strength he could muster. Because the civil rights movement had set off an avalanche that didn't stop with civil rights. It careened through the rest of the 1960s, changing American life in a thousand different ways.

37

THE AVALANCHE

IT WOULD BE NATURAL to think of the civil rights movement growing much as a snowball rolls downhill, gaining size and speed as more and more people join in. But that's not quite the way history works. Rosa Parks did spark a movement by not giving up her bus seat in 1955. But in 1883, when Ida Wells refused to leave a segregated railroad car, her protest had much less effect. American society was not ready then for a civil rights revolution. So instead of imagining a snowball, consider an avalanche. Days and even weeks pass as snow builds up on a mountainside. Then one day, though the world seems sunny and quiet, the crunch of a single ski is enough to start the snowpack tumbling in every direction. Individual actions play a key part. But conditions have to be right. In Ida Wells's day, most African Americans still worked on isolated southern farms, making it hard to unite with others in protest. But during the twentieth century, millions of blacks left their farms for cities in both the North and South. The first sit-ins and Freedom Rides were signs of pressures that had been building for decades.

And the avalanche that followed shook every corner of society, not just civil rights. Americans of all sorts began asking again questions that have been debated over the years: What does it really mean to be free? To be equal? Where is the path to get there in the midst of disorder and disruption?

To begin with, the avalanche split the civil rights movement. The violent attacks on Freedom Rides, sit-ins, and marches led some to cast aside Martin Luther King's nonviolent ideals. The Nation of Islam, a black religious group, had long rejected integration and called on African Americans to carve out their own separate space. "The day of nonviolent resistance is over," proclaimed Malcolm X, the group's most famous leader. Malcolm was gunned down by rivals, but other African Americans took up the cry. "We been saying freedom for six years and we ain't got nothin'," protested Stokely Carmichael, one young black leader. "What we're gonna start saying now is Black Power!"

These views spread well beyond the South. Northern states had no legal system of segregation, but the practice was nevertheless widespread there. Most northern blacks were prevented from moving into the tidy white suburbs around cities. Instead, they were pushed into decaying downtowns where unemployment was high and hope scarce. As southern protests spread, northern anger boiled over, too. In the weeks after King's Birmingham march, over 750 disturbances rocked cities across the nation. Stores were looted, cars were burned, buildings were set afire. Over the next few years, large riots shook Chicago, Newark, and Los Angeles.

At the same time, the civil rights avalanche swept beyond African Americans. Similar pressures had been building among Mexican Americans. Hispanics, of course, had been living in America long before newcomers from the United States conquered the Southwest. Later immigrants had come north from Mexico to work on farms, build railroads, and take jobs in cities. Like black civil rights leaders, Mexican Americans built their movement over decades. In South Texas, Latino lawyers including Gustavo Garcia pressed to end segregation in the courts and in schools. Gus had been his high school's valedictorian and served in the army during World War II before becoming active in civil rights. His opponents argued that Mexicans were not segregated in Texas. They were considered white, not black. If so, Garcia countered, why had no Latino in South Texas served on white juries in over twenty-five years? Why did the "colored" restroom in the very courthouse where they were speaking have a Spanish sign that read, *Hombres aqui* (Men here)? When the case went all the way to the Supreme Court, Garcia and two other lawyers made the trip to Washington to argue it. They were a real "country bumpkin" law team, he joked—they could barely afford the bus fare and hotel room, where Garcia slept on the couch. But two weeks before the Supreme Court heard the more famous case of *Brown v. Board of Education* in 1954, Garcia's arguments won the day in his own case, *Hernandez v. Texas*. The court ruled that Latinos and other ethnic groups could not be discriminated against.

In 1965 the avalanche reached the grape fields of California, with a protest begun by a soft-spoken labor leader named César Chávez. Chávez knew farm work. During the Great Depression, when César was only six, the family had been forced to sell their farm. From then on, the family took one low-paying job after another, driving the family's battered Chevy to follow the crops as they ripened. Migrant laborers stooped all day in the sun picking California lettuce or grapes; others harvested beets in Iowa or hoed cotton in Arizona. They were made to live in rundown shacks or tents, and considered themselves lucky if they had clean drinking water and toilets. Few Americans were willing to take such jobs; most of the work was done by Mexican laborers or other recent immigrants, such as Filipinos.

Chávez watched as time and again the owners of huge farms blocked unions from organizing their workers to demand better working conditions and higher wages. The farm owners always had the upper hand, but one night, in a dream, Chávez realized that the owners weren't all that powerful; it was only "that we were weak. And if we could somehow begin to develop some strength among ourselves . . . we could begin to equal that." Along with another activist, Dolores Huerta, Chávez led a strike of grape pickers. Adopting Martin Luther King's nonviolent tactics, the workers marched 250 miles to Sacramento, California's capital, to call attention to their cause. As the protesters walked, they sang "Nosotros vencerernos"—the Spanish version of the civil rights song "We Shall Overcome." Chávez called on all Americans to stop buying supermarket grapes, a tactic that hit the growers in their wallets. Dolores Huerta directed the grape boycott. Though the strike lasted five years, the big farms eventually agreed to sign contracts with Chávez's union, the United Farm Workers.

The early sit-ins and Freedom Rides depended on youth for their success, and the avalanche now spread to young people everywhere. After white students from the North helped register southern black voters, hundreds returned to college with new ideas about their own lives. Many condemned "the system" that packed them into large impersonal classes in huge universities. They rejected dress codes that told them what they could or could not wear and curfews that required them to return to their dorms by a certain hour. Universities often outlawed political protests as well. So, the students asked—it was all right to demonstrate for freedom in the South but not at school?

Some students occupied college buildings and refused to leave until their demands were met. Others left school entirely. San Francisco and Berkeley, California, attracted many such free spirits, nicknamed hippies. They grew their hair long, wore bright tie-dyed T-shirts, love beads, and bell-bottom jeans. Some formed utopian communities, much as reformers in the 1840s had lived together at Brook Farm or the Mormons had gathered at Nauvoo. The new generation of dreamers hammered together shelters made by connecting a framework of aluminum triangles. Known as geodesic domes, their outer skins resembled an arching, angle-edged giant soap bubble. "Everyone rushing to get their dome built," reported a commune leader in California's Santa Cruz Mountains. "Things moving along of their own accord, no one directing. . . . One sink, washing machine, kitchen for 50 people. . . . Many problems . . . but if you can ride with it for a while, you'll learn a fantastic amount about yourself, and others."

From the beginning, women like Rosa Parks and Dolores Huerta had played a large part in the civil rights crusade. Many northern volunteers registering voters in the South were young women who came despite the protests of their parents. "It is very hard to answer to your attitude that if I loved you I wouldn't do this," one daughter wrote home. "There comes a time when you have to do things which your parents do not agree with." Many women began to consider whether they could really be free or equal if society's customs didn't allow them to do all the things men did.

World War II had marked the first time many women took jobs away from home. At war's end, most of these working women wanted to keep their jobs, but they were forced out as millions of soldiers returned home. And the growing baby boom of the 1950s kept mothers busy raising children. "This wondrous creature," gushed *Look* magazine, "marries younger than ever, bears more babies and looks and acts far more feminine." Not all stay-at-home moms were happy. "Hobbies, gardening, pickling, canning . . . I can do it all, and I like it, but it doesn't leave you anything to think about," one woman confessed to Betty Friedan, a journalist. Even women with jobs outside the home were treated like second-class citizens. Men discouraged women from becoming doctors and lawyers: these careers weren't "women's work." Newspapers listed separate want ads for "Male Help" and "Female Help." When women did work at the same jobs as men, they were paid much less. Betty Friedan wanted to write a story about the limits that hemmed in modern women. But the male editors of women's magazines rejected her idea. "Betty has gone off her rocker," said one. So Friedan wrote a book instead, *The Feminine Mystique.* Its popularity proved that feminism—a movement led by women and for women—had the power to create an avalanche of its own. Friedan and several friends formed NOW, the National Organization for Women, to push for political reforms.

You might think that civil rights reformers would want to join a campaign for women's rights. But little had changed since 1840, when male abolitionists kept Lucretia Mott from taking part in their antislavery conference. In 1967, when one feminist asked members of a convention titled New Politics to push for women's equality, the man with the microphone patted her on the head and said, "Move on, little girl. We have more important issues to talk about." Some younger women decided that in order to change the wider world, women had to first free themselves. These reformers hit on the idea of meeting in small groups—"consciousness-raising" sessions—to explore the ways that women remained unequal. Why were boys encouraged to become scientists and athletes while girls were expected to play with dolls? Why did so few women lead businesses? Even language seemed to favor men. A committee head was a chair*man*, people who kept order were police*men*. Such matters might seem trivial, but the words people used encouraged them to think of such jobs as men's, not women's.

Inevitably, the avalanche of ideas and action tumbled over into politics. President Kennedy had sent his civil rights bill to Congress, but before it could be enacted, he was assassinated during a visit to Dallas, Texas, by a sniper taking aim from a warehouse window. (The motives of the troubled shooter, Lee Harvey Oswald, remain unclear.) As the nation mourned, Americans could not help wondering what course the new president would set. Kennedy had been a northerner from Massachusetts; Lyndon Baines Johnson hailed from the Hill Country of Texas. As Senate majority leader during the Eisenhower years, Johnson had been known as a fixer. He rounded up the votes of lawmakers by flattering, jawboning, and arm-twisting them. Six feet, four inches tall (tied with Lincoln as the tallest president), Lyndon leaned into people when he talked, grabbed their suit coat lapels, and gave them "the Johnson treatment" until they agreed to his requests. As a white southerner, he might have been expected to oppose civil rights. But Johnson saw that times had changed. If he didn't support the civil rights bill, he said, "I'd be dead before I could ever begin." Furthermore, women added a provision to the bill that female job seekers could not be discriminated against, either.

After that law passed, Johnson proposed the Voting Rights Act, which banned literacy tests and other tactics used to keep African Americans from voting. The bill was "one of the most monumental laws in the entire history of American freedom," Johnson boasted. And he was right. After it passed, African Americans voted in numbers not seen since the days of Reconstruction.

If any politician could harness the energy of an avalanche, it was Johnson. He was determined to pass laws so historic they would surpass Franklin Roosevelt's New Deal. Even during the prosperity of the 1950s, over 40 million Americans remained poor—and the number was growing. The president proposed a war on poverty. New laws rolled out of Congress one after another as the Johnson treatment did its work. Loans to poor farm folk passed. So did aid to migrant farm workers and a Job Corps to teach new skills to those out of work. Johnson remembered from his days as a young teacher that many Mexican American students had come to class "without breakfast, hungry. Somehow you never forget what poverty and hatred can do when you see its scars." Now, the president called on Americans to build a "Great Society" that would give every individual a truly equal chance in life. New programs helped needy public schools to buy books and equipment. Project Head Start prepared poor children for elementary school and even funded an educational television series that became known as *Sesame Street.*

Among older people, illness was the key cause of poverty. Johnson created new health insurance programs that created a safety net for the elderly in a system called Medicare. He created a similar program called Medicaid for the poor. Within two years of Johnson becoming president, Congress had passed fifty laws— truly another avalanche. In the rush to remake the nation, more than a few programs missed their mark or wasted money. But the Great Society marked the high point of a movement toward active government begun by the Progressives.

If anyone could ride an avalanche, it was Johnson. But the truth is, no one can. Johnson learned that bitter lesson when he tried to deal with what seemed at first a small war in a distant nation in Asia.

38

A Conservative Turn

COMPARED TO THE CRISIS OVER Cuba, the distant conflict in Vietnam seemed like a minor distraction. There, a Communist revolutionary named Ho Chi Minh had worked tirelessly for over thirty years to throw out the French and make Vietnam independent. Finally, in 1954, his forces won a decisive battle in the valley of Dien Bien Phu. The long struggle had left Ho with gray hair, a wispy beard, missing teeth, and "skin like old paper." But his victory was not complete. An international treaty divided the country into North Vietnam and South Vietnam, with Ho controlling the north and expecting to win upcoming elections to be held in the south. Then America's ally, South Vietnam's president Ngo Dinh Diem, refused to hold elections. So Ho's supporters, known as the Vietcong, began a guerilla war to unite the country. President Eisenhower worried that if South Vietnam turned Communist, neighboring nations would soon follow suit. "You have a row of dominoes set up," he explained. If "you knock over the first one," then the rest "go over very quickly." Eisenhower dispatched seven hundred military advisers to Vietnam and later John F. Kennedy sent thousands more in the hope of combating the Vietcong. But Diem was a dictator unloved by his people and even by his generals. They kidnapped and murdered him only three weeks before President Kennedy himself was shot in Dallas.

Lyndon Johnson was of two minds about Vietnam. On the one hand, he wanted his "fellas" there to "get out in those jungles and whip hell out of some Communists." On the other hand, he worried about how long the conflict would take to win. He felt like a catfish, he said, that had just "grabbed a big juicy worm with a right sharp hook in the middle of it." Still, the Vietcong kept advancing—and Johnson, like the catfish, was hooked. The president began to "escalate" the war—that was the word used in 1965. First he sent aircraft to bomb the Ho Chi Minh Trail, a route used to send supplies south to the Vietcong. But that meant building air bases in South Vietnam, and the airbases needed soldiers to guard them. Johnson sent in several thousand Marines. And—like an escalator that just kept heading up—the war escalated. Next, forty thousand troops went over—so the army could take the offense. A few months later General William Westmoreland, in charge of the fighting, asked for another fifty thousand soldiers. Young American men were given draft cards so they could be called up to serve in the army. By 1968 over five hundred thousand troops were in Vietnam. The U.S. air bases became the busiest airports in the world. The war was costing the United States $2 billion every month.

Despite all the money and men, victory was nowhere in sight. How could it be achieved? Bomb from the air? The thick jungle made it hard to see soldiers and supply caravans along the Ho Chi Minh Trail. Drive the Vietcong from the villages? Fine. But Americans couldn't stay forever in a thousand and one hamlets. The Vietcong faded into the jungle, then returned once the Americans moved on. General Westmoreland began to measure success not by how much land had been conquered but by how many Vietcong had been killed. As this "body count" kept growing, the general promised he could "see light at the end of the tunnel." These were the very words, it so happened, that a French commander had used in 1953—before Ho Chi Minh defeated *him*. In 1968, during the New Year holiday in Vietnam known as Tet, the Vietcong launched a series of surprise attacks, including one on the American embassy itself. The strikes were beaten back, but suddenly the light at the end of the tunnel seemed much farther away.

At home, the war bitterly divided Americans. "Hawks" agreed with Eisenhower's domino theory, arguing that Communism had to be stopped or it would spread. "Doves"—many of them college students already marching for civil rights—called for peace. They argued that the United States was doing little more than propping up a dictatorship. It was also dropping more bombs on Vietnam than it had used in all of World War II. Eventually even Robert McNamara, Johnson's secretary of defense and at first a supporter of the war, changed his view, resigning his position. "The picture of the world's greatest superpower killing or seriously injuring 1,000 noncombatants a week, while trying to pound a tiny, backward nation into submission . . . is not a pretty one," he confessed. Like protesters of the civil rights movement, opponents of the war grew so strong that Johnson announced he would not run for reelection in 1968. The liberal reformer had become an unpopular war maker.

And finally the shock waves from one avalanche collided with waves from the other. Martin Luther King widened his campaign for civil rights to include protests against the war. In April a segregationist shot and killed him in Memphis. The news of his death sparked riots in over thirty cities, including the nation's capital. Robert Kennedy, brother of the slain president, had also come out against the war and was running for president. Two months after King's death, he, too, was shot and killed, by a young Palestinian angry that Kennedy supported the state of Israel. At the Democratic convention in Chicago that summer, protesters and the police clashed. Demonstrators threw eggs, rocks, and balloons filled with paint. Some officers took off their badges and pushed into the crowd, swinging nightsticks as they chanted, "Kill, kill, kill." A journalist watching the mayhem scribbled four words in his notebook: "The Democrats are finished."

He was right. A Republican, Richard Nixon, won the 1968 election. During the 1950s Nixon had eagerly hunted Communist spies and then run for president in 1960. He lost then, but eight years later he prevailed, proclaiming himself the "new Nixon" who could bring about "an honorable peace" in Vietnam. Nixon understood that many Americans were tired not only of the war but of much more: the apparently unending stream of protests in the streets, the rioting and the violence, the long-haired hippies chanting and demanding change, seeming to mock old-fashioned values. Nixon reached out to those he called "forgotten Americans . . . the non shouters, the non demonstrators." Jabbing at Johnson's Great Society, he promised not to pour "billions of dollars into programs that have failed." His victory showed that the revolutionaries of the 1960s could not continue their campaigns indefinitely. The election in that tumultuous year of 1968 marked a turning point toward more traditional, conservative values.

But that turn was neither complete nor quick. Unlike avalanches that crash down mountainsides in minutes, the tremors that shake societies take years to work out. Nixon was more of a practical politician than a deep-dyed conservative. He was quite willing to adopt progressive ideas if he thought they would help. When the economy slumped and the price of gas and groceries soared, he issued an order freezing all prices and wages for ninety days. What conservative would use the government to do that? In foreign affairs, he had long agreed that America should shun Communist China. Yet he became the first American president to visit that nation and improve relations with it. Soon after, Nixon signed a treaty with the Soviet Union to slow the nuclear arms race. By easing tensions with these Communist powers, he hoped that both the Chinese and the Soviets would lean on Communist Vietnam to make peace with the United States. Victory in Vietnam was what Nixon wanted; but at the very least, peace was what he needed.

"I've come to the conclusion that there's no way to win the war," he admitted privately. "But we can't say that, of course. In fact, we have to seem to say the opposite." As Nixon *seemed* to wind down the war by gradually bringing home American troops, he actually widened it by attacking North Vietnamese hideouts in neighboring Cambodia. Again protests at home erupted. Worse, the new attacks and increased bombing of North Vietnam didn't break that nation's will to fight. With no U.S. victory in sight, Nixon was forced to sign a treaty to end America's involvement in the war. Only two years after American troops came home, the South Vietnamese government fell. Ho Chi Minh hadn't lived to see his victory, but then, Richard Nixon didn't survive as president, either. As it happened, his downfall needed no avalanche to bring about. His inner demons did the work on their own.

Despite the president's support of traditional values, he placed little faith in human nature. He suspected that his political opponents would do anything and everything to defeat him—so he felt justified in being ruthless with them. He kept an "enemies list" and plotted ways to get revenge. During his reelection campaign in 1972, five men with White House connections were caught breaking into Democratic Party headquarters, located in Washington's Watergate plaza. Nixon claimed to know nothing about the incident. "What really hurts is if you try to cover up," he explained. But he was doing just that. Senators investigating the Watergate break-in discovered that secret White House microphones had recorded the president talking about paying hush money to "take care of the jackasses who are in jail. . . . You could get a million dollars" to pay them, he told his aides. "And you could get it in cash. I know where it could be gotten." When the full story came out, Nixon faced being the first president to be impeached by Congress and convicted in a Senate trial. He resigned instead.

The Watergate scandal had been a "national nightmare," admitted Gerald Ford, the new president. Though honest, Ford tried to put Watergate behind the nation by pardoning Nixon for any crimes he had committed. It was a sign of how disillusioned people had grown that Jimmy Carter, the Democrat who beat Ford in the election of 1976, won respect by promising voters, "I'll never lie to you." Carter, a former governor of Georgia, was honest, too—perhaps a little too honest to do well as a politician. He told Americans that they faced a "crisis of confidence" that "strikes at the very heart and soul and spirit of our national will." "We were sure that ours was a nation of the ballot, not the bullet, until the murders of John Kennedy and Robert Kennedy and Martin Luther King Jr. We were taught that our armies were always invincible and our causes were always just, only to suffer the agony of Vietnam. We respected the presidency as a place of honor until the shock of Watergate."

New problems added to the sense of crisis. Much of the world's supply of oil came from the troubled Middle East, where Arab nations for a time refused to sell it to countries that had supported Israel when it was attacked by Egypt and Syria. In the United States this embargo on Arab oil sent gas prices skyrocketing. Further trouble erupted in Iran, where revolutionaries stormed the American embassy and took fifty-three hostages. Night after night, the televised evening news showed the United States powerless to rescue its diplomats. Night after night, Jimmy Carter's popularity sank. In the election of 1980, Republican Ronald Reagan challenged him by asking Americans a simple question: "Are you better off than you were four years ago?" To many, the answer seemed obvious. Reagan swept into office just as Iran released the American hostages.

Reagan's victory marked the final turn toward conservative government that had been building for a decade. The new president's success owed a great deal to his personality. Where Nixon had been awkward, suspicious, and consumed by envy, Reagan was easygoing and good-natured. Where Jimmy Carter had warned sadly of a "crisis of confidence," Reagan spoke of a proud nation "standing tall." He won support from two groups that had often aided Republicans. The first were businesspeople who believed that success should depend on the efforts of the individual—luck and pluck, as Horatio Alger would have put it. They rejected the progressive belief that government should support less fortunate citizens through New Deal or Great Society programs. The second group was made up of evangelicals—"born-again" Protestants who wished to set religion firmly at the center of American life. Evangelicals particularly objected to recent Supreme Court rulings that forbade official prayers in public schools and gave women the right to end a pregnancy through abortion. They celebrated the Puritan vision of a holy commonwealth and played down the American tradition that kept the affairs of church and state separate.

Though Reagan liked to recall John Winthrop's city on a hill, he was never much of a churchgoer, devoting more energy to the business side of his program. "Government is not the solution to our problem," he insisted; "government *is* the problem." And in his cheerful, optimistic way, he proposed a method of cutting taxes while actually bringing more money into the government. Tax cuts would leave businesses more money to invest in their companies. As companies grew, the economy would improve—and then businesses would actually pay more taxes on their new profits. Within half a year, Congress lowered tax rates, especially for the rich and for investors in stocks. Meanwhile, the president hacked away at government programs. Supporters cheered him for getting rid of "red tape" so business could recharge the economy. Critics complained that citizens would suffer, as key programs were being cut, such as food stamps and Medicaid.

Unfortunately, lower tax rates didn't bring in more money. Reluctantly, Reagan put new taxes in place, though he was careful to call them "revenue enhancements" in order to ease the pain. The economy, which had been dragging, bounced back. Even so, the government was spending $200 billion a year more than it collected in taxes because the defense budget skyrocketed. Unlike

Nixon, Ford, and Carter, who had begun to ease Cold War tensions, Reagan considered the Soviet Union an "evil empire" that was stirring up "all the unrest that is going on." The new missiles, submarines, bombers, and other weapons Reagan ordered produced the highest deficits in the nation's history.

That might have been bad news for the United States, but it was worse news for the Soviet Union. Its Communist economy had never supplied citizens with many consumer goods, and it had spent billions on foreign aid, including its own Vietnam-style guerilla war in Afghanistan. Trying to keep up with Reagan's defense spending nearly ruined it. In 1985, a younger leader named Mikhail Gorbachev began a policy of *glasnost,* or openness, which called for greater freedom at home and an end to the Cold War abroad. Reagan joined in, working out new arms agreements that destroyed hundreds of nuclear missiles piled up by each side. One by one, eastern European nations under Communist rule rose up in protest. Gorbachev let them go. In 1991, the Soviet Union itself broke apart into individual republics. The Cold War that had lasted for forty years sputtered to an end. Not only had the conservative revolt taken the United States in a new direction at home, a long era in foreign affairs had also come to a close.

39

CONNECTED

AT THE BEGINNING OF this book, I asked you to stretch out an arm and imagine that the fourteen thousand years of human life in North America extended from your shoulder to the end of your hand. Now we've nearly arrived at the present—standing, like tiny figures, atop the far ends of your fingertips. And the view from this perch is rather different. Here, current events loom large. Presidents are elected, laws debated, riots put down, and hurricanes mopped up. All these happenings seem important as we live through them. But in writing a history that spans five hundred years, it's hard to judge what to include and what to leave out. In 1969, the entire world watched two Americans, Neil Armstrong and Buzz Aldrin, become the first humans to reach the moon—a remarkable triumph. That same year, nobody paid attention to another government project tying four computers in Utah and California into a simple network called ARPANET. The first communication sent over it was *lo*—two letters. The message was meant to be *login,* but the network crashed before the last three letters could

be sent. Which event was more important? The answer seems obvious, but fifty years later our journeys to the moon have ended, while
ARPANET has grown steadily until it has become the Internet. It
now speeds billions of e-mails, web pages, business transactions, and
video worldwide.

And the World Wide Web is only one of many forces connecting the United States more tightly with the globe's nations and peoples. In one sense, all of American history can be seen as the story
of increasing connections. Columbus was first to bring together
the two halves of the world, and the hemispheres have only grown
closer over the centuries. In order to separate the more important
pieces of recent history from the clutter of current events, I suggest
we take a few steps back and consider instead the paths traveled
by three very different individuals. Each journey shows, for better
and for worse, how closely the United States has become bound up
with the rest of the world.

The first journey begins in the 1980s with a tall, lanky guerilla
leading a band of fighters high in the mountains of Afghanistan.
Mujahideen, the guerillas are called; and this band is one of many
trying to drive the Soviets from Afghanistan. But its young leader
is not Afghan; he is a devout Muslim from nearby Saudi Arabia.
The secret services of that country, the United States, and Pakistan have helped some thirty-five thousand Muslims from all over
the world to join the war, providing them with millions of dollars
and thousands of weapons. This guerilla leader has used his own
money, too, to recruit volunteers from the Arab world and even
from the United States. In 1986 he opens an office in Tucson, Arizona, where many Arab Americans live, offering $300 a month to
all who will fight. The mujahideen are so successful that the Soviet
Union withdraws from Afghanistan. The Cold War is finally winding down.

And now the young man must decide: what next? Though the
war is over, he gathers even more recruits. He can well afford to, as
he is the seventeenth son of a billionaire Saudi Arabian business-

man. His name is Osama bin Laden. In 1990, he meets with high
officials in Saudi Arabia and offers to lead an attack on neighboring
Iraq, which has just invaded the oil-rich kingdom of Kuwait. "I am the
commander of an Islamic army," he boasts, whose name is al Qaeda.
But Saudi Arabia prefers to work with the United States. In the conflict
that follows, known as the Gulf War, President George H. W. Bush
leads an alliance of thirty-two nations. They force Iraq to withdraw
from Kuwait. Bin Laden is outraged. Why should Muslim Saudi
Arabia allow infidel Americans to launch attacks from its soil,
birthplace of the prophet Muhammad? He returns to camps hidden in Afghanistan's mountain caves and there plots a holy war—a
jihad—against the United States.

The blow is years in the making: George H. W. Bush is succeeded as president by Bill Clinton, then Clinton by Bush's son,
George W. Bush. But on September 11, 2001, bin Laden is ready. Al
Qaeda agents hijack four commercial airliners and fly two of them
into the World Trade Center, twin 110-story skyscrapers in New
York City. (The third plane is flown into the Pentagon in Washington, while the passengers on the fourth plane rise up and cause
it to crash in Pennsylvania.) The attack, the most devastating on
American soil since Pearl Harbor, leaves over twenty-seven hundred dead amid flames and billowing smoke. Such is one journey:
connecting caves in Afghanistan with twin towers in New York.

When the Cold War ended, hopes rose that a calmer era would
replace the world of dueling superpowers and the threat of atomic
war. Instead, a different kind of conflict emerged. Al Qaeda was
no superpower. It possessed no stockpile of missiles, tanks, or vast
armies. Its weapon was terror, a tactic of the weak and desperate
rather than the powerful. But terrorism can spread chaos in a world
so tightly connected. Such a world depends on economies running
smoothly, electrical grids supplying power, and transportation net-
works moving people quickly and safely. The World Trade Center
hummed with global connections. Citizens from over fifty nations
died there on September 11, and the world broadcast the news.

British television was on the scene by the time the second plane hit the towers, TV Azteca in Mexico televised President Bush's statement, China Central began coverage soon after. The world, not just the nation, felt that it had been struck by tragedy.

Osama bin Laden was driven into hiding, his location unknown for years. American intelligence finally tracked him to a compound in Pakistan and in 2011 navy SEALs carried out a helicopter attack, killing him in the assault. Even hiding from the world, bin Laden had watched TV via satellite dish and depended on computers and hard drives. In death as in life, his journey demonstrated the unexpected connections of the modern world—and the threats such connections can bring.

Halfway around the world, a very different young man, Juan Chanax, began a journey. Born in 1956, one year before bin Laden, Chanax lived in the highlands of Guatemala. Two thousand years earlier, his ancestors had forged one of the continent's first civilizations. Now the Maya in his village worked as farmers on terraced fields or as weavers, like Chanax and his father. Juan heard tales of villagers who had headed north to find better-paying jobs. He knew little of the United States but had seen striking photos of astronauts and tall buildings. His relatives had little good to say of the place. "All you will eat there will come out of cans and the only job they will give you is sweeping trash." Chanax decided to go anyway. He left his village one morning in 1978 at 5:00 a.m., looking a bit like Ben Franklin, who had set out from Boston for Philadelphia carrying so little. Juan brought only a tiny suitcase with two pairs of pants, two pairs of underwear, and a shirt. That, and the phone number of two women from his town who had moved to the United States.

On the way he was robbed, then picked up by the U.S. Border Patrol twice while attempting to cross the Rio Grande from Mexico. But he kept trying, and once in Houston, he found a job at Randall's Supermarkets packing grocery bags and cleaning floors. He was well liked and made enough money to send home as much as $100 a week to his astonished family. When Randall's needed another worker, Chanax immediately contacted his uncle. And when another opening appeared . . . and another . . . Juan sent word home again. Eventually, the people at Randall's knew to come to him whenever they needed good workers. Within fifteen years, two thousand Guatemalans—from a population of four thousand in his village—had followed Juan to America. Most settled in a Houston suburb called Las Americas. Over time they founded three separate churches. Juan Chanax started a soccer league that gradually expanded to encompass twenty-six teams.

This was a network of a different sort: a connection of villagers and relatives across sixteen hundred miles, held together by letters, telephones, word of mouth, money orders, and extra beds in living rooms. Historians call it a migration chain, where one newcomer carves out a path that others from the home country follow. Of course, the Irish and the Germans followed similar paths in the 1840s, as did the Slavs, the Chinese, and many other peoples half a century later. The flood then became so great that Congress passed laws restricting immigration during and after World War I. As the drive for American "purity" and segregation spread during those years, a new quota system limited the number of people admitted from each country. Northern European nations were favored, southern and eastern European countries were not.

But the reforms of Lyndon Johnson's Great Society finally overturned these limits, opening the way for newcomers from Asia and Latin America as well as Europe. Castro's revolution pushed many Cubans to seek refuge in Florida. Mexican immigrants were joined in the 1980s by new groups of Central Americans. Then, too, the Vietnam War unsettled Southeast Asia, causing half a million people to flee to America. Previously, most Asian Americans had come from Japan, China, or the Philippines. After the war they were joined by Asians from India, Cambodia, Laos, Vietnam, and Korea. By 2010, more Latinos lived in the United States than African Americans. There were 5 to 8 million Muslim Americans as well as 1.5 million Hindus and about as many Buddhists.

In such a diverse nation it became more common for Americans to trace their family connections worldwide. Here is the family tree of one citizen: a mother from Kansas, a father from Africa, a stepfather from Indonesia. One grandfather a member of the King's African Rifles in World War I, another grandfather an American army sergeant in World War II. A Hawaiian grandmother, an Irish great-grandfather, a great-grandmother who was part Native American. And, very possibly, a great-great-great grandfather who was one of the first slaves in Virginia. These are only a few of the family relations of Barack Obama, who in 2009 became the first African American president of the United States. One family's global connections hold a mirror to American life as it evolves in the twenty-first century.

Even so, there are connections that stretch wider than a migration chain and reach deeper than a guerilla fighter's cave. One woman who called attention to them was finishing her own journey, as it happened, about the time Juan Chanax and Osama bin Laden were growing up. For two decades Rachel Carson gained fame as a nature writer who made woodlands, rugged shores, and ocean tidal pools come alive for readers. "You find yourself taking an enormously friendly interest in all sorts of spiny and slime-wreathed creatures," a New York Times reviewer commented of one of her books. The lure wasn't just the details about this red jellyfish or that spiny crab. Carson painted the bigger picture: the way every creature is part of nature's "intricately woven design." Changing one part of the chain of life could alter the rest of it in unexpected ways. "In nature, nothing exists alone," she insisted. Somewhat to her surprise, in the late 1950s she found herself working on a project much less likely to please her nature-loving readers—one that she called "the poison book."

At that time the United States had become the world's greatest superpower, and its scientists looked confidently toward the future. They had split and harnessed the atom—for bombs, yes, but also with dreams of nuclear power plants and perhaps, one day, even atomic spaceships and automobiles. Research labs were turning out a host of new chemicals, including the insecticide DDT, which promised to banish diseases like malaria, spread by mosquitoes. The slogan of the DuPont chemical company said it all: "Better things for better living . . . through chemistry." On beaches, trucks sprayed clouds of DDT as children played in its fog. "Harmless to humans," read one truck's sign. Crop dusters dropped even stronger chemicals on southern farms to kill off fire ants. Could insects be exterminated? "I give an unqualified yes to the question," boasted one agriculture official.

As Rachel Carson wrote about nature, she couldn't help hearing stories about these chemicals. A friend reported dozens of dying birds around her feeder after planes sprayed a nearby bird sanctuary with insecticide. She corresponded with physicians whose research suggested that pesticides could cause leukemia and other cancers in humans. So she began the most challenging work of her life. It was difficult partly because she knew that the chemical industry, and even many scientists, would bitterly attack her claims that man-made chemicals were altering the balance of nature. It was even more difficult because she learned that she herself was dying of cancer. Despite nausea and fatigue from radiation treatment and surgery, she pushed on. When *Silent Spring* was published in 1962, critics called her a "faddist," a "pseudo-scientist," a "spinster with no children," and "probably a communist." But Carson rose above her attackers, testifying in Congress and earning many honors before illness took her two years later. Friends scattered her ashes across her beloved Sheepscot River on the Maine coast—"Here at last returned to the sea," a plaque explains.

Her campaign was only the beginning of a larger journey for Americans. Others joined in investigating how humans had abused the earth and air. Factory smoke and smog from car exhaust hung over cities. Chemical wastes were dumped into streams. So much pollution filled Ohio's Cuyahoga River that the river itself caught fire in 1969. But that was old news. The Cuyahoga caught fire regularly: in 1868, 1883, 1887, 1912, 1936, 1941, 1948, and 1952. Private industries had little incentive to clean up their toxic waste, for it cost them nothing to use the air and rivers as dumping grounds. Both the liberal Lyndon Johnson and the more conservative Richard Nixon recognized that government had to act to protect the public interest. Congress passed laws establishing the Environmental Protection Agency as well as standards for clean air and water.

But the world is threatened by more than pollution hot spots. Scientists have used weather sensors on land and sea to monitor temperatures and space satellites to track the size of the earth's ice caps. In 2014 some three hundred American scientists summed up the research of thousands more. The earth's climate is warming and humans "are now the primary cause of recent and projected future change." The rise comes because coal-burning plants and gas engines have lofted carbon dioxide into the air, and the gas acts to trap heat in the atmosphere. At the same time, forests—which absorb carbon dioxide—are being cut down. The effects of global warming can be seen in the increasing number of extreme weather events: wildfires caused by drought, flooding caused by hurricanes. "It seems we have the storm of the century every year," commented the governor of New York. As ice caps melt, ocean levels rise. Scientists predict that by the end of the twenty-first century, coastal cities from Miami, Florida, to Alexandria, Egypt, and Ho Chi Minh City in Vietnam will be threatened by flooding.

"It was pleasant for me to believe," Rachel Carson wrote, "that much of nature was forever beyond the tampering hand of man—he might level the forests and dam the streams, but the clouds and the rain and the wind were God's." Not so—not on a shrinking planet where the human and the wild were ever more tightly connected. As Carson put it, "The present is linked with the past and the future, and each living thing with all that surrounds it." That link between the past and the future is the subject of our final chapter.

40

The Past Asks More

HOW DO YOU MAKE HISTORY? That's the question that began
this book, and I suggested then that history can be made by living it or by writing it. But it's not a question of either/or. To make
history by living it—to *act*—requires knowing where you've come
from, for the past has shaped every one of us. So even if we don't
actually write history ourselves, we piece together stories of who
we are, what we believe, and the principles we hold dear. Strange as
it may seem, moving forward requires looking back.

That's *how* we make history. But why? Why spend so much time
in the past?

The first answer is simple but true: because the time spent is so
riveting and entrancing. The "damned human race," as Mark Twain
once called it, is endlessly inventive. Even the best novelists would
be hard-pressed to think up the things real people do. William
Bradford gets a foot stuck in a deer trap on his first day exploring
America. Jonathan Edwards watches spiders unreel their webs in
the breeze, while young Benjamin Franklin uses the same zeph-

yrs to get himself towed across a pond by a kite. The infant Andrew Carnegie eats his oatmeal with two spoons, calling for "Mair!
Mair!" A conquistador pens his slogan: *More and more and more
and more.* The Dutch march the Swedes out of their fort with bullets
in their mouths. Dirt falls on the heads of senators as visitors prop
their feet up in the balcony. Charles Sumner is beaten unconscious
on the Senate floor. A brakeman scrambles up his train ladder as
snow whirls about his pant legs. An eight-year-old named Phoebe
slices her thumb open in a sardine factory. Harriet Tubman carries
a pair of live chickens to distract suspicious villagers from noticing
the fugitives she leads north. Jay Gould buys up all the cows in Buffalo to outsmart Cornelius Vanderbilt. Teddy Roosevelt lowers his
children by rope from the second floor of the governor's mansion.
Philadelphians dangle a boy over George Washington to place a
crown of laurels on his head. Girls play knucklebones in the Old
World; boys buy Kix atomic rings in the New. GIs fight their way
onto Normandy beaches on D-Day in 1944. A thousand children
march into harm's way for Dr. King on Double-D Day in 1963. Migrating birds guide Columbus to America. Dying birds lead Rachel
Carson to warn of the earth's peril. Five hundred astonishing years.
A body could long wander with pleasure such Elysian fields.

But the past asks more of us. It pushes us to think closely about
certain ideas that circle our story, turning up regularly even in unexpected places. Martin Luther King didn't know he was about to
make history when he drove with a friend, Elliott Finley, to the first
bus rally in Montgomery. The traffic got worse and worse until the
two men ditched their car and started walking. Then it dawned on
them: the *meeting* had caused the traffic jam. "You know something,
Finley," King said, "this could turn into something big." History
is more than fascinating stories; it can have vast personal consequences. It can turn, as King discovered, into something big.

Two big ideas echo through American history, circling and ever
returning: *freedom* and *equality.* And the two are drawn together,
like the nation itself, by the motto first engraved on the Great Seal

in 1782: *E pluribus unum.* We are free, we are equal, we are one. The words echo so often, they are taken for granted.

But the motto seems a sham. When in human history have the lands that encompass the United States ever truly been one? Columbus dropped anchor at the edge of a continent already divided among hundreds of native cultures and languages. The arrival of Europeans and Africans over the next three centuries only added to the patchwork quilt. Yamasee, Iroquois, Arapaho, Pueblo, Chumash, Spanish, French, English, Dutch, Swedish, Scottish, Ibo, Gambian, Angolan, and so many more. As the Republic grew, the flood increased, bringing Irish and Germans and, later, Poles, Slavs, Russians, Italians, Chinese, and Japanese. The latest wave has been truly global, encompassing Indians, Thais, Vietnamese, Filipinos, Mexicans, Salvadorans, and Guatemalans. Can we ever truly create one from so many?

Yet that has been the dream, right from first contact in 1492. Europeans recalled the tales of a golden age when all people lived together as one: innocently and at peace. Columbus would give the Indians red caps and glass beads and get them to wear the right sort of clothing; and the Indians would give him gold and become Christian and work willingly. Or so Columbus wished. Puritans dreamed of a holy commonwealth where the saints would rule and the strangers in their midst would learn righteousness. Jonathan Edwards saw the Great Awakening as the first fruit of "those glorious times" predicted in scripture, when divisions and conflicts would disappear. These dreams of unity and harmony have propelled the peoples of America for centuries.

But the divisions didn't disappear. Madison thought long and hard about that problem as he worked on the Constitution. A republic would always have divisions, he decided—factions, he called them. And they arose not just because people came from different parts of the world. The causes of faction were "sown in the nature of man." Humans make mistakes in reasoning things out. Their passions are easily aroused. They are influenced by "self-love," which blinds them to the viewpoints of others. More important, people naturally divide because of their different circumstances in life. Most often, said Madison, divisions arise because of "the various and unequal distribution of property. Those who hold and those who are without property have ever formed distinct interests in society. Those who are creditors, and those who are debtors. . . . A landed interest, a manufacturing interest, a mercantile interest . . . " It was wishful thinking to believe that humans would ever find a golden age so gentle, a millennium so peaceful, or a common-wealth so holy that disagreements would disappear. Or, as Madison put it, no government would ever manage to give "every citizen the same opinions, the same passions and the same interests."

No, if there was to be a "more perfect union" binding together the people and provinces of the United States, it would have to come from crafting a government that allowed factions to work out their different interests—through debate, through a fair system of representation, through compromise, through laws passed. The trick was to put all that into the Constitution and still hold tight the values that the Declaration of Independence had proclaimed: *freedom* (*liberty* was the other word used) and *equality*.

At first even Madison hoped that such a system would work without needing political parties to represent different interest groups. But that, too, proved an unattainable golden age. After the War of 1812, the Federalist Party faded away. But once the presidency of James Monroe ended—the last of the founding generation—a new system of political parties sprang up. As Martin Van Buren recognized, parties had come to stay. They gave energy to the new democracy and brought more voters to the polls than ever before. The "common people" had strong ideas about what it meant to be free and equal. Why should only those who owned a certain amount of property be allowed to vote? Why shouldn't ordinary Americans run for office, not just the well-to-do? And, some few dared to ask, why shouldn't women be free to vote? Weren't they the equals of men?

The least free Americans, of course, were slaves. Madison, a southerner, realized from the beginning that the Union's greatest danger lay in the division between northern and southern states, "principally from the effects of their having or not having slaves." Washington went to his grave convinced that "nothing but the rooting out of slavery can perpetuate the existence of our union." It was not just that slavery deprived those in chains of the freedom and equality every individual deserved. The institution of slavery also gave the owners of human property a great deal of wealth and power. It allowed a strong interest to grow up, determined to keep slavery. Strange to say, as the United States grew more democratic in the era of Andrew Jackson, slavery also grew stronger, became rooted more deeply with every acre of cotton planted in the South and every yard of cloth machine-woven in the North.

Over time, northern states abolished slavery and it became the South's peculiar institution. The parties struggled to compromise by drawing lines: slave states on one side and free states on the other. But the Constitution's federal system was not able to resolve the conflict, even as the lines were redrawn again and again: the Three-fifths Compromise, the Missouri Compromise, the Kansas-Nebraska Act, the Compromise of 1850. The lines were all about freedom and equality—and the lines never held. Slaves themselves regularly crossed them by voting with their feet. Only a bloody conflict could settle the disagreement and save the Union. The Civil War was the political system's biggest failure.

Beyond slavery, Madison pointed to the unequal distribution of property in general. And the gap between the richest and poorest Americans increased sharply after the Civil War, as the new systems of industry allowed the United States to become richer and more powerful than any nation in the world. The captains of industry who scrambled to the top of this new heap praised laissez-faire, the policy of leaving individuals alone. They had become splendidly successful through luck and pluck, through the survival of the fittest. Wasn't that what was meant by equality of opportunity?

"Every man shall be free to become as unequal as he can." "Daft" Andrew Carnegie, like Ragged Dick, showed what a boy with pluck could accomplish; and in old age he was generous with his riches, giving away millions. "A man who dies rich, dies disgraced," he said.

But when the depression of the 1890s left millions unemployed, out of a home, or even starving, people like Jacob Coxey begged the government to act. His call harked back to the vision of John Winthrop's commonwealth, a community knit together for the common good. Opportunity was hardly equal when people lacked a basic living or the chance at a decent education, nor when huge corporations used their power to crowd out smaller businesses and free competition. Even Carnegie granted that the government needed "to legislate on behalf of the workers, because it is always the worst employers that have to be coerced into what fair employers would gladly do." Progressives, New Dealers, and Great Society reformers all agreed with Franklin Roosevelt that the definition of freedom had to be enlarged. "True individual freedom cannot exist without economic security and independence."

The pattern of boom followed by bust had repeated itself since the first rush for tobacco in Virginia. But the ups and downs grew ever steeper and more frightening. The depression of 1892 exceeded any that came before it because the systems driving big industry had become more closely linked. The failure of one big bank or mammoth factory led to the ruin of many more. Then the imperial nations of Europe, in their own scramble for bigger and better, tumbled into the Great War and pulled the United States in as well. When the guns at last went silent, Woodrow Wilson promised a peace to end all wars—but no. The pattern repeated. The roaring economy of the 1920s turned out autos and radios and created a standard of living never before matched, followed by a crash and depression also never equaled, ending in a world war unlike any in human history. After 1945, another boom commenced, this time accompanied by tail fins and televisions. For a frightening month in 1962, the damned human race seemed ready to leap into the atomic abyss. Instead, the Cold War sputtered on, eventually exhausting the United States in Vietnam and the Soviet Union in Afghanistan.

Can we stop the circle from coming round again? And still hold close our freedom and equality? In 1910 Teddy Roosevelt warned of the gap between rich and poor; between ordinary laborers and the "small class of enormously wealthy and economically powerful men, whose chief object is to hold and increase their power." A century after Roosevelt, that gap had returned, stretching wider than nearly any time in the nation's history. By 2010 half of American families collectively owned only 1 percent of the nation's wealth. American workers found it harder to get ahead—to change a blue collar for a white one—than workers in most other developed nations. Equality of opportunity seemed threatened.

As for freedom, that was easier to define in Ben Franklin's day. You could vote with your feet, running away to start a new life, as Franklin and many other apprentices and slaves did. But as the world has grown more connected, that sort of freedom has become harder to find. It's not just that the radioactive fallout lofted on high can reach anywhere someone might walk, nor that the world's center of commerce can be wounded from caves halfway around the world. Those threats are sobering, but the biggest threat of all is the one we humans pose to ourselves. We are steadily warming the planet we live on. The danger has mounted gradually, but it possesses the power to make not a heaven on earth but a hell.

Do we have the resolve to stop that final circle from coming round at last? The United States has been called an exceptional nation and so it is, though perhaps not in the way many imagine. It's quite common for nations to consider themselves exceptional. "God has chosen you," the Bible told the Hebrews, "to be a people . . . above all peoples who are on the face of the earth." The Aztecs considered themselves divinely singled out, as did the Dutch and the British, to name only a few. Certainly Americans have been exceptional at *bragging* about how exceptional they are—as humorist

Finley Peter Dunne recognized in 1898. On the eve of the Spanish-American War, Dunne wrote a series of stories about a fictional Irish American bartender, Mr. Dooley, including one in which his friend Hennessey stoutly declares that Americans are a great people. "We ar-re that," Mr. Dooley agrees, in his fine Irish lilt. "An' th' best iv it is, we know we ar-re." It's all too easy for a chosen people to think of themselves as different, better, purer. But that path leads toward separation rather than union. To remain pure, best wall yourself off in a smaller settlement, where everyone thinks the same. Roger Williams tried, but soon discovered the problem with making purity the job of the state. A truer vision of the American union is Walt Whitman's: "Here is not merely a nation but a teeming nation of nations." The United States is exceptional because its continental union is political. It welcomes diversity. It is not a union based on all citizens thinking alike.

We are free, we are equal, we are one. The past calls us to think how this is so. Looking back, we acknowledge the wisdom of those who have gone before; else why bother with history? But respect is not blind. "Some men look at constitutions with sanctimonious reverence, and deem them like the ark of the covenant, too sacred to be touched," Jefferson wrote in 1816. "They ascribe to the men of the preceding age a wisdom more than human." He understood that "as new discoveries are made, new truths disclosed . . . institutions must advance also, and keep pace with the times. We might as well require a man to wear still the coat which fitted him when a boy."

The world we inhabit surely includes perils the founding generation could not have foreseen. And the American political system, as it has evolved, seems so divided, so disconnected from an intimately connected world that the term *gridlock* is frequently applied. Will the union hold? Will we discover new ways to remain free and equal and one?

Enough questions. The past asks more of us because the future deserves more. It's your history now, to write and to live. You tell me.

Acknowledgments

For me, the writing of history has very often been collaborative. The list of colleagues and coauthors I've worked with in the making of American histories is too long to include, to say nothing of the hundreds of scholars whose work I have drawn on in writing this tale. But I owe a particular debt of gratitude to those who read this *Little History* in draft: Mark Lytle, Christine Heyrman, Michael McCann, John Rugge, Ken Ludwig, Mary Untalan, and Antonia Woods. Chris Rogers, my friend and steadfast editor at Yale Press, provided more than one close reading, while Margaret Otzel and Erica Hanson eased my way through production. I owe a special thanks to Gordon Allen. Forty years ago, he executed the drawings for my first book, a guide to wilderness canoeing written with John Rugge. It is especially satisfying to have him back, pen in hand, once more.

Index

American Revolution, 90; Civil War ignited by, 158–63, 306; climate and, 8; decisions entailed by, 126–27; economics of, 58, 125; emancipation of, 125, 160; extent of, 90; founders' views of, 85; Indians subjected to, 18, 19, 28, 39; migration and, 123–24; Northern views of, 130; representation and, 96–97; territorial expansion and, 147–56

Sledge, Eugene, 250–51

smallpox, 25, 29, 70, 76, 110–11, 140

Smith, John, 46–47

Smith, Joseph, 133, 134, 143

social Darwinism, 208

socialism, 134

Social Security, 243

Society of Friends (Quakers), 56–58, 62

Society of Jesus (Jesuits), 67

Socrates, 61

Sonoran Desert, 13

Sons of Liberty, 77, 78, 79

South Carolina, 97, 175; black population in, 59; cotton growing in, 124; nullification proclaimed by, 121–22; rice cultivation in, 53, 58, 124; secession of, 156

South Dakota, 202

Southeast Asia, 248, 298

Southern Christian Leadership Conference (SCLC), 273, 275

South Korea, 260

sovereignty, 97

Soviet Union: Afghanistan invaded by, 293, 295, 308; collapse of, 293; containment of, 258; détente with, 289–90; nuclear arsenal of, 260, 261, 269; as superpower, 255, 256; in United States provoked by, 264–68; World War II, 249, 250, 256

Spain, 139, 226, 265; Catholicism in, 34; England vs., 37, 75; as global power, 35, 37; North America discovered and settled by, 1, 3, 17–29, 67; sugar crops and, 46

Spanish-American War, 225, 226, 271, 309

Spencer, Herbert, 208–9

spices, 2, 18, 45, 46, 53

Squanto (Wampanoag Indian), 39

Stalingrad, Battle of, 250

Stalin, Joseph, 250, 256, 258, 259, 261

Stamp Act, 77, 78

Standard Oil Company, 180–81

Stanton, Edwin, 171

Stanton, Elizabeth Cady, 137, 187

steamboats, steamships, 116, 124, 132, 138, 140, 224

steam engine, 132, 231

Steel, Ferdinand, 125

steel industry, 177, 181, 184–85

Stephens, Alexander, 170

stock market, 181–82, 235–36

Stowe, Harriet Beecher, 153

Strauss, Levi, 14

strikes, 189, 209–10, 215, 216, 281

Strive and Succeed (Alger), 206–7

Student Nonviolent Coordinating Committee (SNCC), 274, 275

submarines, 228

suburbia, 265

subways, 194

sugar, 46, 53, 73, 90, 124, 176, 265

Sugar Act, 77

Sumner, Charles, 154, 303

Sutter, John, 200

Sweden, 53, 112

Swift, Gustavus, 194

Syria, 291

Taft, William Howard, 222

Taino, 18, 19

Tallmadge, James, 149–50

Tanaghrisson (Half King; Iroquois chief), 66, 71

tariffs, 121, 122

taxation, 78, 223, 234, 239, 292

Taylor, Zachary, 146, 151–52

tea, 46, 78–79, 224

telegraph, 143, 179, 224

television, 265